THROUGH CHINA

WITH A CAMERA

BY

JOHN THOMSON, F.R.G.S.

AUTHOR OF
"THE ANTIQUITIES OF CAMBODIA"
"ILLUSTRATIONS OF CHINA AND ITS PEOPLE" ETC. ,

WITH NEARLY 100 ILLUSTRATIONS

1898

INTRODUCTION.

HAD the great Venetian traveller, Marco Polo, been able to confirm by a series of photographs his story of the wonders of Cathay, his fair fame would have escaped the discredit cast upon it for centuries, and indeed until comparatively recent investigation confirmed his story.

Since the time when I made my first journey into Cambodia to examine its ancient cities, it has been my constant endeavour to show how the explorer may add not only to the interest, but to the permanent value of his work by the use of photography.

The camera has always been the companion of my travels, and has supplied the only accurate means of portraying objects of interest along my route, and the races with which I came in contact. Thus it came about that I have always been able to furnish readers of my books with incontestable pictorial evidence of my "bona fides", and to share with them the pleasure experienced in coming face to face for the first time with the scenes and the people of far-off lands.

Some parts of this volume have been published in a more costly form. In the present instance the photographs have been reproduced and transformed into printing blocks by a most effective half-tone process, so that nothing in the original plates is lost. The letter-press has been carefully revised and brought up to date and in part re-written. I have kept myself "au c ourant " with the course of events in " Further Asia." But in China and in Chinese institutions there is no well-defined change to place on record. Western civilisation with its aggressive activities appears to be opposed to the genius of the people, who fain would be left alone to follow their time-worn methods social and political.

To those of my readers interested in photography I may add a note on my method of working.

All my negatives were taken by the wet collodion process, a process most exacting in its chemistry, especially in a land where the science is practically unknown.

Some of my troubles are recounted in these pages, and may prove interesting to the amateur who works along the line of rapid plates and films, and who after making his exposure, may retain the plate with its latent image for an indefinite period before development. With such plates and films ready to his hand the explorer ought to be in a position to produce work of the highest artistic and scientific value.

I must here thank my former publishers, Messrs. Sampson Low and Marston, for their courtesy in allowing me to make use of such matter as I required for the present volume.

January, 1898.   J. THOMSON.

CONTENTS.

LIST OF ILLUSTRATIONS.

THROUGH CHINA WITH A CAMERA.

CHAPTER I.

A BRIEF SKETCH OF THE CONDITION OF CHINA, PAST AND PRESENT.

"THE Chinese are so ancient in the world that it fares with them, as to their original, as with great rivers whose source can scarce be discovered." It is over two centuries since this was written by Le Comte, and the origin of the Chinese is still wrapped in the obscurity that preceded the dawn of authentic history. It is held by native scholars that Chinese history supplies a fairly accurate record of the Kings and Emperors who have reigned for the past four thousand years, and that their annals, dealing with an earlier period are largely mythical. The primitive sovereigns of the race are represented as the sources of the wisdom and probity, which are supposed to characterise the Government of the present day. They were certainly not without influence in moulding the political and social institutions which have kept the Chinese together for so many centuries in independence and isolation. The cause, however, of the permanency of the Chinese Government, in its main outlines has afforded ample scope for controversy to sinalogues and students of history, some affirming that it is solely due to the principle of paternal authority that forms the basis of the Chinese System, while others attribute its continuity to the traditional method followed in selecting officials. "It is solely owing to a principle which the policy of every successive dynasty has practically maintained, in a greater or less degree,—viz., that good government consists in the advancement of men of talent and merit only, to the rank and power conferred by official posts."

This view Mr. Meadows supports by the authority of Confucius, who says:—"Good government depends on obtaining proper men. Justice is what is right in the nature of things, its highest exercise is to honour men of virtue and talent."[1]

But other maxims are not wanting in the works of Confucius to prove that good government, to be enduring, must be based on the duties of universal obligation between "Sovereign and minister, between father and son, between husband and wife, between elder brother and younger brother, and those belonging to the intercourse of friends."[2] It would appear, therefore, that the persistency of the Chinese system of government must be attributed to more causes than one, in some measure to the patriarchal system, as well as to the principle embodied in selecting the most accomplished scholars for the service of the state. Be that as it may, the reader is probably aware that the system of government examination for civil and military preferment is one of the most ancient institutions of the Empire. All official posts, theoretically, are open as the rewards of distinguished scholarship. Examinations are periodically held in the chief cities of the Empire, and the subjects for examination, and methods followed by the examiners, are practically the

[1] Meadow's Notes on China.
[2] Chinese Classics, vol. I, page 103.—Prof. Legge.

CIVIL MANDARIN IN OFFICIAL CHAIR.

same as they were two thousand years ago, with this difference, that a thorough scholarly acquaintance with the classics takes now first rank, while the result of the moral teaching of the sacred text-books is hardly recognised, and is left to the somewhat elastic conscience of the successful candidate for office.

These examinations are open to all grades of society, excepting the most depraved sections of the community, and those having no recognised social status. On the surface, this appears to be the one democratic institution of the country, but in its practical operation proves no exception to the purely conservative basis upon which all Chinese institutions are reared.

Literary graduates, when selected for the Imperial service, are at once cut adrift from the people, and form a caste by themselves, whose sole interest lies in maintaining the ancient policy of the Government, to the exclusion of such measures of progress and reform as would bring the country abreast of the times, and foster the permanent interests of the community from which they sprang. The system is nevertheless popular, and the examination-hall full of infinite possibilities, affording a strong incentive to parents to educate their children, with the result that the schoolmaster is found in every village in the Empire. He is himself a student, an expectant, or unsuccessful candidate for office, who is treated with the honour befitting the dignity of his position, and supported with much self-sacrifice by the villagers. Judging from personal experience, few Chinamen are wholly illiterate, while the majority are too poor to procure anything beyond elementary training. It is from this untutored class that our colonial settlements draw their supplies of labour, the class "par excellence" showing capacity and determination to adapt themselves to new surroundings and to profit by the methods of Western progress. They are naturally free from the retarding influence of cultured prejudice, which characterises the Chinese "literati." It is to this humbler section of the race, engaged in trade, and tillage, that one is forced to look for the ultimate regeneration of China, rather than to the accomplished followers of Confucius. It is within my knowledge that some of these emigrants and their descendants, the latter having been trained in foreign schools, have risen to opulence and launched successfully, on foreign lines, abroad and in their own country, commercial undertakings of great magnitude and importance. In the hands of such men as these, perchance, lie the destinies of China, which must either move forward, or drift and be dismembered by powers over which she has no control. The experience of the last quarter of a century, and especially the results of the last war are far from reassuring, and do not encourage the hope that China at the eleventh hour will "set her house in order." She would have to re-organise her whole system of administration, excepting her Imperial Maritime Customs under Foreign Commissioners, which might well serve as a model, or an honest foundation upon which to rear the new fabric of government. In regard to the pressing necessity for reform of a drastic type, the reader may draw his own conclusions from a perusal of the recent "Times" correspondence, or still more recent British Consular Report, on "The Revenue and Expenditure of the Chinese Empire." The political as well as the fiscal outlook are there set down in the most sombre colours. Will China face the position boldly and at once? A native scholar once remarked that it takes more than a thousand years to introduce a new tone into the Chinese language. Should this estimate afford some clue to the ratio of political and social progress, it is difficult to limit the time required to cast off the chrysalis

MILITARY MANDARIN.

of antiquity in which the Empire is shrouded. Signs of forward movement, however, have not been wanting, but they are solely due to pressure from without, not unfrequently applied at the point of the bayonet. There has been no spontaneous advance. The efforts of the Chinese have been spent, and their resources exhausted, in futile endeavours to safeguard their ancient institutions. Arsenals, Naval and Military Schools and Colleges have been founded, a fleet and armaments purchased, and untold wealth lavished on useless defences which have left the Empire at the mercy of her foes. Still with all these reluctant and costly innovations the Chinese to-day place implicit faith in their time-worn methods of training for government service, civil and military. The nine books of the Classics are the Examination Text-books, just as they were two thousand years ago, and on them they have staked their existence. Five of the books were written before the days of Pythagoras, and the remaining four compiled by Confucius and his immediate disciples. In these sacred tomes the authors are supposed to have completed the circle of human knowledge, and left to their countrymen a store of wisdom sufficient for all time. All discoveries in Science and Art should conform to, and be tested by these primitive standards, sources which were frozen up during what may be termed the glacial epoch of Chinese progress. Confucian philosophy stands at the opposite pole to that of Bacon, and if not inoperative as a means of cultivating the mind, is useless for all work of human development. It is the modern Great Wall, hedging round the ignorance and superstition of the race. The moral maxims of Confucius "are excellent, but they have not made the Chinese a moral people." [1] While his doctrine is full of faultless ethic-

[1] The Religions of the Chinese.—Dr. Edkins.

al teaching, it is placed on record that the teacher himself failed in his integrity when personal interest was involved "He broke an oath he had sworn at a place called Pfoo, on the plea that it was a forced oath, and the Spirits do not hear such." [1] He also enjoined concealment of truth, if by that means a father or friend might escape the consequences of their own misdeeds. This touches upon a phase of national character which accounts for much official malfeasance. The cultured disciples of Confucius have not failed to profit by the few isolated passages which record the back-sliding of the Master, while the scrupulous correctness of his conduct as a whole, and excellence of his moral teaching have had little or no effect in moulding the character of his modern followers.

If the ancient rulers of China were remarkable for wisdom and probity, the morality of the modern Mandarin is mainly confined to polite phraseology and posturing. This outer semblance of virtue and integrity presents a phase of Asiatic character, with which foreigners in their Chinese experience are not unfamiliar. It is the polished husk presented to the outer barbarians with all due ceremony, and which has proved so unsatisfying as to have led to reprisals which have brought China to the verge of bankruptcy. But foreigners are not the only sufferers by such methods of official procedure. The provincial Governors enjoy a quasi-financial independence in the collection and administration of a large part of the Imperial revenue. Foreign and native trade alike suffer from the irregular mode practised in levying and collecting taxes. The policy of the provincial officials in dealing with the revenue is to retain as much as possible for local expenditure, and to

---

[1] The Chinese Classics, vol. I, p. 101.—Prof. Legge.

remit as little as possible to Peking. Things are made to appear what they are not; a considerable portion of the revenue never finds its way into the official returns, while many of the large items set down for military and naval expenditure are so manipulated as to leave a large residue in the pockets of the provincial rulers and their numerous retainers. For this the Government is in some measure responsible, as the official salaries of Mandarins are merely nominal. That, for example, of the governor-general of a province about equals the salary of a city clerk, while his supplementary allowances are indefinite and elastic, affording ample scope for the exercise of predatory habits. It is indeed difficult, and, from the oriental point of view, impossible, for the official to carry on his administration with clean hands. Besides, his tenure of office is short, while his present and prospective wants are immeasurable.

The safeguarding of a system that tolerates this state of official corruption accounts in part for the native dread of innovation, and their intolerance of foreigners and foreign intercourse.

The one branch of the Imperial service carried on with honesty is, as I have noticed, the Imperial Maritime Customs, under the direction of Sir Robert Hart. This yields an ever increasing revenue. The average annual return is over 23,000,000 taels, while the native Customs, with many more stations and irregular imports, produce about 10,000,000 taels, an amount which always remains about the same, irrespective of war, famine, pestilence, or fluctuations of trade. In the Kwang-tung province the foreign Customs collect at four ports 3,000,000 taels, while the native Customs returns from forty ports and stations less than half a million taels. [1] The work accomplished

[1] Far Eastern Question.—Val Chirol.

by the Foreign Commissioners has met with scant appreciation
at the hands of the Chinese, and although it supplies the most
important item of revenue of the Central Government, has led
to no reform in other branches of the administration. Corruption
is still the rule, sapping the strength of every modern effort,
whether in re-organising the army, founding arsenals, or the
purchase of a fleet.

In justice, however, it must be recorded that the ruling classes
are not wholly corrupt. There are exceptions; men in authority
who are famed for honesty rather than for stores of ill-gotten
gain, and men like the Viceroy of Hupeh and Yunan, Ching-
Chi-tung, who, in a patriotic attempt to benefit his country, squandered his fortune in founding gigantic iron and steel works,
which were to provide the railroad plant of a line from Hankow
to Peking. The works were to be managed entirely by Chinese,
while the foreigner was to look on with mingled envy and apprehension. But, as might have been foreseen, for lack of knowledge the project had to be abandoned. It may be noticed that
this Viceroy, so it was said, was not wholly unacquainted with
the promoters of the pseudo-republican rising in Formosa, which
gave the Japanese some trouble when they entered into possession of that island. Since the close of the war with Japan,
reforms are in the air, just as they were a quarter of a century
ago. A new fleet is to be purchased, and the Chinese navy
organised under a British officer, Commander Dundas, R.N.
The army too, is to be re-modelled by English and German officers.
It is to be supposed before this step was taken, that a suitable
guarantee was obtained that the officers in question will be
accorded better treatment by the Chinese Government than fell
to the lot of Captain Lang, who became simply a naval instructor,
subordinate to the native officials, who embraced every oppor-

tunity of misapplying funds, supposed to be devoted to rendering the fleet efficient. If the new fleet, yet to be purchased, and the army, yet to be formed, are to be of service, the funds set apart for their organisation and maintenance should be administered by Europeans as a guarantee that they will be wholly applied to the purpose for which they are intended. Should this precaution fail to be taken, history will repeat itself, as the next war will prove. What has become of the army of 600,000 fighting men, supposed to have existed before the war with Japan, an army sufficiently organised to require regular rations and payments. In travelling all over the country I saw no evidence of the existence of any great military force. In the official pay-sheets it figures as a very formidable host. Apart from the numerical strength named, a considerable force does exist in the North, brought together and maintained by Li Hung Chang, when Viceroy of Pechili.

The navy, before the war broke out, numbered about one hundred vessels of all sorts, from sea-going ironclads to torpedo boats. This fleet, which does not now exist, will probably be recreated at great cost, and before officers or men can be trained for service. But this is a matter, which does not disturb the Chinese mind. I do not know what the last navy cost the Government, but I do know that neither ships, officers nor crews were ever fit for fighting. The Chinese trusted entirely, after the manner of their renowned Chieftains of ancient history, to the outward show of force, rather than to force itself, to defeat their foes. As for the army, on paper it is a costly machine. In the provinces and capital a considerable part of the revenue is annually expended on this line of defence, and yet in order to make some show of resistance during the war, the force herded to the front was mainly from the fields; men engaged in tillage, who had never handled a weapon more formidable than a hoe, were pushed forward, musket in hand, and many of them left to raid their own countrymen for rations, until brought to the shambles on the battlefields, or disbanded.

Reform, one would suppose in the case of China, to be effective, would begin, not in wild schemes for arming the the Empire in defence of the very institutions which are the cause of her impotency, and of a system of corruption which would render her land forces and fleet useless in a struggle against any third-rate power, but begin with the government itself. The system of administration must be made worthy of respect, so as to be supported by the patriotic endeavour of the whole nation.

This can never be the case in China so long as the government figures as one in the first rank of Asiatic despotisms, so long as there are no railways, no public press, no public opinion, no modern facilities for intercourse, and no encouragement for the development of great industries, except what China has been forced to concede by Treaty stipulations, notably by clauses contained in the Treaty of Shimonosaki, which has thrown open some new ports to trade. Under Article VI, it is stipulated that Japanese subjects shall be free to engage in all sorts of industries in the cities and open ports of the Empire, and be free to import all sorts of machinery for manufacturing purposes. By the provisions of the Treaty of Tientsin, Great Britain and all other powers under the most favoured nation concessions, share in the benefits conferred upon Japan. China, indeed, has again been reluctantly thrust forward as the direct result of her own immobility. But in order that she may hold together, and voluntarily proceed along the path of progress, it is essential first that the Government should conduct its affairs with honesty and discretion. For this end there ¦should be a central fiscal administration, accountable for the whole income and expenditure of the Empire, and a Court of Exchequer having a thoroughly experienced foreign Chancellor, as a guarantee of efficiency. This would naturally lead to a complete revision of official salaries, which would be so supplemented as to remove the necessity for peculation, and would secure the whole revenue for the purposes of the Government, measures which would at once place China in a sound financial position, enabling her not only to meet all the liabilities resulting from the late war, but to have a considerable surplus in reserve. It is estimated that from one-half to two-thirds of the revenue disappears in the process of collection and transmission. Other essential reforms should follow, such as a complete survey of the land, in order to secure a proper adjustment of the land tax and return of the legitimate proceeds accruing from that source. The unification of the whole of the Customs under the present Imperial Maritime Customs Commissioners would sweep away the system of farming inland transit dues, and levying illegal imposts on foreign goods, by which they are so burdened as to become unsaleable in many of the inland marts. The total abolition of native collectorates would add greatly to the internal resources, as returns from those quarters are always much below actual collection. [1] The entire revenue of the Central Government of China, roughly speaking, is about one-fourth of that of India, although in area of productive soil and in population India is at a disadvantage, while at the same time the burden of taxation borne by the people under British rule is lighter and less oppressive, and is not subject to fluctuations

[1] See British Consular Report. Parl. 1897.

arising from the necessity, caprice or avarice of local officials. It must be noted that the money paid to the central Government falls far short of the amount actually collected by the provincial authorities.

In India every facility is afforded for the development of the resources of the country, and for the expansion of trade, by a network of railways and trade routes, and by the safeguarding of the interests of the entire population. In China there are no facilities for inland transport save by river and canal navigation, which the Chinese discovered to their cost during the late war, no railroads of any commercial importance and no roads worthy of the name. This in a land having boundless stores of wealth in coal, iron and minerals of all sorts, and an unlimited supply of efficient labour; a land famed for the minute economy of its people, who derive warmth and fuel from charcoal and millet stalks, while millions of tons of coal lie undisturbed beneath their feet. The people are remarkable for their utilisation of waste products in food and in tillage, while their rulers can boast of the waste of their country's resources. Mandarins hold commerce in contempt, and may not stoop to trade at the peril of losing caste, and yet some there are who add to their wealth by a quasi-connection with trade, as in the case of Li Hung Chang and the China Steam Navigation Coy., and who, while denouncing foreign opium as a curse to the people, foster the cultivation of the native drug for their individual profit. Li Hung Chang has acquired great wealth by methods sanctioned by custom and best known to himself. He is also not without fame as the figure-head of the modern school of China, from whom better things were expected than the complete collapse of her armaments, for which he is held in a great measure responsible. It can hardly be expected that the Government will so warily guide the helm of state as to clear the shoals which beset their course on all sides. On the north and north-east, Russia, who used her influence successfully in modifying the Treaty of Shimonosaki and who guaranteed part of the indemnity exacted by Japan, has not failed to advance her interests by obtaining a concession to continue her Trans-Siberian railway through Chinese territory to the seaboard; there she will have a naval station with an open sea at all seasons. The arrangement is ostensibly temporary, but Russian diplomacy may be safely left to secure its permanency. Along the coast of China the land lies open to attack at all points, while on her south-western border the French and ourselves are busily at work, contesting the right to widen the ever extending sphere of influence, and to tap the trade of two of the richest provinces of the Empire. In this region the British have been treated to another example of bad faith in the Chinese ceding territory to France, the small state of Maung U, which by treaty stipulation was never to be transferred to a third power. Negotiations regarding this double dealing have terminated satisfactorily, and one important result for British commerce has been secured in opening the western river of Kwang-tung to trade. By this concession we obtain a direct route to Kwangsi and Yunan. France has permission to carry her railway from Tongking as far as Liuchow in Kwangsi, but Britain may safeguard her interests by the completion of the Mandalay railway to Kun-lung ferry, whence little difficulty would be encountered in continuing the route to a point above the French limit on the Mekong. Given these routes and a fair field for trade, one need not dread the results of the competition of our gallant neighbours, whose trading capacity is far outstripped by their chivalrous desire for Empire in the East. There is no reason why we should not work in harmony, as the French cannot dispense with our services in commerce, unless indeed, they foster a more intimate relationship with our German rivals. On the other hand, the Germans have every reason to encourage French colonial expansion as a factor not to be under-estimated in securing peace on their European borders. It is a sort of blood-letting of the military power of the latter, by which war fever is allayed and forces are spread over an extremely wide and unhealthy area.

Regarding the modern movement of China which had for its object the defence of the Empire, one of the most daring departures from her conventional and time-honoured institutions was promoted by the Viceroy of Hupeh and Yunan, Ching-Chi-tung, already noticed, by the erection, at a cost of about six million dollars, of rolling mills and arsenals at Hanyang. The plant covered seventy acres, and had its railroad, half a mile in length, from the Yangtize Kiang to the works. The arsenal was destroyed by fire soon after its completion, and finally the effort of this Chinese patriot had to be abandoned. He proposed not only to supply the Government with abundant, up-to-date munitions of war, manufactured by natives alone, but to produce the plant, steel rails included, and to build a trunk line from Hankow to Peking. The scheme proved a ruinous failure as had been predicted, Ching-Chi-tung having determined to dispense with the help of European experts and workmen, his own object being to prove, once and for all, that China, alone and unaided could supply herself with all that was requisite to sustain her position as the paramount power in the Far East. The money required for this disastrous venture came from the private purse of Ching-Chi-tung, how he came to be possessed of such vast resources has not been revealed. His

latest venture is framed on more modest lines—viz., the erection
of a Mint at Hankow; the dies for the coinage were sent from
Birmingham. This institution will possibly share the fate of the
Canton Mint, set up some seven years ago, and which turned
out dollars and smaller coins, but the dollars never got into
circulation, as no two batches proved of like value owing to
defective assay. Small coins are still struck, and find a market
as charms against malign influences.

The railway from Tientsin to Peking, constructed under the
direction of H. E. Hsu, should be completed before this work
sees the light.   The more important trunk line from Hankow
to Peking is still in abeyance. But it is reported that a Belgian
Syndicate has secured the privilege of advancing £ 4,500,000
sterling to be spent on the construction of the line, and the
right to supply materials and engineers. As the line is to figure
as part security, and the money is to be expended by Belgians,
one would expect that this much needed and long projected
railway would be built forthwith and finished with all speed.
I hope that the report may prove well-founded, and that the
Syndicate may ere long reap the reward of an enterprise so
daring and not unattended with risk. This loan it would appear
has been authorized by Imperial Edict, and the contract signed
by Ching-Chi-tung and Sheng Taoti at Wuchang, also by the
members of the Tsungli Yamen Peking. Sheng secured for himself a most unenviable reputation during the War, and has since
posed as the promoter of the Chinese Imperial Bank Scheme,
and financier of the Hankow-Peking railway. It is said that the
Belgians were not alone in their offer of capital for the enterprise,
but that the Chinese were fain to close with Belgium, being a
small power without a fleet. It is quite possible, notwithstanding,
that French and Russian financiers are not wholly uninterested

in the loan, and that, in the event of misunderstanding, Belgium might not be left to settle matters singlehanded.

As I close this review of the position and prospects of China, news has arrived of the opening of the West River of Canton, and for this great boon to commerce we are in a great measure indebted to the energy and diplomacy of Sir Claude Macdonald. The opening of the ports on the west branch of the Pearl river, has not been secured for ourselves alone, but for all foreign nations, and this I may say is truly characteristic of the liberal spirit of British diplomacy. The opening of this route is a step which must have a far-reaching influence, not only on foreign trade, but on the future of this part of the Chinese Empire. Steamers now run from Hongkong to Wu-Chau-fu three times a week, carrying passengers and produce.

I have alluded to the cession of Maung U, in the valley of the Nam U, to France in violation of the understanding with Great Britain. This breach of faith has been atoned for under the new Anglo-Chinese Convention ratified in Peking on June 5th of this year. By this agreement the Chinese cede to Great Britain the Shan State of Kokang on the South of Yunan. The State appears to be in form triangular, its base resting on the British Shan States, and its apex piercing Yunan. The Salwin flows through its centre, from the northern limit to Kun-lung ferry, thus opening a route from the ferry, a point to which the Mandalay railway will soon be completed. From Kun-lung to the Yunan frontier in a straight line, is about sixty miles. Gold is said to exist in the country, but the interior of Kokang is practically unknown to Europeans. In addition, a small territory has been added to the west of the Swali river, which ought to prove important, as it points to a possible trade route from Bahmo, by Kwitu, to the Shewli.

I will conclude this introductory sketch by expressing the hope that China may awake from her lethargy before it is too late, and pursue a policy of progress and enlightenment, and so banish for ever her antiquated usages and bring herself abreast of the times. The great trunk railway piercing the most populous part of the Empire, will prove of incalculable service, not only in opening new fields for commerce, but in breaking the fetters of superstition which for centuries have bound China and her people.

CHAPTER II.

Chinese Guilds—Hongkong - Native Boats—Shopkeepers—Artists—Music Halls.

My experience of the Chinese was not wholly confined to their native land. Before travelling through China I obtained some knowledge of the people in the Straits of Malacca, Siam, Cambodia and Cochin China. Although it forms no part of my scheme to recount in detail my impressions of the Chinaman abroad, yet a brief outline of his condition and prospects as one finds him outside the limits of his own land may assist the reader in forming a fair estimate of his character and capacity. He has been regarded as a non-progressive type, moving like a planet in an orbit of his own, from which he may not diverge without disaster to the political and social system of his nation. The conclusion is not without reason, as in his own country he is fettered by ancient tradition and the stern rule of a despotic government. His sacred books are the classics of antiquity in which are stored the tests of all human knowledge; there he must find the light of his life to guide him in his career from birth to burial. He may not, and seemingly cannot, conceive of the existence of a brighter and better philosophy, where evolution and progress reign supreme. He is nevertheless charged with latent energy and intelligence, which, as we shall see only requires change of condition and fitting opportunities for their liberation. The Chinaman out of his own country, enjoying the security and prosperity which a more liberal administration confers, seems to develop into something like a new being. No longer chained to the soil, he finds wide scope for his energies and high rewards for his industry. In Singapore, I found him filling positions of honour and trust, figuring as a member of the Legislative Council, as a contractor, builder, handicraftsman and labourer, and so full of resource as to render his services indispensable to the European community, having indeed no equal among Asiatics. But the love of combination, of the guilds and unions in which all Chinamen delight, tempts him at times too far. His countrymen combine among themselves to get as much out of each other as they possibly can, and when practicable to monopolise trade and rule the markets; and feeling the strength of organisation, the societies so formed set up laws for themselves, for the rule and protection of their members, in defiance of the local government. The congsee, or guild, thus drifts from a purely commercial into a semi-mercantile, semi-political league, and more than once has menaced the power of petty states, by making efforts to cast off the yoke which rested so lightly on its shoulders. These societies are imitations of similar institutions existing in every province of the Chinese Empire, where the people combine to resist government oppression, and the peasantry unite in clans and guilds to limit the power of local officials and of their employees, and to promote their own commercial and social interests. Such societies are frequently the cause of local disturbances, when the Sam-sings, or fighting men, resist the interference of the police. The Sam-sings are thus described by an old Chinese resident. "They live by looting and are on the watch for any excuse for exercising their talents. Each hoey, or society, must have so many of them, but I don't know any means of ascertaining their numbers. They are a regular fighting people and are paid so much a month. If there is any disturbance these people go out in looting parties; whether ordered by the head men or not, I cannot say; perhaps they do it on their own account." I was present on one occasion in a village in Penang which had been sacked and burned by hired ruffians belonging to an opposing clan, and it required strong measures on the part of the Government to put down the faction fight. This sort of warfare, as we shall see when we reach the "Flowery Land", the Imperial Government in the south of China has, at times, been either unable or unwilling to suppress. This class of Chinese immigrants cast upon the shore of a friendly state do not unfortunately confine their attention to faction fights; they organise gang robberies and the wealthier Chinese are rarely, if ever, the victims of their raids; they indeed enjoy an immunity which would appear unaccountable if we knew nothing of native guilds. Chinese thieves are thorough experts at their profession, adopting the most ingenious devices to attain their infamous ends. I recollect a burglary which took place at a friend's house, when the thief found his way into the principal bedroom and deliberately used up half a box of matches before he could get the lamp to light; his patience being rewarded at last, he proceeded with equal coolness in the plunder of the apartment, not forgetting to search beneath the pillow, where he secured a revolver and a watch. These Chinese robbers are reported to be able to stupify their victims by using some narcotic known only to themselves. I have no doubt this was done in the case referred to by the agency of the Chinese house-servants, who perhaps introduced the drug into my friend's bed. The Malays have told me of cases, as they averred, where the cunning Chinese thief passes the doorway of the house to be pillaged, and tosses in a handful of rice impregnated with some aromatic drug. This drug soon sends the inmates off into deep repose, from which they seldom awake till long after the robber has finished his undertaking, and that in the complete and deliberate style which suits the taste of the Chinese; for I must tell you that they at all times object to vulgar haste, whatever be the business they are pursuing, and they prefer if possible to avoid sudden surprises and unexpected attacks. The slightest sound will make them take to flight, dropping their booty and their garments, if any, in order to facilitate escape. But when they have a daring robbery on hand they go quite naked, with the body oiled all over and the queue coiled into a knob at the back of the head and stuck full of needles on every side. The following adventure with a Chinese burglar befel an acquaintance of mine. About midnight as he lay awake in bed, with the lamp extinguished and the windows open to admit the air, he saw a dark figure, silhouetted against the sky, clamber over his window rail and enter the apartment. He lay motionless, till the intruder, believing all to be safe, had reached the centre of the room, and then sprang out of bed and seized him; both were powerful men, and a furious struggle ensued, but the robber had the advantage, for his only covering was a coat of oil, so that at last, slipping like an eel from the grasp of his antagonist, he made a plunge at the window and was about to drop over, when his pursuer caught him by the queue. The tail, stuck full of need-les, and alas! a false one too, came away, and was left a worthless trophy in the hands of the European.

The Chinese guilds have been a fruitful source of trouble to the government of the Straits Settlements, but I believe that they are now well under control.

One element which operates successfully in maintaining order in China is the superstitious reverence which the Chinese have for their parents. Should a son commit a crime and abscond, his parents are liable to be punished in his stead. This law, even supposing it were put in force in a foreign land, would not affect the immigrants, as they seldom bring their wives or parents with them; and to this fact alone—that is, the absence of the strong family ties held so sacred by the race—we may attribute much of the difficulty encountered by our own author-ities in dealing with the crime and vice of this section of the population. A few of the Chinese immigrants marry native women, but the majority remain bachelors. If any one perchance is unable to realise the hope of returning to his native village, if he should die on foreign soil, his friends expend the savings of the deceased in sending his body back to mingle with the dust of his forefathers in China. Thus we find a steady stream of the living and the dead passing to and fro between the Straits Settlements and the southern provinces of China.

The foregoing presents a somewhat sombre sketch of the Chinaman abroad, but it portrays some of the worst phases of his character, and applies most particularly to the "mauvais sujets" who have left their country for their country's good, and some of them, embracing the opportunities afforded for engaging in honest and remunerative labour, depart from their evil ways and become useful members of the community. On

the other hand, there is a large and ever increasing body of
patient, orderly and industrious labourers flowing southwards from
the parent source, who meet with every inducement to settle
in the undeveloped regions of Borneo, Sumatra and the Malayan
Peninsula; these men not only engage in tillage, but are the
most successful traders in the East. The mercantile section
have established for themselves connections in almost all the
islands to which our foreign commodities are carried; their
agents reside in Sumatra, Java, Borneo and on the Indo-Chinese
mainland, collecting produce by barter with the natives, to
whom they are not infrequently related by social, as well as
commercial ties. In this way much of the produce shipped
from the East passes through the hands of Chinese middlemen,
or they forward it direct to their agents in Europe and America.
The great majority of the Chinese who emigrate to the Straits
Settlements are natives of the island of Hainan, or of the Kwang-
tang or Fukien provinces. Should they intermarry with the
Malays, the children of such parents assume the dress and
acquire the language of the father in addition to an English
education in the Government schools. They also obtain commercial
training under the compradors employed by European firms to
deal directly with the natives in buying and selling produce,
and the result of this is that a large percentage of the direct
trade has passed into the hands of the Chinese. They have
indeed adopted the philosophy of Bacon, which differs from that
of Plato and Confucius, its sole aim being "to provide man
with what he requires while he continues to be man," while
that of the Platonic and Chinese philosophy was "to raise us
far above vulgar wants." The aim of the Baconian philosophy
was "to supply our vulgar wants," and this is the business to
which the immigrant from Cathay devotes his energies, when

freed from the guidance of his sages, "which began in words
and ended in words." [1]

Having touched lightly on some points of character in the
Chinese as one finds them abroad, I will now proceed to pass
them in review as I saw them on their native soil in Hongkong.
This spot, moored to our little island by an electric cable that
sweeps half round the globe, rises like a political beacon out of
the China Sea, and has by no means been without its influence
in preventing the Tartar dynasty from foundering, in maintaining
peace and casting the light of a higher civilisation over some
dark corners of the Flowery Land. It stands alone on the
fringe of the great continent of Asia, with its mixed population,
its British rule, its noble European edifices and Chinese streets,
its Christian Churches and Buddhist Temples, a Crown Colony
of which we have no reason to be ashamed. The geographical
position of the island, its climate, its mineral and material products are so well known as to require no comment at my hands,
but its native population present some curious phases of life
and character, and with these I propose to deal. On its hospitable shores we again find the Chinaman free to follow the
lucrative channels of commerce and of labour. His industry, his
thrift and his placid contentment with his surroundings cannot
fail to impress the most casual observer. The city of Victoria
with its solid granite buildings, its magnificent esplanade and
palatial residences are the handiwork of this much maligned
alien; by his labour the island rocks have been hewn and fashi-
oned and reared into a city that has no equal in Eastern Asia.
The initiative lay with the Government, with the British architects
and designers, but the practical details and solid work are

[1] Macaulay, vol. I, page 399.

The Kwangtung Slipper-Boat.

Chinese. Since 1843 when we hoisted our flag, the progress of
the colony has experienced no serious check, and the native
population, despite local disturbances caused by the influx of
the scum of Chinese cities, has contributed in no small degree
to its general prosperity. The natives, the best of whom still
cling to their old superstitions, are in the mid-stage of evolution;
their inborn prejudice against up-to-date foreign methods of
dealing with crime and insubordination, and the not infrequent
waves of zymotic disease, such as cholera and the black plague,
rouse them to most determined resistance. They stubbornly
refuse sanitation as a body, or as individuals. But of this we
have examples much nearer home, in the centres of congested
population in our large towns. The low-lying quarters of Hongkong, where the poorest and most depraved class of Chinese
reside, present the most favourable conditions for the growth of
zymotic disease, especially during the hot months of the year.
Poverty, insufficient and unwholesome food, a humid atmosphere
and temperature over 90 deg. in the shade, account in a great
measure for the frequent visits of cholera and the black plague.
These scourges of unsanitary humanity invariably limit their
ravages to such localities as I have indicated, while the wealthier
and more cleanly localities are free from the disease. Under
these circumstances it is surprising to find, even among the
educated Chinese, a rooted objection to our modern methods
of sanitation and our treatment of disease; they regard the
drastic operations enforced as utterly barbarous and quite unsuited to a cultured, if not cleanly people. There are of course
many notable exceptions among the old resident natives, who
have learned wisdom by experience, and who have aided the
Government in dealing with their unruly countrymen. Many of
the unlettered natives have a notion that England is a small

settlement on the borders of China, and that we as a people are wholly engaged in commerce with that Empire, and that Hongkong represents our greatest possession. The floating population must not be overlooked. There are in Hongkong waters many thousands of such people, who make their homes in their boats, and earn their subsistence by fishing, or attending upon the ships in the harbour. These folk carefully study the indications of the weather, and can calculate with great shrewdness the near approach of a storm; they usually verify their own observations by ascertaining the barometrical changes from foreign ship-captains in port, and when they have settled in their own mind that a typhoon is at hand, they cross the harbour *en masse*, and shelter in the bays of Kowloon until the fury of the hurricane is past. The men in the boats are naked to the waist and bronzed with constant exposure, but the women are decently clothed and are pretty and attractive-looking. Some of them, if we may judge by their pale skins, their finely formed features and their large lustrous eyes are not of purely Chinese blood.

The sedan chair, in use all over China by the official classes, was the favourite mode of conveyance in Hongkong, and afforded remuneration to a large number of stalwart coolies. This has been replaced by the jimricksha from Japan, a hand-cart on wheels with a man motor between the shafts. The change is not without significance, as the Japanese are destined by modes less gentle, if all the more sure, to drive their neighbours over paths of progress hitherto unexplored. I may here note that in a former work I made a fairly accurate forecast of the recent conflict between the Empires of China and Japan and its issue. The jimricksha men, who take the place of our cab-drivers, make it their study to find out the habits of European residents,

CANTON BOAT-GIRL.

CHAU-CHOW-FU FEMALE.

so that a new-comer only requires to be about a week in the place, and it is ten chances to one, should he dine out and hail the first vehicle to take him home, the coolie, without a word spoken on either side will land him at his domicile. Nay, more, they have learned something of his personal character, and whether they ought to trust him and accept the paper which he offers. It is customary in most transactions with the Chinese to pay them with an order on the Schrof, or Chinese cash-keeper, of the house to which one belongs, and the Schrof in honouring these cheques, whenever he has the opportunity, will discharge the debt in light dollars and charge full weight to his employer's account. This is the first sample of the system-atic squeezing and overreaching process which is the keynote of Chinese society over the whole land. The system is as minute as it is perfect in its ramifications.

Chinese shopkeepers are a class apart, and vie with each other in their display of costly wares, Canton silks, carved ivory, jewellery, porcelain and paintings. Entering a Cantonese shop, one is welcomed by the proprietor himself, a Kwang-tung gentle-man speaking English; his attire is a jacket of Shan-tung silk, dark crape breeches, white leggings and velvet embroidered shoes, and he displays all the ponderosity and ease of a pros-perous Chinaman. His assistants are dressed with equal care and stand behind ebony counters and glass cases, the latter of spotless polish and filled with curiosities. One side of the shop is occupied by rolls of silk and samples of grass matting, all labelled and priced; the floor above is taken up with a cleverly arranged assortment of bronzes, porcelain, ebony furniture and lacquered ware. These men, as a rule, are fine specimens of their race, generally fair in their dealings, and will supply the cheapest toy with as great politeness as if receiving an order for a ship-load of embroidered silks. In the market-place in the Chinese quarter the chief business of the day is concluded by about seven in the morning. Here the avenues are rendered picturesque by painted and gilded sign-boards, inscribed with Chinese or English characters, though the dealers are all of them Chinamen. Thus, Ah-Yet, Sam-Ching, Canton Tom and Cheap Jack announce that as ship compradors, they are prepared to supply poultry, beef, vegetables and groceries of the best quality at the lowest rates, and solicit a trial, or at least an inspection of their stalls. Such men keep monthly market-books for their customers, and these with each item supplied and price jotted down, are settled at the end of each month. Apart from the well-fitted shops of these useful members of society there are stalls which supply special commodities, preserved European provisions, fruit, fish and so forth. Perhaps the most interesting of these is the fishmonger's, whose establishment consists of a number of tanks or aquaria, filled with clear running water and teeming with living sea or river fish, for the most part reared in the Canton fish-breeding ponds and brought to market in water-boats. The purchaser stands over the tank, selects some finny occupant which he fancies, and this is at once caught and supplied to him. The fish are of great variety and beauty, as may be gathered from an inspection of Mr. Reeves' collection in the British Museum. Then at the butchers' stalls sundry delicacies are met with, unknown to the European palate, and in which the natives delight; rats strung up by their tails, temptingly plump, and festoons of living frogs, fattened for the epicure. Here and there one may see small ribs and legs, undoubtedly canine; these are exceptional and are more commonly exposed for sale in purely Chinese cities. As a rule the Chinese are not par-

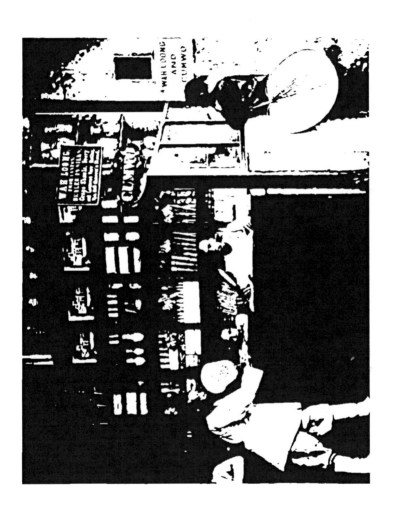

ticular as to the kind of food they eat, but they are cleanly in their modes of preparing it, and we might well learn some valuable lessons from them in this branch of domestic economy; thus they are skilled in making palatable and nutritious dishes out of odds and ends, and are far less wasteful and extravagant in the use of their food than we are. A number of the best European vegetables are sold in the Hongkong market; beef, mutton, fowls, eggs, fish and game are also to be procured at prices which seldom exceed what we pay for the same commodities at home. Besides, there are about fifty different kinds of fruit, nearly half of them indigenous and peculiar to China.

Following the main thoroughfare, one notes the display of sign-boards, each one glowing in bold Roman letters with the style and title of some Chinese artist, such as "Chin-Sing, portrait painter", "Afong", "Ating" and many others, which make up the list of the painters and photographers of Hongkong. Some of the specimens of photographic art displayed in doorways are fairly good, while others are the most hideous caricatures of the human face that it is possible for the camera to produce. A Chinaman will not suffer himself to be posed so as to produce a profile or three-quarter face, his reason being that the portrait must show him to possess two eyes and two ears and that his round face is perfect as a full moon. The same observance of symmetry is carried out in the entire pose of the figure; the face too must be as nearly as possible devoid of shadow, or if there be any shadow at all, it must be equal on both sides. Shadow they say should not exist, it is an accident of nature and therefore should not be portrayed, as it does not represent any feature of the face; and yet they all of them carry fans in order to secure that very shade so essential to existence in the south of China. They fail to recognise

that, in conjunction with light, they are indebted to shade for
the visible appearance of all things animate and inanimate which
make up the Chinese Empire. These desultory notes would be
incomplete were I to omit an account of the portrait and miniature painters of the Colony. They have no Academy or periodical exhibitions, in which one may inspect their work, it is
therefore necessary to visit the studios. The walls of Ating's
atelier are adorned with paintings in oil, and at one extremity
of the apartment a number of artists are at work, producing
large coloured pictures from small imperfect photographs. The
proprietor has an assistant, whose business it is to scour the
ships in port in search of patrons among the foreign crews.
Jack desirous of carrying home a souvenir of his visit to the
wonderful land of pigtails and tea, supplies a photograph of Poll
or Susan, and orders a large copy to be executed in oils. The
whole to be finished, framed and delivered in two days, and is
not to exceed the contract price of four dollars, or about one
pound sterling of our money. The work in this painting-shop,
like many things Chinese, is so divided as to afford the maxi-
mum of profit for the minimum of labour. Thus one artist
sketches, another paints the face, a third does the hands, and
a fourth fills in the costume and accessories. Susan is placed
on the limner's easel and is covered with a glass bearing the
lines and squares which solve the problem of proportion in the
large work. A strange being the artist looks, he has just roused
himself from a long sleep, and his clothes are redolent of the
fumes of opium ; he peers through his large spectacles into
poor Susan's black eyes, and measures out her fair proportions
as he transfers them to the canvas,—then she is passed from
hand to hand, until at last every detail has been produced with
pre-Raphaelite exactitude, and a glow of colour added to the

A VENERABLE STUDENT.

CHINESE ARTIST.

whole far surpassing nature. But let us examine the finished
picture. The dress is sky blue, flounced with green; chains of
the brightest gold adorn the neck, there are bracelets on the
arms and rings on the fingers, gleaming with gems. The hair
is pitchy black, the skin pearly white, the cheeks of vermilion
and the lips of carmine; as for the dress, it shows neither spot
nor wrinkle, and is as taught, her lover would say, as the
carved robes of a figure-head. Jack proudly hangs the picture
above his bunk, but still, at times, he has his grave misgivings
about the small hands and feet and about the rainbow-hued
sailor's goddess into which Susan has been transformed. Ating's
miniature work on ivory is conducted on the same co-operative
and commercial lines, and is decidedly better than when the
copies are enlarged. The paintings are always minute, but
during my stay in the Colony I fell in with only one man who
could venture with any success beyond a mere servile imitation
of a photograph. He was a sort of genius in his way, and at
the same time a most inveterate opium smoker; when I first
knew him, he was a good-looking dandy, in full work as a
miniature painter, fond of good company and high living, a
frequenter of music-halls and the gambling clubs of Victoria.
He first smoked opium in moderation, but this habit gained
upon him to such an extent, that when the hour for the pipe
came on, no matter where he was, he had to rush off and
abandon himself to the use of the drug, which soon brought
him to his grave.

The lower quarter of the town to which I have alluded, em-
braces "Tai Ping Shan", or the Hill of Great Peace. The
name is a fine one, but a fine name will not hide the sins
of the place; it is inhabited almost wholly by Chinamen; as
for the women, they are numerous enough, but of the lowest

type. There are strange hotels in this quarter, besides music-halls and lodging-houses, the haunts of vagabonds known to the police. I once accompanied an inspector of police on one of his periodical rounds through this region of darkness, and I should shrink from describing everything I saw there; but it proved to me that all that has been alleged of the immorality of this section of the native population is perfectly true. On the other hand, the more respectable part of the community had there many places of rational amusement, with which one could find no fault whatever. Among the largest music-halls, one may serve as a type of the great majority of the others. At the entrance there stood an altar, crowned with votive offerings dedicated to the god of pleasure, whose image surmounted the shrine. To the right and left of this hung scrolls, on which high moral precepts were inscribed, sadly at variance with the real character of the place. Half a dozen of the most fascinating of the female singers were seated outside the gate; their robes were of richly embroidered silk, their faces were enamelled, and their hair bedecked with perfumed flowers and dressed, in some cases, to represent a teapot, in others, a bird with spread wings on the top of the head. On the ground floor all the available space was taken up with rows of narrow compartments, each one furnished with an opium couch and all the appliances for the use of the drug. Here were girls in constant attendance, some ready to prepare and charge the bowl with opium, and others to strum upon the lute and sing sweet melodies to waft the sleeper off into dreamland, under the strangely fascinating influences which, ere long, will make him wholly their slave. On the first floor, reached by a flight of steps, there is a deserted music-room showing traces of the revel of the preceding night, in faded garlands which still

CHINESE HOUSES, HONGKONG.

festooned its carved and gilded ceiling. There were two more stories to the edifice, both of them partitioned off in the same way as the ground floor. At another house we visited we found a goodly company in the music-saloon; the interior had been freshly decked with flowers, festooned from the ceiling, or suspended in baskets made of wattled twigs, while mirrors, paint, gilding and all the skill of Kwang-tung art had been lavishly bestowed on the more permanent wall decorations. At a table spread with fruits and delicacies, sat a merry throng of Chinamen, young, middle-aged and old; hot wine in bright pewter pots was passing freely round the board, and the revellers were pledging each other in small cups of the steaming draught. We had dropped in upon a dinner-party, where, under the influence of native wine, melon seeds and pretty women, the guests were engaged in a noisy, but at the same time friendly, contest in the art of versification. Behind each guest, as is customary at such gatherings, a young girl sat; many of them might fairly claim to be called handsome, while all were prettily dressed in the fashionable silks of Canton; their hair was wreathed with flowers, and their faces painted until they resembled their native porcelain ware. An old Chinese merchant present, whom I knew, informed me that these women were all highly respectable. That might be the case; at any rate, he assured me that they were not infrequently carried off by the visitors and raised to the rank of second wives or concubines. Music was being performed in the four corners of the room by four independent female bands, each accompanying the shrill piping voice of an old woman, who sang the adventures of a hero of romance, a personage famous alike for his prowess and his ardent and amorous heart.

3

CHAPTER III.

Gambling—Typhoons—The Floating Population of Hongkong—North Branch of the Pearl River.

GAMBLING is a phase of Oriental vice to which the Chinese are peculiarly addicted, and was at one time farmed by the Government, but the ordinance was eventually suppressed. The licensing system, during its short career, contributed about 14,000 dollars a month to the Treasury; and judging from local statistics, naturally aided in the suppression of crime. It was, besides, supposed to maintain a higher moral tone among the native police, who, when secret gambling-houses flourish, are seduced continually by bribes into dereliction of duty and corruption. One of the difficulties in carrying out the plan was the conscientious scruple, which, apparently, even affected the promoters of the measure, as to the application of a constantly accumulating fund derived from a source so polluted. It was even suggested to drop it silently into the sea and have done with it. All I would say is, if the policy of sheltering this particular vice, in order to effect a diminution of crime in the Colony, was sound, the proceeds of the gambling-farm might have been worthily employed in rendering the police-force

Street Gambling.

st ill more efficient, and in lightening the burden of taxation borne by the colonists. But, as I have no desire to criticise government measures, I will simply state that, on the same lines, the policy adopted of bringing disorderly houses under the direct supervision of the government by licensing, had also to be abandoned, although the results, as far as statistics show, proved the wisdom of the measure.

During the time when gambling-houses were under supervision, they became the open resort of most respectable-looking Chinese; patterns one would suppose of native virtue. It took me by surprise, when visiting a gaming-house, to find one or two native shopkeepers, otherwise noted for respectability, busily engrossed at the table. The room in which I found them was nearly square, and the ceiling had been pierced with an opening leading to the next floor or gallery. This gallery was filled with a silent party of players, some of whom were bending over, looking down upon a long table spread before us. A close-shaven, placid Chinaman on the right of the table acted as banker, and before him an orderly array of coins and bank-notes were spread out on the table. It was surprising to note the speed with which he reckoned up the winnings and interest on the smallest sums, deducting a seven-per-cent commission from the gains of every transaction; behind him an assistant weighed the dollars, broken silver and jewellery of the players, then at his side was the book-keeper, and on the left the teller. On the centre of the table lay a square pewter slab crossed with diagonal lines, and the sections thus formed bore the numbers, one, two, three and four respectively. The player was at liberty to stake on any of these numbers, when, unless he ventured on two numbers separately and at once, he would have three to one against him, plus seven per cent on his winnings should he succeed. Some men spend the entire day in the house, and on starting, open an account with the bank, which is kept carefully posted on a pewter slab before them, and balanced at the close of the day. When the stakes are made, some are dropped from the upper gallery in a small basket attached to a cord. The teller, who conducted the vital part of the business, sat there serene and stolid, closely watched in spite of his seeming probity and honour. His sleeves were short, nearly up to his arm-pits; before him, on the table, lay a pile of polished cash, from this he took a handful, placed it on a clear space and covered it with a brass cup. After the stakes were made, the cup was removed, and the teller proceeded with the extreme end of an ivory wand to pick out the cash in fours, the remaining number being that which wins. Before the pile is half counted, provided there are no split coins or trickery in the game, a habitual player can always tell, with puzzling accuracy, what the remainder will be, and at this stage of the game one observes a striking peculiarity in the Chinese character. There are no passionate exclamations, no noisy excitement, no outbursts of delight, no deep cursing of adverse fate. It is only in the faces of the players one can see the signs of emotion, or the sullen determination to carry on at all hazards, until Fortune smiles once more, or leaves them beggared at the board.

Native gambling is not confined to gaming-houses, it is carried on in clubs and private abodes, in the highways and at the corners of streets by labourers in their leisure moments; even children will form a ring round a vendor of sweets and stake their cash in the attempt to win a double share of his condiments. Lotteries are also in great vogue in China at all times; for these, tickets are sold on which a series of numbers are engrossed; the purchaser pays his cent and marks ten of

Pepohoan Woman, Formosa.

Cantonese Girl.

the numbers, those which by some secret process of his own he selects as the lucky set. The marked ticket is then paid in, and the holder receives a duplicate marked in the same way. On the day of drawing, the numbers are supposed to be dealt with by a mystic being or spirit, whose abode is darkness; he who holds three of the winning numbers gets back his money in full, and he who holds the ten numbers gets back six thousand times his stake. This banker not unfrequently pockets fifty per cent as his profit for managing the lottery. Although gambling is a popular Chinese vice, it does not, so far as I am aware, meet with recognition from the Chinese Government, and this is all the more astonishing as it might be made to contribute largely to the Imperial revenue.

I have already noticed the floating population of Hongkong, a community which suffers great loss during the storms or typhoons common to the region. I had long been anxious to witness a typhoon, and I had my wish gratified on more than one occasion. The force of the wind at such times is more than I thought possible. It whirls ships helplessly adrift from their moorings, and I have seen them emerge from the storm with canvas torn to shreds, spars carried away, and masts broken off nearly flush with the deck. In Hongkong, the wind, with a sudden blast, has riven roofs from houses and blown them far inland, and has sent solid brick corners and projecting verandahs flying across the streets. Once while the tempest was at its height, I ventured down to the Praya, in time to see the crowd of Chinese boats and sailing craft that had been blown inshore and piled up in a mass of wreck below the city, at the western end of the beach. One or two intrepid foreigners had been there and had rescued a large number of the natives, but many more had gone down with their boats. The sky was dark and leaden, and there were moments when the wind abated only to gather fresh violence, catching up the crested waves and sending them in long white streaks of vapour across the scene, through which dismantled ships were dimly descried, drifting from their moorings, and steamers with steam up, ready for any emergency. Blinded by the waves as they leapt over the road and dashed against the houses, and lying forward on the wind, I at length reached the east end of the Praya, joining a number of foreigners who were attempting to rescue two women from a small Chinese boat. These women, seemingly greatly exhausted, were putting forth their last efforts to keep their tiny vessel in position and to prevent it from being dashed to pieces against the dislodged, jagged blocks of the Praya wall. Advantage was taken of a slight lull to fire off line-rockets, but these were driven back like feathers, against the houses; then long-boats were dragged to the pier, but the first was wrecked in launching, the second met with a like fate and its gallant crew were pitched into the sea. Every effort proved abortive, and as darkness set in the poor women were reluctantly left to their fate.

The Chinese as I found them at home, under their own paternal Government, proved in some material respects different from their fellow-countrymen abroad. The large majority are engaged in manual labour of some sort, chiefly tillage, not because of its lucrative nature, but because Mother Earth was the only friend they could trust to yield them subsistence for labour. Their rulers, represented to them by the nearest Mandarin and his crafty Yamen-runners, collectors of revenue, legitimate and otherwise, could be trusted only to gather their spoil. They were the far-reaching antennæ of the Government, trained to a degree of scientific nicety to leave blood enough in the body of

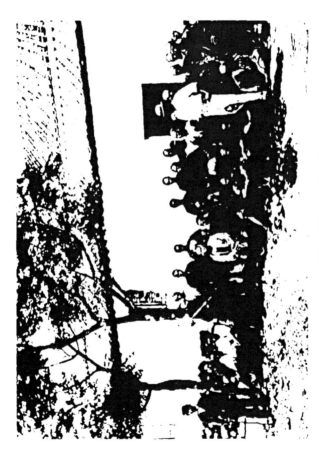

Group of Chinese Labourers, Hong Kong.

the patient husbandman, to enable him to continue his toil without fainting, to supply his own modest wants and to fill the local treasury. But some seasons the crops fail, and the farmers having no resource whatever, perish in multitudes, of famine and disease. In some of the Western provinces, the people, noted for their independence, resist extortion by the ruling classes and live in comfort and even affluence. This limitation also applies to the merchants at the ports open to foreign trade ; many of them amass wealth and enjoy the protection of the local authorities, who, some of them, have money profitably invested in native commercial enterprises. The bulk of the officials, however, while they view commerce with contempt, do not scruple to levy extortionate exactions on trade, and to accept bribes to condone offences against the law, even to the extent of permitting a criminal to procure a substitute to suffer capital punishment in his stead. [1]

My first excursion into China proper was an ascent of the north branch of the Pearl river of Kwang-tung, accompanied by three Hongkong residents. This northern affluent joins the main stream at a point called "San Shui," or Three Waters, lying above Canton, about forty miles inland. To reach it we must pass through the Fatshan Creek, where Commodore Keppel fought his famous action in 1857. The town of Fatshan exceeds a mile in length; the Creek passes right through its centre, and it is the nucleus of the great manufacturing districts of Southern China. Cutlery and hardware are the two chief industries, hence it is said to be the Sheffield of Cathay. It appeared strange to me after examining the native wares, that similar articles of superior English make had done so little to supplant the industry of the

[1] Meadow's Notes on China.

Fatshan factories. This is partly caused by the cheapness of Chinese labour and the suitableness of the articles manufactured to local popular requirements. Chinese scissors, for example, are quite different from those in use with us, and if we were to attempt to cut with them, we should be apt to tear the cloth. In the hands of a native tailor they are made to work wonders, and indeed use has taught the latter to prefer them to our own. The iron used in this district is mainly imported from abroad, although it is said that ore abounds in the Ying-ping district of the province, of a quality so good as to yield 70 per cent of the metal. [1]

But the "Feng-shui" superstitious dread of natives, fostered by the Mandarins, to opening mines is gradually giving way before the pressure of foreign intercourse and a practical popular awakening to a knowledge of the wealth stored up in the land. Contiguous to the iron deposits are also coal-beds of un-known extent and value. So long, however, as "Feng-shui" and Government opposition hold their sway, mines are certain never to be opened up. Some progress has been made in this direction; the coal mines of Kaiping, eighty miles north-east of Tientsin, are worked with European machinery, and connected by a railroad with the Peh-tang river, twenty-one miles distant. As we pass through the city we notice numerous edifices sub-stantially built of brick, the residences of native merchants, temples with a sculptured granite façade, and a large customs station; but the houses in the suburbs which border the creek are raised above the water, on piles, and their temporary, miserable appearance is in striking contrast to the abodes and evidences of wealth which we encounter in the heart of the town. The Creek

[1] China Review, 1873, p. 337.

CHINESE SAWYERS.

CHINESE PEDLAR.

is the principal thoroughfare, and is crowded with thousands of junks and boats, all busily engaged in loading or discharging cargo, or else in bearing passengers to and fro along the extremely narrow channel which winds its way through this floating Babel where endless discord reigns. This creek is evidently much too contracted for the traffic of the place; and I can readily imagine how, forty years ago, the Chinese squadron, fleeing before a handful of British tars in their small boats, drew up like a wall across this narrow passage, and poured a hail-storm of shot upon their gallant assailants, spreading death and destruction among the little band. As for the Commodore, with his boat shot away from under him, "with his coxswain killed, and every man of his crew wounded, [1] he retired to await reinforcements, and returned at last from a severe attack, with five of the largest junks in tow." The Chinese themselves, who are by no means destitute of courage, are said honestly to have acknowledged their admiration for the pluck and daring of the man who started with seven small boats to capture Fatshan and its 200,000 inhabitants, and who destroyed their entire fleet—the terror, as was supposed, of the "foreign fire-eating devils," who were held never before this to have fought a fair fight; but to be always taking their foes in the rear of 'their forts, instead of bravely coming to the front and taking the guns which had been set up with so much pains for the very purpose of receiving their assaults.

Whenever a block-up among the boats in the creek takes place—which happens frequently, and is protracted indefinitely for a long period of time—one has leisure to notice the numerous floating tea and music saloons, and many flower barges

[1] China, p. 35.—G. Wingrove Cooke.

moored close against the banks. These boats carry elevated
cabins on their decks, and are very prettily carved, painted,
gilded and decorated throughout. The windows and doors are
curtained with silk; and through one of these, which stood
conveniently open, we could discern gaily-dressed young dandies,
and even elder Sybarites, flirting with gaudily painted girls, who
waited upon them with silver pipes or Chinese hookahs, or
served up cups of tea. There were pleasure boats, too, fitted
up with private cabins, in which families were being conveyed
into the country to enjoy a glimpse of the green rice-fields and
orchards.

At San-shui we entered the north river, passing into a picturesque district, in some places not unlike the Scottish lowlands,
covered with ripening fields of barley. Halting not far from
the town of Lo'pau, at Wong-Tong village, on the right bank
of the stream, I prepared to take a photograph, and my intention was to include a group of old women who were gossiping
and drawing water; but when they saw my instrument pointed
towards their hamlet, they fled in alarm, and spread abroad the
report that the foreigners had returned and were preparing to
bombard the settlement. A deputation soon set out from the
village, led by a venerable Chinaman, the head man of the clan,
and to him we explained that we had come on no hostile errand,
but only to take a picture of the place. He gave us a hearty
welcome to his house, spreading tea and cake before us. This
was one of those many instances of a simple, genuine hospitality
which I experienced all over the land; and I feel assured that
any foreigner knowing enough of the language to make his immediate wants understood, and endowed with a reasonable, even
temper, would encounter little opposition in travelling over the
greater part of China. But there is always a certain amount of

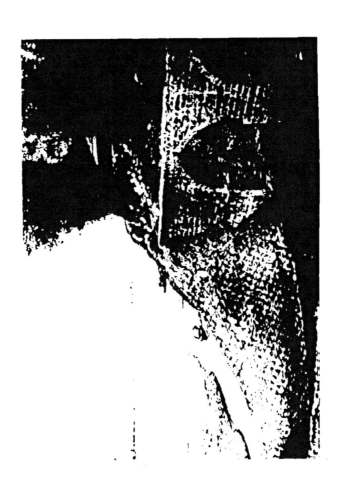

danger in the larger and more populous cities. We offered one or two small silver coins to the children of the house, but the old gentleman would not permit them to be accepted, until it had been carefully explained to him that they were simple gifts to be worn as charms, and not intended as a recompense for his hospitality.

On the bank of the river in the Tsing-yune district, I narrowly escaped sinking into a quicksand. We spent a night before Tsing-yune city, but were kept awake by the noise of gongs and crackers, by the odour of joss-sticks, and by the smoke of cooking from the adjoining boats. At length we reached the Buddhist monastery of Fi-lai-sz, perhaps the most picturesque, and one of the most famous of its kind to be seen in the south of China. The building is approached from the brink of the river by a flight of broad granite steps; this conducts us to an outer gate, whereon is inscribed in characters of gold, "Hioh Shan Miau." The monastery has been built on a richly wooded hill-side, and half way up to it, on the verge of a mossy dell, we reach the Fi-lai-sz shrine. Three idols stand within this shrine, one of them representing, or supposed to represent, the pious founder. A favourite resting-place this for travellers, one where they are hospitably entertained, and where the monks, with impious sympathy for human weakness, supply their guests with opium, and sell carved sticks, cut from the sacred temple groves, as parting relics of their visit.

The Tsing-yune pass, in which the monastery lies, is in great repute as a burial-ground. There, thousands of graves front the river and stud the hill-slopes to a height of about 800 feet. To every grave there is a neat facing of stone, something in the form of a horse-shoe, or like an easy chair with a rounded back. The interior of the temple cloister is paved with granite and decorated with flowers set out in vases and ornamental pots; thus art lent its aid to a scene of natural loveliness, the most romantic and beautiful. On the opposite bank of the stream a narrow path leads to a wooded ravine, whither the monks retire when they ought to abstract themselves from the world, forgetting existence, with its pleasures and sorrows, and cultivating that supreme repose which will bring them nearer Nirvana. It seemed to me, when I inspected the cell-like chambers of these devotees, that some among them were not unfamiliar with the fumes of the opium-pipe, and that they must, poor frail mortals! at times endeavour to float away to the western heavens steeped in the incense of that enslaving drug.

We next halted at a village called Lien-Chow-Kwong. It was a miserable specimen of its kind, planted in a desolate neighbourhood, and with an air of poverty and destitution pervading both it and its inhabitants. The passes in this river present some bold rock and hill scenery, while the short reaches and sudden bends of the stream remind one of Highland lochs. In other places the hills slope gently downwards towards the water, and terminate in a bank of glittering sand, not unfrequently a mile broad. These sand-banks glare like miniature deserts beneath the blazing mid-day sun, but are happy in the association of a refreshing stream which flows clear and cool along the margin. The Mang-Tsz-Hap, or Blind Man's Pass, is one of the finest on the river. Here the bold crags shoot up in precipices that are lost in shreds of drifting mist, as if the heavy clouds, sweeping across jagged pinnacles of rock, were riven into a hundred vapoury fragments. The weather was now cold and stormy, but fitful gleams of sunshine broke in upon the darkness. Once, caught in a rapid by a sudden gust of wind, our boat seemed like to have been shattered in the breakers;

but her crew in a twinkling slipped the tracking line, and she
drifted safely down mid-stream.

The Chinese get the credit of being exceedingly temperate,
and in the majority of cases this is true; but at the same time,
among the lower orders, especially the boating population, tem-
perance is only observed because sheer necessity compels re-
straint; and many of the boatmen on the rivers along which I
have travelled will drink sam-shu to excess during the cold
weather, whenever they can win a few extra cash. These men
are about as poor and miserable a class as one can meet in
the most poverty-stricken districts of the land. In the southern
provinces their sole food is steamed rice, flavoured with salt,
or rendered more savoury with a fragment of salt fish; and
when times are good, they even indulge in the luxury of a
little bit of pork fat. It is surprising how they stand the cold,
more especially in the northern regions, and how a drop of
spirits will send the warm blood tingling through their veins
and cause them to display a muscular power and a strength of
endurance not easily accounted for, when one considers the
simple nature of their food. Millions of these hardy sons of
toil live from hand to mouth, and are only kept from starving,
from piracy, and from rebellion by the cheapness of their staple
food, and by the constant demand for their labour. But there
are pirates to be found in this very river; our crew themselves
told us of it, and added, that for anything they knew to the
contrary, there might be a swarm of them in the boats among
which we moored at night.

At Ying-Tek city I fell in with a spectacle which fully
affirmed this assertion, and at the same time produced in me
a sensation of horror that it will be impossible ever to forget.
Ying-Tek stands on the right bank of the stream; beneath

its outer wall there stretches a bank of reeking filth and garbage, which at mid-day must pollute the air for miles round.
We picked our way over slimy, treacherous paths and across
putrid-looking pools, till we passed through the gateway into
the main street of the town. It was an exceedingly narrow
thoroughfare, and had at one time been paved, but the pavement was now broken and disordered; while, as to the people,
they looked sickly, sullen and dispirited. But it was in the
market-place that we beheld the most shocking sight of all :—
there the bodies of two men were exposed to the public gaze,
their position indicated by swarms of flies, and the air telling
that decomposition had already set in. One of these male-
factors had been starved to death in the cage in which he
stood, and the other had been crucified.

Beyond the rapids of this part of the river we reach vast
cultivated plains, out of which isolated limestone rocks and
parallel ranges of mountains rise up in shapes most fantastic,
and disorder most picturesque. It was from a hill above the
Polo-hang temple that we obtained the finest views of the
country. The cultivation hereabouts was of a kind I had never
seen before; in the foreground were a multitude of fields,
banked off for the purposes of irrigation, but already shorn of
their crops; here and there was a mound covered with temples
and trees, and beyond, reaching to the base of the distant
mountains, were groves of green bamboo, rocking their plumage
to and fro in the wind, like the waves of an emerald sea.
The bamboo is reared in this and other districts, and forms a
valuable article of commerce, the wealth of a farmer being
frequently estimated by the number of clumps which he has
on his estate. It requires neither care nor tillage, and is a
source of wealth in this part of the country.

When looking on this scene my old Chinaman, Akum, came up. I do not think he has yet been introduced to my readers. He was a faithful servant, or boy, as they are here called, about forty years of age, who had been in my employment in Singapore, and afterwards turning trader, had lost his small capital. " Well," he said, " what are you looking at, Sir ?"— "At the beautiful view," I replied.—"Yes," he said; "I wish I had the smallest of those hills; I would settle there, on the top, watching my gardeners at work below, and when I saw one labourer more industrious than the rest I would reward him with a wife."

He spoke to me often afterwards about this ideal hill on which he hoped one day to sit and reward the virtue of his servants. He was a disciple of Confucius.

Hereafter I may say something as to the multitudinous uses to which the bamboo can be applied. There is good snipe and pheasant-shooting in this quarter.

We noticed quantities of the reeds employed for making Canton mats. Mats of this sort are manufactured extensively in three places—viz., Tun-kun, Lintan and Canton; they afford occupation to many thousand operatives, and are indeed an important industry of the province of Kwang-tung. About 112,000 rolls, measuring 40 yards apiece, are said to be annually exported from Canton.

About two hundred miles above Canton we visited the most remarkable object which we had encountered in the course of our journey. This is the celebrated grotto of Kwan-yin, the goddess of mercy, formed out of a natural cave in the foot of a limestone precipice which rears its head high above the stream. The mouth of the cavern opens on the water's edge, and the interior has been enlarged in some places by exca-

vation, and built up in others, so as to render it suitable for a
Buddhist shrine. A broad granite platform surmounted by a
flight of steps leads us into the upper chamber, and there the
goddess may be seen, seated on a huge lotus-flower; sculptured, so they tell us, by no human hands, and discovered *in
situ* within the cave. The priests placed implicit faith in the
story, but they could not be persuaded to believe that the
flower might be the fossil of a pre-historic lotus of monstrous
dimensions. Barbarians might credit such childish fables as that
flowers or fishes can be turned into stone, but not the
enlightened followers of Buddha. No; they say the lotus was
created in the cave for Kwan-yin to sit upon; there was no
getting over that.

According to their account this goddess of mercy has a
marvellous history. She first appeared on earth in the centre
of the world, that is China, as the daughter of a Chinaman
named "Shi-kin," and she was made visible to mortal eyes as
a child of the Emperor Miao-Chwang. The sovereign ordered
her to marry, and this she stedfastly refused to do, thus vio-
lating the native usages, whereupon the dutiful parent put her
remorselessly to death. But this measure, contrary to Miao-
Chwang's expectation, only caused his daughter to be promoted
into the proud position she now fills. Afterwards Kwan-yin
is said to have visited the infernal regions, where the presence
of such transcendent goodness and beauty produced an in-
stantaneous effect. The instruments of torture dropped from
the hands of the executioners, the guilty were liberated, and
hell was transformed into paradise itself. The goddess now
looks down with a benign expression from her seat upon the
lotus throne, but she seems to be urgently in need of repairs.

The priests who dwell within the cave, sit overlooking the

Buddhist Monks.

river from an opening in the upper face of the rock, which serves the purpose of a window. As we see them with the sun at their backs they appear like a row of badly preserved dolls, so motionless do they sit, and so unconscious, to all seeming, of the presence of foreigners. But when we confront them and display a bright coin, they wake up and manifest an unholy zeal to appropriate it.

The money is offered and accepted, and then a venerable member of the order shows us through the interior of the cave. A number of smaller idols, the attendants of Kwan-yin, are ranged along niches in the rock; a little lighted taper burns in front of each, while cups of sam-shu and votive offerings of food are spread out before them. A group of stalactites hangs in front of the window; above and around them hover a number of pure white doves, that descend at the call of the aged priest and feed out of his hand. It was interesting to notice the outstretched hand of the old man; it was withered, shrunken, and encumbered by a set of long yellow nails, that looked dead, and were already partly buried beneath the unwashed encrustation of a lifetime.

It is harvest-time, and the grain in many places is already cut, and has been piled up in farm-yards in stacks, to be thrashed with flails, or trodden beneath the heavy-footed ox. The season has been a plenteous one, and the farmers are full of joy, praising the god of agriculture for the abundance of this their second crop from a soil which has yielded produce during centuries of constantly recurring harvests. The Chinese are careful farmers, and were probably the first to understand that their land requires as much consideration as their oxen or their asses; that the substance which it gives up to a crop has to be replaced by manure, and that it requires a time of rest

4

after a season of labour, before it will yield its greatest increase. How the Chinese acquired this knowledge, and at what epoch, are questions which Confucius himself would probably have been puzzled to answer. There is no doubt that they succeed in raising green crops and grain alternately from their fields at least twice in the year. But this extraordinary fertility is due in part to the small size of their farms, which are, most of them, of so limited an area that the proprietors can cultivate them personally with unceasing care, and part also to the abundant use of manure in fashion among the peasants of China. We see evidence of the social economy of the people in a multitude of instances and a variety of ways. Thus, when the farmer is near a town he pays a small sum to certain houses for the privilege of daily removing their sewage to his own manure-pit. This sewage he uses, for the most part in a fluid state, often to fertilise poor waste lands which have been leased to him at a low rental. If his farm is some distance from villages or towns, he is careful to use every opportunity for securing cheap supplies of the manure which he so much needs, and accordingly erects small houses for the use of wayfarers, along the edge of his fields. His neighbour is equally careful to have houses of the same description; and they vie with each other in keeping them as clean and attractive-looking as possible.

I returned to Canton alone from San Shui, in a small boat, leaving my friends to find their own way leisurely back. At one place there were only a few inches of water above the bed of the stream, so I had to hire an open canoe, while my baggage was carried overland to the next bend of the river. In this canoe I descended, or rather raced, down to Fatshan, amid a number of similar craft whereon Chinese traders were embarked. The distance was about twenty-five miles. We contrived to reach the town about half an hour ahead of the rest, and passed at once down the narrow channel between the crowded boats. This was by far the most disagreeable experience of the journey. Attempting to land quietly and take a photograph of the tower, I was assailed on the bank by a mob of roughs, who drove me into the river, where I was taken into a boat by a couple of good-natured women, and by them rowed down stream till I could succeed in engaging a fast boat to convey me as far as Canton.

CHAPTER IV.

CANTON AND KWANG-TUNG PROVINCE.

Tea—Foreign Hongs and Houses—Schroffing.

CANTON and the Kwang-tung province, as my reader is doubt-less aware, continued for many years to be almost the only places in the vast Chinese Empire with which Europeans were acquainted. I need hardly do more here than refer those of my readers who take an interest in the obscured and chequered history of Canton, to an elaborate and interesting account, translated and published in China by Mr. Bowra, of the Imperial Customs. In this narrative it is stated that the first authentic notice of Kwang-tung province is found in the native writings of the Chow dynasty, B. C. 1122. The fifth century of our era is set down as the date at which Buddhist missionaries introduced their religious classics, and not only founded the sect which now predominates in the country, but led to the establishment of commercial relations between the Empires of India and China. Until recently, for the last two centuries foreign trade was confined to Canton, and nearly all

the knowledge of China possessed by Western nations was limited to that city and its neighbourhood. The foreign trade of Canton was one of sufferance, maintained by the aggressive perseverance of traders and their disregard of the repeated slights and indignities of the local authorities, who looked upon trade and traders with contempt and reported accordingly to the Government at Peking. But the Treaty of Tientsin placed the course of trade beyond the control and caprice of local Mandarins. The people are now allowed comparative freedom to indulge their trading inclinations. Although in some degree modified, the native prejudice against foreigners and their wares still flows in a deep undercurrent, which comes to the surface, conceal it as they may, in their contact with Europeans.

The city of Canton stands on the north bank of the Chukiang or Pearl river, about ninety miles inland, and is accessible at all seasons to vessels of the largest tonnage. Communication between the capital and the other parts of the province is afforded by the three branches which feed the Pearl river, and by a network of canals and creeks. A line of fine steamers plies between the city and Hongkong, and the submarine telegraph at the latter place, has thus brought the once distant Cathay into daily correspondence with the western world. It is a pleasant trip from Hongkong up the broad Pearl river; from the deck of the steamers one may view with comfort the ruins of the Bogue forts, and think of the time and feelings of Captain Weddell, who in 1637 anchored the first fleet of English merchant vessels before them. The Chinese cabin in the Canton steamer is an interesting sight, too. It is crowded with passengers every trip; and there they lie on the deck in all imaginable attitudes, some on mats, smoking opium, others on benches, fast asleep. There are little gambling parties in one corner,

and city merchants talking trade in another; and viewed from
the cabin-door the whole presents a wonderfully confused per-
spective of naked limbs, arms and heads, queues, fans, pipes,
and silk or cotton jackets. The owners of these miscellaneous
effects never dream of walking about, or enjoying the scenery
or sea-breeze. I only once noticed a party of Chinese passengers aroused to something bordering on excitement, and it was
in this Canton steamer. They had caught a countryman in an
attempt at robbery and determined to punish him in their own
way. When the steamer reached the wharf, they relieved the
delinquent of his clothing, bound it around his head, and tied
his hands behind his back with cords: and in this condition
sent him ashore to meet his friends, but not before they had
covered his nakedness with a coat of paint of various tints.

My readers will remember the celebrated Governor Yeh of
Canton, who was carried prisoner to Calcutta. He would almost
be forgotten in this quarter were it not for a temple erected to
his departed spirit. It may be seen on the bank of a suburban
creek; a very pretty monument it is to remind one of our
lively intercourse with the notorious Imperial commissioner in
1857, an intercourse marked by trouble and bloodshed throughout,
and which ended in the capture of that unfortunate official in
an obscure Yamen.

The Fatee gardens, so often described were still to be found,
almost unchanged, at the side of a narrow creek on the right
bank of the river. These gardens were nurseries for flowers,
dwarf shrubs and trees. Like most Chinese gardens they covered
only a small area, and were contrived to represent landscape
gardening in miniature. Some distance below the Fatee creek,
on the same side of the river, a number of Tea Hongs and
tea-firing establishments are to be found. To these I now

venture to introduce the reader, as he must needs feel more or less interest in the tea-men, and their mode of preparing this highly-prized luxury. Passing up the creek, along the usual narrow channel, between densely-packed rows of floating craft, we land on a broad stone platform, cross a court where men are to be seen weighing the tea, and enter a large three-storied brick building, where we meet Tan King Ching, the proprietor, to whom we bear an introduction from one of his foreign customers. One of the clerks is directed to show us over the place. He first ushers us into a large warehouse, where thousands of chests of the new crop are piled up, ready for inspection by the buyer. The inspection of this cargo is an exceedingly simple process ; the foreign tea-taster enters and places his mark on certain boxes in different parts of the pile and these are forthwith removed, weighed and scrutinised as fair samples of the bulk. The whole cargo is shipped without further ceremony should the parcels examined prove satisfactory ones ; and, indeed, nowadays it seldom happens that shortcomings in weight and quality are at the last moment detected, for the better class of Chinese merchants are remarkable for their honesty and fair dealing. I am the more anxious thus to do justice to the Chinese dealers, because the notion has got abroad that, as a rule, they are the most notorious cheats ; men who never fail to overreach the unsuspecting trader when an opportunity occurs, and upon whose shoulders must fall the full weight of the charge of preparing and selling spurious or adulterated teas which have reached this country in a condition not fit for human food. It seems clear to me that the Chinese manufacturer of this sort of rubbish is by no means the most reprehensible party in the trade. He it is, indeed, who sets himself to collect from the servants of foreigners or natives, and from the restaurants and tea-saloons, the leaves that have been already used, and to dry them, cook them and mix them with imitations of the genuine leaf. This process completed, he next adds pickings, dust and sweepings from the tea-factory, and mixes the whole with foreign materials, so as to lend it a healthy surface hue. Lastly, he perfumes the lot with some sweet-smelling flower—the chlorantus, olea, aglaia and others; and thus provides a cheap, fragrant and polluted cup ·for the humble consumers abroad. This evil has been to a great extent cured by the competition which has sprung up in the cultivation of tea. China still holds a market in the finer sorts of tea, but her trade has greatly fallen as a whole, and is threatened with extinction unless, by improved methods of culture and preparation, she can rival the cost and quality of the full-flavoured leaf of India and Ceylon. In 1895, as compared with the previous year, the export of black teas to Great Britain and the United States had fallen off 150,000 piculs.

The tea-trade in China is more or less a speculative one, always full of risks (as some of our merchants have found out to their cost); and though a vast amount of foreign capital is annually invested in the enterprise, it is probably only every second or third venture that will return, I do not say a handsome profit, but any profit at all.

We will now proceed to another apartment and see the method adopted in the manufacture of gunpowder teas. First the fresh leaves of black tea are partially dried in the sun; these are next rolled, either in the palm of the hand, or on a flat tray, or by the feet in a hempen bag, then they are scorched in hollow iron pans over a charcoal fire, and after this are spread out on bamboo trays, that the broken stems and refuse may be picked out. In this large stone-paved room we notice the leaves in different stages of preparation. The

labour required to produce the gunpowder leaf is the most curious and interesting of the many processes to which the plant is subjected. We are surprised to notice a troop of able-bodied coolies, each dressed only in a short pair of cotton trousers, tucked up so as to give free action to his naked limbs. One feels puzzled at first to conjecture what they are about. Can they be at work, or is it only play? They each rest their arms on a cross beam, or against the wall, and with their feet busily roll and toss balls of about a foot in diameter (or the size of an ordinary football), up and down the floor of the room. Our guide assures us it is work, and very hard work too. The balls beneath their feet are the bags packed full of tea leaves, which by the constant rolling motion assume the pellet shape. As the leaves become more compact, the bag loosens and requires to be twisted up at the neck and again rolled; the twisting and rolling being repeated until the leaf has become perfectly globose. It is then divided through seives into different sizes, or qualities, and the scent and bouquet is imparted after the final drying or scorching. I feel convinced that the introduction of the best machinery for rolling, cooking and preparing the leaf is only a question of time, and will follow in the wake of railways and silk and cotton mills, after the manner of the Japanese.

Most of the tea shipped from Canton is now grown in the province of Kwang-tung; formerly part of it used to be brought from the "Tung-ting" district, but that now finds its way to Hankow. Leaves from the Taishan district are mostly used in making "Canton District Pekoe" and "Long-Leaf Scented Orange Pekoe," while Loting leaf makes "Scented Caper and Gunpowder" teas.

In order to see the foreign tea-tasters prosecuting a branch of science which they have made peculiarly their own, we must cross the river to Shameen, a pretty little green island, on which the foreign houses stand; looking with its villas, gardens and croquet-lawns and churches like the suburb of some English town. We ascend a flight of steps in a massive stone retaining wall with which Shameen is surrounded,—and this done we might wander for a whole day and examine all the houses on the island, without discovering a trace of a merchant's office, or any outward sign of commerce at all. Those who are familiar with the factory site, and who can figure what that must have been in olden times, when the foreign merchants were caged up like wild beasts and subjected to the company and taunts of the vilest part of the river population, and to the pestilential fumes of an open drain that carried the sewage of the city to the stream, will be surprised at the transformation that has, since those days, been wrought.

The present residences of foreigners on this grassy site (reclaimed mud flat, raised above the river) are substantial, elegant buildings of stone or brick, each surrounded by a wall; an ornamental railing, or bamboo hedge, enclosing the gardens and outhouses in its circuit. Except the firm's name on each small brass door-plate, there is nothing anywhere that tells us of trade. But when we have entered, we find the dwelling-house on the upper story, and the comprador's room and offices on the ground-floor; next to the offices the tea-taster's apartment. Ranged against the walls of this chamber are rows of polished shelves, covered with small round tin boxes of a uniform size, and each bearing a label and date in Chinese and English writing. These boxes contain samples of all the various sorts of old and new teas, used for reference and comparison in tasting, smelling and scrutinising parcels, or chops, which may

SUBURBAN RESIDENTS, CANTON.

be offered for sale. In the centre of the floor stands a long table bestrewn with a multitude of white porcelain covered cups, manufactured specially for the purpose of tasting tea. The samples are placed in these cups, and hot water of a given temperature is then poured upon them. The time the tea rests in the hot water is measured by a sand-glass; and when this is accomplished, all is ready for the tasting, which is a much more useful than elegant operation.

The windows of the room have a northern aspect, and are screened off so as to admit only a steady skylight, which falls directly on a tea-board beneath. Upon this board the samples are spread on square wooden trays, and it is under the uniform light above described that the minute inspection of colour, make, general appearance and smell takes place. All these tests are made by assistants who have gone through a special course of training which fits them for the mysteries of their art. The knowledge which these experts possess is of the greatest importance to the merchant, as the profitable outcome of the crops selected for the home market depends, to a great extent, on their judgment and ability. It will thus be seen that the merchant, not only when he chooses his teas for exportation, but at the last moment before they are shipped, takes the minutest precautions against fraudulent shortcomings, either in quality or weight. It is possible, however, for a sound tea, if undercooked or imperfectly dried, to become putrid during the homeward voyage, and to reach this country in a condition quite unfit for use. This I know from my own experience. I at one time was presented with a box of tea by the Taotai of Taiwanfu, in Formosa, and when I first got it I found that some of the leaves had a slightly green tint and were damp. I had intended to bring this tea home to England; it was of good

quality, but it spoiled before I left China. Judging from the
quantities of tea that have been condemned, the importation of
spurious cargoes can hardly be a lucrative trade.

Although Chinese commercial morality has not run to such
a very low ebb as some might imagine, yet the clever traders
of the lower orders of Cathay are by no means above resorting
to highly questionable and ingenious practices of adulteration,
when such practices can be managed with safety and profit.
Thus the foreign merchant finds it always necessary to be vigil-
ant in his scrutiny of tea, silk and other produce, before
effecting a purchase. But equal care requires to be observed
in all money transactions, as counterfeit coining is a profession
carried on in Canton with marvellous success; so successful
indeed, are the coiners of false dollars that the native experts,
or schroffs, who are employed by foreign merchants (Mr. W.
F. Mayers assured me), are taught the art of schroffing, or
detecting counterfeit coin, by men who are in direct communication with the coiners of the spurious dollars in circulation.

In many of the Canton shops one notices the intimation
"Schroffing taught here." This is a curious system of corruption,
which one would think would be worth the serious attention
of the Government. Were counterfeiting coining put down,
there would be no need for the crafty instructors of schroffs;
and at the same time the expensive staff of experts employed
in banks and merchants' offices could be dispensed with.

But the dollar in the hands of a needy and ingenious Chinaman is not only delightful to behold, but it admits of a
manipulation at once most skilful and profitable. The art of
"schroffing" or detecting spurious coin and ascertaining the
difference in the value of dollars of various issues, is studied
as a profession by hundreds of young Chinamen, who find em-

SCHROFFING DOLLARS.

ployment in banks and merchants' offices. The establishments where schroffing is taught are well known to be in direct communication with counterfeiters of Mexican dollars and other coin, and it has often been said that the existence of schroffs and false money are mutually indispensable to each other. If the amount of counterfeit coin in circulation were less, the necessity for a multitude of schroffs would not be so severely felt, and if the establishments where schroffing is taught did not exist, the counterfeiters would lose the principal means of passing false money into circulation.

CHAPTER V.

Its general Appearance—Its Population—Streets—Mode of transacting Business—Signboards—Work and Wages—The Willow-pattern Bridge—Juilin, late Governor-General of the two Kwang—Clan Fights—Hakkas—The Mystic Pills—Dwellings of the Poor—The Lohang-tang—Buddhist Monastic Life—On board a Junk.

CANTON is by no means the densely packed London in China which some have made it out to be. The circuit of the city wall very little exceeds six miles, and if we stand upon the heights to the north of the city, and turn our faces southward, we can trace the outline of these fortifications along a considerable portion of their course. This, then, is the entire area strictly included in the limits of the town; but there are large straggling suburbs outside the walls which spread for no little distance over the plain. In these suburbs there are many open spaces; some, shaded by trees and orchards, form the parks and gardens of the officials; others, again, display the carefully tended produce of the market-gardener; while military parade grounds, rice-fields, and ponds where fish are bred, are scattered at intervals between more thickly populated ground. There is,

FEMALE COIFFURE, CANTON.

indeed, nothing in the whole picture of this southern metropolis suggestive of a teeming land population, save the centre of the city itself. But to the south of the wall there is the broad Pearl river, and communicating with this stream a network of canals and creeks, the whole more densely populated perhaps than the city. In the boats which crowd these waterways a vast number of families pass their lives, and subsist by carrying merchandise or conveying passengers to different parts of the province. The population of Canton is computed at about a million souls, although the official census returns it at a figure considerable higher.

As in Peking, so at Canton, the space within the walls is divided into two unequal parts, the one occupied nominally by the Tartar garrison and official residences only, and the other containing the abodes of the trading Chinese population. But the descendants of the old Tartar soldiers, too proud to labour, and too haughty to stoop themselves to the mean artifices of trade, have become impoverished in process of time, and have disposed of their lands and dwellings to their more industrious Chinese neighbours. As to the houses themselves, they everywhere preserve one uniform low level, but the monotonous appearance thus produced is at rare intervals broken by some tall temple, which rears its carved and gilded roof from amid a grove of venerable trees, or by the nine-storied pagoda, or lofty quadrangular towers that mark the pawnshop sites. The pawnshops in this strange city rear their heads heavenwards as proudly as church steeples, and indeed at first we mistook them for temples. What was our surprise then, to discover in them the Chinese reproduction of that money-lending establishment which is found in the shady corners of our own bye-streets, beneath a modest trinity of gilded balls, and whose private side

entrance stands invitingly open. In Canton they are square
bold-looking edifices, lifting their benevolent grey-brick heads
to a height which positively, in Chinese eyes, invests them
with sanctity.

Ah-sin and Ah-lok, indeed, look up with something akin
to veneration at their plastered walls, narrow stanchioned windows, and at the huge rock boulders poised on the edge of
the roof above, ready to drop down upon any robber who
might dare to scale the treasure-sheltering sides. I recollect
visiting one of these places for the purpose of seeing within,
and to obtain a view of the city. Armed with an introduction
from a leading Chinese merchant, I presented myself one morning before an outer gate in the high prison-looking wall, which
encircled the tower. My summons was answered by a portly
gate-keeper, who at once admitted me inside. Here I found
a number of military candidates going through a course of
drill; the porter was himself an old soldier, a sort of drill-
sergeant, and was now instructing pupils in the use of the bow
and how to lift up heavy weights. After exhibiting one or two
specimens of their powers, we were taken to a narrow barred
gate at the base of the tower. The office for transacting business was on the ground-floor, and above this, a square wooden
scaffolding, standing free of the walls, ran right up to the roof.
This scaffolding was divided into a series of flats, having ladders
which lead from one to the other; the bottom flat was used
for stowing pledges of the greatest bulk, such as furniture or
produce; smaller and lighter articles occupied the upper flats,
while the one nearest the roof was devoted to bullion and
jewellery. Every pledge from floor to ceiling was catalogued,
and bore a ticket denoting the number of the article and the
date when it was deposited. Thus anything could be found

and redeemed at a moment's notice. Such towers are places
for the safe custody of the costly gems and robes of the wealthy
classes of the community, and are really indispensable institutions in a country where bridgandage and misgovernment
expose property to constant risks. Besides this, a licensed
pawnbroking establishment makes temporary advances to needy
persons who may have security to lodge; the charge being three
per cent per month on sums under ten taels, save in the last
month of the year, when the interest is reduced to two per
cent. If the amount of the loan exceeds ten taels, the rate is
uniformly two per cent per month. The pledges are kept for
three years in the better class of pawnshops; it is customary for
the poor to pawn their winter and summer clothing alternately,
redeeming each suit as it may be required.

Not far below the Heights in the Tartar quarter of the city,
is the British Consulate, or Yamen. This edifice stands in the
grounds of what was once a palace, and is made up of diverse
picturesque Chinese buildings, environed by a tastefully laid out
garden and deer park. Hard by is the ancient nine-storied
pagoda ascribed to the reign of Emperor Wu-Ti, in the middle of
the sixth century of our era; it is octagonal in shape and 170 feet
high. In 1859 some British sailors, weary of shore life and
longing to go aloft, managed, at the risk of their necks, to
scale this crazy-looking monument—an event which greatly
disgusted the Chinese, for they hate to have their dwellings
overlooked from a height, more especially by a pack of foreign
fire-eating sailors. Descending from the height, and passing
southwards down to the main street of the town, we are struck
by the appearance of the closely-packed shops, which differ
from anything we have ever seen before. We observe that
the folks who lounge about, even in the meanest-looking

5

dwellings, are, most of them, good-looking—the men of average height and shapely, and the women seldom disfigured by small bandaged feet. There are also a number of soldiers, not far from the parade-ground—fellows who, erect and muscular, carry themselves with a dauntless military air. These are the remnants of the once powerful Tartar camp. They have been instructed in foreign drill, and are said to make good soldiers; they certainly contrast favourably with many of the troops I saw in other quarters of the Empire. As to the shopkeepers, they are all Chinese, but their small-footed consorts are nowhere to be seen; the fact is, they keep them strictly secluded. Some of these handsome Tartar matrons have their children seated in bamboo cages at their doors, and pretty little birds they make, too.

One is almost bewildered by the diversity of shops and the attractive wares they display. Then the shopkeepers are so very fascinating in their manners. Have a good look at them; they are about the best class of men in China—industrious, contented and refined-looking, some of them. A short time back a curious, though not uncommon, sort of lottery was got up among the shopkeepers of Canton. Wang-leang-chai of the Juy-Chang boot shop in Ma-an street, seized with a passion for poetry, organised a sort of literary lottery, and offered the stakes as prizes to the successful composer of the best lines on five selected subjects. [1]

Frequently, on entering a Canton shop, you will find its owner with a book in one hand and a pipe or fan in the other, and wholly absorbed in his studies. You will be doomed to disappointment if you expect the smoker to start up at once, all

[1] See China Review, 1873, p. 249.

PHYSIC STREET, CANTON

smiles and blandness, rubbing his hands together as he makes a shrewd guess of what he is likely to take out of you, and receiving you obsequiously or with rudeness accordingly. Quite the reverse. Your presence is apparently unnoticed, unless you happen to lift anything; then you hear that the fan has been arrested, and feel that a keen eye is bent on your movements all the while. But it is not till you enquire for some article that the gentleman, now certain that you mean to trade, will rise without bustle from his seat, show you his goods, or state the price he means to sell at—with a polite yet careless air, which plainly says, "If it suits you, we make an exchange." After all, by adhering to this independent style I believe they sell more, and make better profits, than if they were perpetually soliciting patronage by word and gesture. On our way homewards we pass through Physic Street, or Tsiang-Lan-Kiai. Here nearly all the shops are uniform in size, a brick party-wall dividing each building from its neighbour. All have one front apartment open to the street, with a granite or brick counter for the display of their wares. A granite base also supports the tall upright signboard, the indispensable characteristic of every shop in China. Opposite the signboard stands a small altar or shrine, dedicated to the god who presides over the tradesman and his craft. This deity is honoured regularly when the shop is opened, and a small incense-stick is lighted, and kept burning in a bronze cup of ashes placed in front of the shrine.

The shops within are frequently fitted with a counter of polished wood and carved shelves, while at the back is an accountant's room, screened off with an open-work wooden partition, so carved as to resemble a climbing plant. In some conspicuous place stand the brazen scales and weights, ever polished and adorned with red cloth. These scales are used for weighing the silver-coin bars and fragments of the precious metal, which form part of the currency of the place. When goods are sold by weight, the customer invariably brings his own balance, so as to secure his fair and just portion of the article he has come to buy. This balance is not unlike an ordinary yard measuring-rod, furnished with a sliding weight. It is a simple application of the lever. But the tendency of this mechanical contrivance is not calculated to elevate the Chinese in our estimation; it proves a universal lack of confidence, which finds its way .down to the lowest details of petty trade, for which the governing classes may take to themselves credit. The people are in this, as in many other matters, a law unto themselves. A ceaseless struggle against unfair dealing has therefore, like other native institutions, become a stereotyped necessity.

It is by no means pleasant to be caught in one of these narrow streets during a shower, as the water pours down in torrents from the roofs and floods the pavement, until it subsides through the soil beneath. The broadest streets are narrow, and shaded above in some places with screens of matting to keep out the sun. So close indeed, are the roofs to each other in the Chinese city, that, viewed from a distance, they look like one uninterrupted covering—a space entirely tiled over, beneath which the citizens sedulously conceal themselves until the cool of the evening, when weary of the darkness and of the trade and strife of the day, they swarm on the housetops to gamble, or smoke, or sip their tea until the shades of night fall, then they retire again to the lower regions to sleep on the cool benches of their shops. Canton boasts no system of drainage, no water supply save the river, no gas works, and no system of street lighting.

Opium Smoking.

The signboards of Cantonese shops are not only the pride of their owners, but they are a delight to students of Chinese. In the high-flown classical, or poetical phrases by which public attention is drawn to the various shops, one fails to see in most instances the faintest reference to the contents of the establishment. Thus, a tradesman who sells swallows' nests for making soup, has on his board simply characters signifying Yun-Ki, sign of the Eternal. But here is a list:

Kien Ki Hao—the sign of the symbol Kien (Heaven) Hwei-chow, ink, pencils and writing materials. This is indeed a very high compliment to literature.

Chang Tsi Tang (Chang of the family branch designated Tsi). Wax-cased pills of select manufacture. Chang is evidently proud of his family connection and probably offers it as a sufficient guarantee for the quality of his pills.

Tien Yih (Celestial advantage). Table-covers, cushions for chairs and divans for sale. Now what "Celestial advantage" can a customer be supposed to derive from table-covers or cushions, unless, indeed, one supposes that the downy ease conferred by the use of these cushions is almost beyond the sphere of terrestial enjoyment. There must be some notion of this sort associated with upholsterers' shops, as we have here another sign embodying a high-flown phrase flavoured with a little common sense.

Tien Yih Shen (Celestial advantage combined with attention). Shop for the sale of cushions and ratan mats.

Yung Ki (sign of the Eternal). Swallows' nests. Money-schroffing taught here.

K'ing Wen T'a'ng (the hall of delight in scholarship). Seals artisticly engraved.

Notwithstanding the narrowness of the streets of Canton, they

are extremely picturesque; more especially those in which we
find the old curiosity-shops, the silversmiths and the silk-mercers,
where the signboards present a most attractive display of brilliant
and varied colours, as indeed, in the one through which we have
just been passing.

Striking thence by a narrow alley into a back lane, we find
ourselves in a very poor neighbourhood with dingy, dirty hovels
filled with operatives, who are busily at work; some weaving
silk; others embroidering satin robes; others again, carving and
turning the ivory balls and curios which are the admiration of
foreigners. Entering one shop we were shown an elaborately
carved series of nine ivory balls, one within the other. It is
commonly believed that these balls are first carved in halves
and then joined together so perfectly as to look solid. But as
we watch a man working on one of them the mystery is gradually solved. The rough piece of solid ivory is first cut into
a ball; it is then fixed into a primitive-looking lathe and turned
with a sharp tool in various positions until it becomes perfectly
round. It is then set again in the lathe and drilled with the
requisite number of holes all round. After this one hole is
centred, a tool bent at the end is passed in, and with this a
groove is produced near the heart of the sphere ; another hole
is then centred, and after that another, the same operation
being carried out with all the holes until all the grooves meet
and a small ball drops into the centre. In this way all the balls,
one within the other, are ultimately released. The next operation
is carving the innermost ball; this is accomplished by means of
long drills and other delicate tools, and in the same way all the
rest of the balls are carved in succession, the carving gradually
becoming more easy and elaborate until the outside ball is
reached, and this is then finished with a delicate beauty that

resembles the finer sorts of lace. Close by these ivory-turners are men designing patterns of birds, butterflies and flowers on satin robes. The wages of the people who do this lovely work are very small indeed. The artist who furnishes the designs receives about £1 5s a month, and the following table gives the average at which skilled labourers are paid.

	£	s	d	
Shoemaker		15	0	a month with food
Blacksmith	1	0	0	„
First-class ivory carver	2	8	0	„
Skilled embroiderer		15	0	„
Silversmith	1	12	0	„
Painter		18	0	„

It takes about ten days to complete the embroidery of a pair of shoes; and these, when soled and finished, fetch fifteen shillings a pair. The wages of the embroiderer, according to this calculation, would amount to six shillings or thereabouts, and the balance, to cover cost of material and making, would leave but a modest profit to the master; but then embroidered shoes are in constant demand, and a lady of rank will require some thirty pairs for her marriage trousseau alone. Some ladies embroider their own shoes, but the practice is by no means a common one. The dress shoes of the men are embroidered too, and are used by all except the poorest class. It will be seen from the foregoing notes that skilled labour is so cheap in China as to give artisans a great advantage in all those various branches of native industry which find a market abroad; and this will one day render the clever, careful and patient China-man a formidable rival to European manufacturers, when he has learned to use machinery in weaving fabrics of cotton or silk.

Many of the beautifully embroidered stuffs we see in our shops at home are made by hand in China, and yet they can be sold in London at prices that defy competition. The opposition to the introduction of the machines used in Bradford and Manchester comes mostly from the operatives themselves. It is noteworthy that the Chinese in this province have adopted Pasteur's method of detecting and eradicating disease in the silkworms. Machinery is also being introduced in reeling the silk, notwithstanding the native dread of innovation. It is perfectly astonishing to see what these Cantonese can accomplish on their own inferior looms. Give them almost any pattern or design, and they will contrive to weave it, imitating its imperfections with as much exactness as its beauties. I like to linger over these shops, and to meditate on these scenes of ceaseless industry, where all goes on with a quiet harmony that has a strange fascination for the observer. Amid all the evidences of toil, the poorest has some leisure at his command; then, seated on a bench, or squatting tranquilly on the ground, he will smoke or chat with a neighbour, untroubled by the presence of his employer, who seems to grow fatter and wealthier on the smiles and happy temperament of his workmen. Here, too, one can see how the nucleus of this great city is more closely populated than at first sight one would suppose. Most of the workshops are kitchen, dining-room and bed-room too; here the workpeople breakfast on their benches; here at nightfall they stretch themselves out to sleep. Their whole worldly wealth is stored here too. An extra jacket, a pipe, a few ornaments which are used in common, and a pair of chopsticks—these make up each man's total worldly pelf; and indeed his greatest treasure he carries with him—a stock of health and a contented mind. The Chinese operative is completely content if he escape the pangs of

REELING SILK.

hunger, endowed with health sufficient to enable him simply to enjoy the sense of living, and of living too in a land so perfect, that a human being ought to be happy in the privilege of residing there at all. It is a land, so they seem to suppose, wherein everything is settled and ordered by men who know exactly what they ought to know, and who are paid to keep people from rising, or ambitiously seeking to quit the groove in which Providence placed them at their birth. Many will say that the Chinaman is not without ambition, and in a sense they will be right. Parents are ambitious to educate their children, and to qualify them for candidature at the Government examinations; and there are probably no men who lust more after power, wealth and place than the successful Chinese graduates, simply because they know that there is no limit to their prospects. If they have interest and genius, the poorest of them may fairly aspire to become a member of the Imperial Cabinet; but then these are the men of letters, and not the poor labouring classes, the populace whom I have just described.

Before I quit Canton I must give some account of a spot there, which I visited more than once, and which was commonly known as the garden of Pun-ting-qua. Pun-ting-qua, or Pun-shi-cheng, the original owner, had been a wealthy merchant at Canton, but his Government ultimately drained him of his wealth, by compelling him to pay a certain fixed sum for the monopoly of trade in salt. Falling into heavy arrears, and being unable to raise the amount, his property was sequestrated, and his splendid garden raffled in a public lottery. A notable instance, this, of the danger of becoming too rich in China. His house, a singularly beautiful place, was sold to the anti-foreign, anti-missionary society of Canton; and at the time of my visit to this quaint pleasure-ground, traces of decay had already set

their stamp upon the curious structures that adorned it. I first
made my way up Sulphur Creek, which sweeps round to the
west of the city, and passed many a strange-looking edifice
rising above the dull water and bending over a frail wooden
jetty which divided it from the stream. Women are washing
and children sit upon the steps and jetties in a way that makes
one tremble for their safety. Dogs bark and snarl at the doorways, domesticated pigs or fowls look out upon the throng of
boats, while the men are busy dipping dark blue cotton fabrics
into the stream. A three-storied pagoda marks the site of
Pun-ting-qua's garden, which we enter through a gateway in
the outer wall. Once arrived inside, we seem for the first time
to realise the China pictured to us in our schoolboy days.
Here we see model Chinese gardening; drooping willows, shady
walks and sunny lotus-pools, on which gilded barges float.
Here, too, spanning a lake, stands the well-known willow-pattern bridge, with a pavilion hard by. But we miss the two
love-birds; there is no dutiful parent, with the fish-tail feet,
leisurely and with lamp in hand pursuing his unfilial daughter
as she, with equal leisure, makes her way after the shepherd
with the crook. I photographed this willow-pattern bridge, but
when I look at my picture, I find it falls far short of the scene
on our soup-plates. Where, for example, is the pavilion which
is all ornaments, the tree above it which grows nothing but
foot-balls, and that other tree, too, on which only feathers
bloom? Where is the fence that meanders across the platform
in the fore-ground? And yet these gardens have a quaintness
all their own. Their winding paths conduct to cleverly contrived retreats; and tunnels cut through mossy fern-covered rocks,
land us in some pavilion or theatre, on the edge of a glassy
pool, where gold-fish sport in the sunshine, and glistening

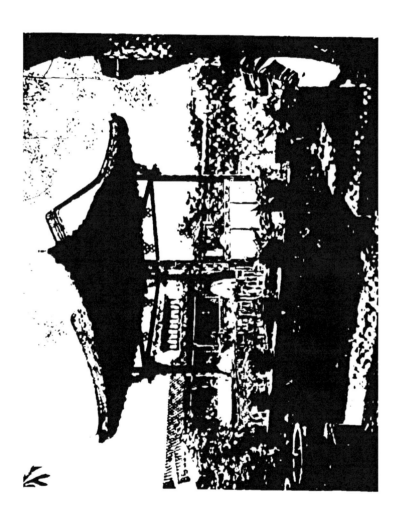

frogs sit gravely on broad dew-spangled lotus-leaves; or else where we discover some spacious open saloon, where a party of native gentlemen, seated on square, cool, marble-bottomed, ebony chairs, enjoy a repast of tea or cake, or listen to the strumming of a lute, and to the shrill song of some lady in attendance.

Juilin, who was governor of the province and of Kwangsi as well, was an officer who had seen distinguished service. A man of marked ability, who did much to promote the prosperity of the two provinces. It was he who organised a steam gunboat service, which made its presence felt among the pirates on the coast, and was also instrumental in suppressing the village clans in Cha-chow-fu, which had for many years set all authority at defiance. These villages were each inhabited by one family, or clan, and were at feud with all the other surrounding villages and clans.

When in Chao-chow-fu, in the Kwang-tung province, I visited several of these villages and got some notion of their style of fighting. Those unfortunates who were carried off as prisoners of war were frequently detained in slavery, or met with a fate even worse than this, for their captors would dispose of them to be sent, as involuntary emigrants, to foreign shores. At harvest-time one village would make a midnight raid upon its neighbour and carry off all the crops; and at Sinchew I found an old feud existing between that village and a number of smaller hamlets. One Aching and his brother, tired at last of fighting, and of being constantly interrupted in more peaceful and profitable pursuits, resolved to go into the Fukien Province, and there to seek for work. With their bundles on their backs they started from their native place, but halted when not far on their journey to fish in a neighbouring stream. While thus engaged, a boat full of their enemies carefully disguised, made its approach, and one of the crew offered to buy their stock of fish. The two brothers falling into the snare, were thus carried off to the hostile village, and there killed and mutilated in an open space in front of the settlement. Aching's heart was cut out, boiled and eaten by his savage captors, under the notion that they would become more daring and bloodthirsty in consequence of this revolting deed.—Another example of native treachery and cunning will suffice. Two men of opposite clans had made up their minds to quit the province with the loot they had gained in war; they, both of them, went to Cheng-lin at the same time, in search of the same object, viz., a boat. The one, hearing of the other's presence, hired a number of ruffians to slay him, promising them six pounds for his enemy's head and heart. The gang, tempted to the crime by the prospect of this liberal reward, soon caught their man; but he, enquiring how much they were to receive for his head, at once offered them, on better security, double terms for the capture of his crafty foe. They had no hesitation in accepting the proposal, and it was their first employer, therefore who fell a victim to their guile. In the end a small army was sent into the provinces, and all who refused to come to terms, and obey the law, were mercilessly put to the sword. So it came about that at the time I visited the place a well-dressed man might walk abroad, and no longer fear lest he should be stripped and sent adrift without a rag to cover him, or else be sold into slavery or even killed.

There is a hardy race of people found in this and several other districts. These are known as Hak-kas, and some are of opinion that they are a people distinct from the Chinese, as they speak a language of their own, and resemble Indians in

BUDDHIST MONK.

physical appearance, rather than the Chinese type. Others, again, hold that the Hak-kas emigrated some eight hundred years ago from the Ning-hwa district in the Fukien province; and a writer in the "China Review" undertakes to prove from the Hak-kas family records that Ning-hwa was really their original home. Be their origin what it may, they have carved out an important place for themselves in the rich province of Kwang-tung. I also met them increasing, multiplying and spreading their industry in the island of Formosa. It was they who, having no sympathies in common with the Puntis of Canton, formed the Coolie corps to the allied troops, and won a high reputation for perseverance and bravery. They have even been known to rescue British soldiers, when wounded and drowning, amid a perfect storm of bullets. Dr. Eitel, who laboured among them for many years, and who kindly furnished me with some of his experiences, described them as the hardest workers and the most industrious men in Kwang-tung; —and when the interests of Hak-kas and Puntis, or natives of the province, clashed, the former have always distinguished themselves by their readiness to fight. For more than two centuries a stream of Hak-ka emigration has been flowing into the Ka-ying-chow department, taking its course more especially through the mountainous and thinly populated parts. This movement is still going on.

The process, in individual cases, is more or less as follows. A couple of Hak-kas come to a Punti village, and there they hire themselves out to labour on the farm. In process of time, when they have laid up a little money, they rent a few acres of mountain land, or unredeemed bog. The insecurity caused by robbers and banditti makes it difficult in sparsely populated districts to cultivate land far from a village. The Hak-kas, therefore, easily find landowners willing to rent their outlying

acres at a merely nominal rate. All further difficulties are
gradually overcome, and at last the persevering Hak-kas send
for their families and friends, and settle down in mud huts,
which they build like forts, surrounding them with ditches, with
thorny thickets and impenetrable bamboo. Success in most
cases follows, the hamlet grows rapidly, and a flock of immigrants from their native province crowd in to plant a settlement
in the neighbourhood. Those scattered settlements form a
confederation among themselves, and forthwith demand a reduc-
tion of the ground-rent. If this be not acceded to, things
will progress pleasantly for a short time longer, until the confederation feels itself strong enough to wage war with the original
owners and refuse to pay any rent. But, lest the Government
should interfere, they are careful to inform the mandarins beforehand that they will pay lawful ground-rent to them. Besides,
in many public offices in the Kwang-tung province, the subordinate employés are Hak-kas. This always enables them to
judge of their own strength, to meet intrigue with intrigue,
and to keep their quarrels outside the limits of Government
intervention. As this class of village wars is looked upon as
harmless by the authorities, they only interfere to squeeze both
parties. The Punti employ bravos to fight for them, while the
Hak-kas fight their battles for themselves, and that is why the
latter always win.

I will now glance at a quarter of the town which has under-
gone improvements. Not far from the old factory site, and
close to the river, there stands a row of well-built brick houses.
In 1869 these houses had not been built, and the ground was
occupied by a strange mixed population of the poorest classes.
Too poor to live in boats, or in the houses of the city, they
squatted on this waste land between the river and the wall,

existing, most of them, nobody knew how. Some of the hovels
in which they dwelt would not have made decent dog-kennels;
and yet, amid all their poverty, they seemed a tolerably contented lot. I remember one hut which had been pieced together out of the fragments of an old boat, bits of foreign
packing-cases inscribed with trade-marks that betrayed their
chequered history, patches of decayed matting, clay, mud and
straw; a covering of odd tiles and broken pottery made all
snug within. In the small space thus enclosed, accommodation
was found for a lean pig that lived on garbage, two old women,
one old man, the old man's daughter and the daughter's child.
A small space in front was arranged as the kitchen, while part
of the roof and one or two pots were taken up with vegetables
or flowers. I have seen the inmates, in the morning sunshine,
breakfasting off a savoury meal of mixed scraps that they had
picked up in their perambulations about the city. There were
many such dwellings in this neighbourhood, and the district
physician lived not far off. The doctor had a very aged look,
as if, at some distant period, he had been embalmed and preserved in a dried-up state, though still alive. He might be
consulted at all hours, and would be found at his doorway
among his herbs and simples, dressed in a pair of slippers and
cotton breeches, and with ponderous spectacles across his
shrivelled nose. But the door and walls of this public benefac-
tor's abode were covered with an array of black plasters, to
which the old man pointed with great pride as incontestable
evidences of his professional skill. These plasters had a wide
celebrity among his poor patients, and many a man, as a token
of deep gratitude for some signal cure, had brought his plaster
back as a certificate to adorn the residence where his deliverer
dwelt.

Leaving this quarter, and striking for the suburbs north of of the foreign settlements, we come upon a temple, perhaps the most interesting in Canton. This is the Temple of 500 Gods; said, in Mr. Bowra's translation of the native history of the province, to have been founded by Bôdhidharama, a Buddhist monk from India, about the year 520 A.D. It is Bôdhidharama whom we frequently see pictured on Chinese tea-cups, as he ascends the Yangtsze river on his bamboo raft. The temple was rebuilt in 1755, under the auspices of the Emperor Kien-lung. It contains the Lo-hang-tang, or hall of saints, and with its temple buildings, its houses for priests, its lakes and its gardens, covers altogether a very large space. Colonel Yule, in his last edition of Marco Polo, says that one of the statues in this temple is an image of the Venetian traveller; but careful inquiry proves this statement incorrect, for none of the images present the European type of face, and all the records connected with them are of an antiquity which runs back beyond Marco Polo's age. The abbot, who is the centre figure in the illustration of a group of chess-players, received us with great cordiality, and showed us into his private apartments, where we enjoyed a repast of tea and cake, and spent some time in examining a collection of dwarf trees and flowering shrubs, which he had arranged in a court in front of his sitting-room. In the centre of this court stood a tank containing fish, and a group of sacred lotus flowers in full bloom. The old gentleman had spent many years of his life in seclusion and seemed to be devoted to his garden, expressing his delight to find a foreigner who could share in his love of flowers. The apartments of this prelate impressed me with a sense of cold squareness and rigid uniformity. The flooring was marble, and the tables and chairs were either wholly of marble, or ebony, or ebony and marble combined. If the chairs sent too

Buddhist Monks at Chess.

rheumatic a chill through your blood, you could test the comfort of a block of polished rock in the corner, or try one or two cold glazed porcelain stools. Sundry texts from the sacred classics were hung about the dim walls; everything was in order and everything scrupulously clean. But at length we discovered, when a number of the monks had joined our party, that the shaven, silent, thoughtful-looking inmates of the cloister could unbend if they chose, and take a natural and ardent interest in the current gossip of Canton. Nay, they conducted us to a snuggery in an inner court, where a table was sumptuously spread, embowered beneath plantain-trees and shaded by their huge waving leaves. Round a lotus-pool, in the centre of this court, ran a paved pathway, and an ornamental railing, draped with the green leaves of a creeping plant. Here we left the monks engaging their venerable abbot in a game at chess, while I took my way to the interior of the shrine to obtain a photograph of the central altar. I found a number of people at worship within, making votive offerings to the idols whose aid they sought. Some ladies were there, decked in their finest silks; and my entrance so startled these fair devotees, that they would have fled but for the intervention of the priests, who gave me a high character, as one in search of knowledge, who had wisely come from an obscure island to view the greatest temple in all Cathay, and to carry pictures of its wonders home.

Wending our way back to the river through narrow tortuous streets, and passing third-rate tea establishments, where men mix the fragrant leaves and toss them about with their naked feet, on mats spread out in the sun, we at length embark in one of the many small boats which ply for hire at the jetties. The crew of the little craft consists of three young girls, and these boatwomen are the prettiest and most attractive-looking of their

6

sex to be met with out of doors in this part of China. They never paint, and are therefore set down by their countrywomen as of doubtful respectability. This is really true of some of them, although in the presence of Europeans who may hire their boats, they behave with uniform modesty and decorum. Their boats are the perfection of neatness, and their dress as simple as it is picturesque. They scull or row with great dexterity, skimming in and out among the crowd of shipping, or along the narrow ways that form the thoroughfares in the floating town of boats, where natives in tens of thousands pursue their various avocations, quite apart from the dwellers on shore. A brisk trade is carried on in many of these narrow avenues, and the small merchants who engage in it have their shops in the bows of their boat and their residences at the stern. If business happens to be dull at one end of the town they move to the other, or else take a tour in the provinces, carrying their whole establishment to a region where the family can enjoy balmy air, and where they will delight the hearts of the rustics with their display of city wares.

Steering clear of a floating market in one of the main alleys of this aquatic Babel, we come in front of a row of flower-boats, the floating music-saloons of this quarter of the stream. It is growing dark, and the numerous lamps which hang round these boats produce a very striking effect. Each saloon rears its head high above the water, and is carved into the most elaborate representations of the animal and vegetable world, of the beauties on earth or the wonders in the heavens above. Through the interstices of the carving we can make out some pretty female faces, and suddenly a crowd of fine young damsels rise above the woodwork, looking like a continuation of the ornaments. Suddenly they again disappear, as a gay group

Chinese Pagoda, Kwangtung Province.

of youths in silken robes step out of a boat and pass into the nearest saloon. Then we hear the warble of the lute and the damsels piping in shrill treble tones; for these maidens have descended from their perch above and are entertaining the city youths, who have come to dine in the saloon, to enjoy a whiff of opium and to bask in smiles so sweet, that they seem like to crack the enamel off the faces of the fair damsels.

Pulling back is hard work for the crew, but they redouble their efforts, for as they say, "Plenty piecee bad man hab got this side, too muchee likee cut throat pidjin," and soon we are once more in mid-stream. Here we pass close under the dark frowning hulks of a fleet of old weather-beaten junks that lie moored in a long double line. As everyone already knows all about these junks—what they look like, with their big eyes set in front to scare off the demons of the deep—I need not attempt to describe them here; but I may inform the reader that the accompanying picture of the deck of a junk was one which cost me some trouble to obtain. I got it under the following circumstances. Two artistic friends and myself were one day pulling about Hongkong harbour, in quest of a good subject for a picture, and after having scrambled by the aid of a convenient rope, on to the deck of a junk at anchor there, we found the crew busy with a complex machinery of ropes, poles and wind-lasses, and indeed on the point of making sail. Suddenly they forsook their work, confronted us with angry gestures and threat-ened to bar our advance. We enquired for the captains, of whom there are not uncommonly half a dozen on board; for these junks are built in water-tight compartments, and each owner of cargo is a captain so far as concerns that compart-ment where his own goods have been separately stored. Thus if the compartments be six, the captains are six, and each cap-

tain has a sixth part of the vessel under his own command.
The result of this equitable arrangement is that the craft is
sometimes required to travel in six different directions simul-
taneously, and to stand for six different points at a time; and
in the end the crew take the steering into their own hands, or
else consult Joss, who stands in his shrine in the cabin un-
moved, though tempests rage. As it happened in our case
there were but two captains on board, the one anxious to be
civil and the other ready to pitch us into the sea. At length
they requested us to remain, while they referred the case to
Joss. The idol, it appeared, gave us a hearty welcome, for
captains and crew returned from the interior to unite in helping
me to get up a successful picture.

CHAPTER VI.

THE charitable institutions of China are far from numerous, and
but ill-organised as a rule. At the time of my visit an establishment under Chinese supervision, and supported entirely out
of Chinese funds, was about to be opened in Canton for relieving the sick and destitute, and supplying coffins to the poor.
The intention of its founders, so it is supposed, was to counter-
act the influence of the hospitals and charities supported by
the foreign Christian Missions in their city.

But when I left Canton the place was still unopened, although
a house had already been bought, which had been occupied as
a private residence by Pun-ting-qua, the last of the Hong merchants, whose property, as I have said already, had been con-
fiscated by Government. This house was one of the finest I

have seen in China, and its magnificent costly decorations conveyed some notion of Pun-ting-qua's great wealth, which had been quietly absorbed by the authorities.

Among the charities in Canton there is a Leper Village. These sort of asylums for plague-stricken men and women are found in various quarters of the Empire, but as I only visited one place of the kind, I shall reserve what I have to say about them for a future page. There are also institutions for the aged and infirm, and a foundling hospital, in which the poor children, who may be left at its door, are nursed on the slenderest fare. Dr. Kerr gave some interesting details as to the management of this hospital, in the "China Review." One wet nurse, so he tells us, has at times as many as three infants to feed, and she must herself be reduced to starvation allowance, as her pay is only about eight shillings a month. Many of the nurslings die, as might be expected, while those who survive are sold for about three shillings apiece. It is mostly female children who are brought to this benevolent institution, for girls are esteemed nothing but encumbrances to poor parents in China, the reproach of their mothers, who ought to give birth to boys alone. These foundlings are bought by the wealthy and brought up as servants or concubines; or else they are disposed of to designing hags, who purchase them on speculation and reserve them for a more miserable fate. This custom of investing in girls as speculative property, and of rearing them carefully till their personal attractions will command a high market value, is one of the worst aspects of that traffic in slaves which is carried on without shame or concealment all over Chinese soil. The evil might be mitigated if we could but persuade the Chinese Government to encourage female emigration by any means in their power, more particularly to

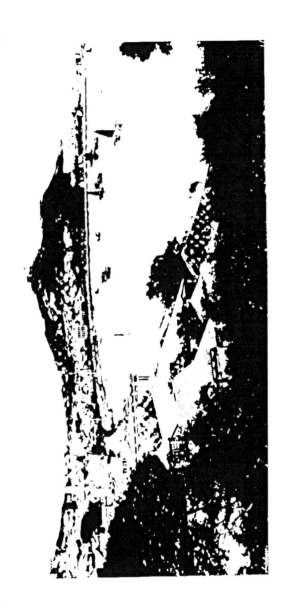

those lands where as yet only males have found their way from
China. Besides this there are countries in which the Chinese
are as yet almost unknown—Africa, for example—where, with
wives and children around them, a congenial climate, and a
rich soil to cultivate with produce, which they have been accustomed to grow, vast tracts of the waste lands of the earth
might be colonised and redeemed. Thus would the parent
country be relieved from the pressure of over-population, which
hitherto has been mainly kept in check by famine, infanticide
and civil war.

Macao is interesting as the only Portuguese settlement to be
found on the coast of China. It may be reached by steamer
either from Hongkong or Canton, and it is a favourite summer
resort for the residents of our own little colony. In that pretty
watering-place we may enjoy the cool sea-breezes, and almost
fancy, when promenading the broad Praya Grande, as it sweeps
round a bay truly picturesque, that we have been suddenly
transported to some ancient continental town. Macao is a
magnificent curiosity in its way. The Chinese say it has no
right to be there at all; that it is built on Chinese soil; whereas
the Portuguese, on their part, allege that the site was ceded
to the King of Portugal in return for services rendered to the
Government of China. These services, however, cannot have
been properly appreciated, for the Chinese in 1573, built a
barrier-wall across the isthmus on which the town stands, to
shut out the foreigners. The place has had a chequered history
since the time of its original foundation, sometimes being under
its own legitimate Government, and at others being claimed and
ruled by the Chinese. But its history, however important to
the parent country, had better be left alone, more especially as
there are passages in it which reflect no great lustre on the

nation whom Camoens adorned. The main streets in Macao
are deserted. The houses there are painted in a variety of
strange colours, some of the windows being fringed with a rim
of red, which gives them the look of inflamed eyes in the
painted cheeks of the dwellings. But there are magnificent
staircases, wide doorways and vast halls, though the inmates
for the most part are a very diminutive race; they are called
Portuguese, but they suffer by comparison with the more recent
arrivals from the parent land, being darker than the Portuguese
of Europe, and darker even than the native Chinese. There
is trade going on the streets, but it is of a very languid
kind, and the gambling-houses, or the cathedral are the chief
places of resort.

The forts are, of course, garrisoned with troops from Europe.
At 4 p.m. or thereabouts, the settlement wakes up; carriages
whirl along the road; sedan chairs struggle shorewards, that
their occupants may taste the sea-breeze; and the mid-day
solitudes of the Praya Grande have been converted into a
fashionable promenade. Ladies are there too, attired in the
lightest costumes and the gayest colours; some of them pretty,
but the majority sallow-faced and uninteresting, and decked out
with ribbons and dresses, whose gaudy tints are so inhar-
moniously contrasted, that one wonders how Chinnery the
painter could have spent so many of his days among a community so wanting in artistic tastes. The young men—for there
seem to be no old men here, at least all dress alike, quite
irrespective of years—are a slender race, but not more slender
than diminutive. But if Macao is interesting as a Portuguese
settlement, and the only one which now remains to Portugal
of those which her early traders founded in China, it can also
. boast of historic associations, giving it a special and independent

Approach to Buddhist Temple, Macao.

attraction. Here the poet Camoens found a retreat, and here too, Chinnery produced a multitude of sketches and paintings, which have really had some influence on art in the south of China.

Swatow is the next place on our route northward, and to reach it we take steamer from Hongkong. There is, I must tell you, almost daily a service of steamers up and down the Chinese coast. The splendid passenger accommodation and the facilities for conveying merchandise, supplied by these vessels, are of a kind not easily surpassed; and considering the nature of the coasts they navigate and the dangerous typhoons to which they are exposed, very few accidents occur.

Swatow is the port of the city Chao-chow-fu, which lies in the province of Kwang-tung. Chao-chow-fu ought really to have been an entrepot for foreign trade, but this idea was given up in consequence of the turbulence of the surrounding clans. The town is built upon the banks of the Han, and the district through which that river flows is one of the most fertile in the province. Swatow has a harbour available even for vessels of the largest tonnage; and so far as that point goes the place is better suited to foreign trade than Chao-chow-fu would have been; for the latter place stands some thirty miles up the river, and can only be reached by lighters of a shallow draught. The foreign settlement, or rather the residences of foreigners, are perched upon a low range of hills, which remind one of the barren cinder-looking hills of Aden. Huge boulders of granite are planted up and down these hilly slopes in the most extraordinary positions; some are like Druidical circles, others resemble great obelisks. Not unfrequently, too, they bear inscriptions in Chinese characters, which are nothing more than the productions of natives, who have sought to gain an un-

profitable immortality by graving their names, or their poetical
effusions, or else a record of some local incident upon the
imperishable surface of these stones. Here the foreign houses
and many of the native ones too, are built with a local concrete,
made of the felspar clay which abounds in the neighbourhood,
combined with shell-lime. In process of time this compound
hardens into a stony substance, producing solid and durable
walls. The interiors of these dwellings are no less remarkable,
for the ceilings are adorned with beautiful stucco cornices, representing birds and flowers in endless variety and profusion.
The men who execute this sort of artistic work are to all
appearance coolies, receiving for their labour but little more
than they could earn by tilling the soil or drawing water; and
yet, to fit themselves for their tasks, they must undergo what
is a fine art training, at least to a Chinaman. When at work
they squat on the floor, with a hod full of stucco before them,
and a sort of small baking-board at their feet. On this board,
with their fingers and a trowel, they model flower after flower—
stems, foliage, fruit and all—besides birds of one or two kinds;
passing the portions, as they complete them, up to a workman,
whose business it is to group the bits together, and fix them
in position. No moulds are used, no wooden pattern of any
sort,—all is done with the unaided hand and eye.

Of the native settlement of Swatow I need only say that it
is more or less like the river quarters of Canton, or Fatshan,
or any other town in the south of China; but I cannot refrain
from introducing the reader to the Swatow fan-painters. There
are a number of fan-shops in the main street, and one which
is perhaps more celebrated for the beauty of its work than
any of the others can pretend to be. To this shop, then, I
repaired in the company of an English merchant, whose warm

hospitality proved him to be no exception to the majority of his associates in China. We were here shown some of the most beautiful and delicate fan-painting that I have ever come across, representing, for the most part, garden scenes. Asking to be introduced to the artists, I was shown into an apartment at the back of the premises, where I found three occupants. Two were seated before a table, engaged in designing on the yet unpainted fans, while the third lay stretched on a couch, indulging in an opium-pipe. They were, all of them, opium-smokers; and it struck me that their most finely imaginative paintings were executed under the influence of the drug. As I have said, the pictures produced by these men were remark-able for their beauty, and that because the drawing and per-spective were good, and the designs full of delicacy. Here, then, we find Chinese art pure and simple, without the ad-mixture of any foreign element, as in Hongkong; and my opinion is that it is a higher class of art than we are apt to suppose the Chinese to possess. But then we must bear in mind that after all we do not know much about China and her art. It was only the other day, when in Peking, that I picked up one or two old pictures which had formed part of the collection of a private Chinese gentleman, and that alone gave me a more favourable opinion of, at any rate, the ancient school of Chinese artists.

One specimen, a series of original sketches representing chil-dren at play, was as remarkable for its quaint humour as for its clever execution; yet the pictures are nothing more preten-tious than unelaborated pen-and-ink sketches. In a postscript attached to his book, the artist modestly tells his readers, " I have made up a portfolio of twelve sketches, consecutively illustrative of the four seasons of the year, beginning with a representation of New Year festivities, and ending with the drawing of the snow lion; and, though I cannot pretend to the perfection of the artists of bygone days, perhaps I may aspire to six or seven tenths of their talent. Written on the 4th day of the 4th month of the year Woo-shin, by Se Hea of Hangchow." There can be no doubt that art has declined in China, and this the Chinese themselves confess, as the above note will serve to show. Moreover, as with ourselves, the wealthy and cultivated classes in China expend large sums of money in collecting the works of the ancient masters, which they carefully preserve. Many of these old paintings have been executed on silk scrolls, and thus a Chinese picture gallery is quite unlike what we should expect to see, for the pictures are not framed and exposed on the walls, but are kept carefully rolled up and protected against the light and air. My friend Mr. Wylie, who is well known to Eastern scholars, when examining several old pictures which I had brought from Peking, made some interesting remarks on this point. He said, "Many anecdotes are on hand regarding the achievements of the old masters. Thus, in the third century we are told of a painter, Tsaou Puh-ying, who, when he had finished a screen for the Emperor, added some flies to the picture by a few touches of the pencil here and there; great was his gratification at seeing his Majesty take up a handkerchief to drive these flies away. Not less celebrated was Hwan Tseuen, who flourished about A.D. 1000, and who introduced several pheasants into a mural decoration in one of the halls of the palace. Some foreign envoys, who had brought a tribute of falcons, were ushered into this hall; and no sooner did the birds of prey get sight of the pheasants on the wall than they made a precipitate dart at their victims, more of course to the detriment of their heads than to the satisfaction of their appetites."

Between Swatow and Chao-chow-fu I have met wayfarers on a hot day stripped to the skin, every article of their clothing bound around the head, and thus marching along, to all appearance without the slightest sense of impropriety. The higher one ascends the Han the more savage-looking are the people we encounter there, but, happily, the clan-fights had been suppressed and peace re-established in the province. At Chaochow-fu I got up one morning before daybreak, to photograph an old bridge across the river there, and I fondly thought that being so early astir, I should get clear of the city mob; but as it happened, there was a market held on the top of the bridge, and even before it was quite light, long trains of produce-laden coolies were pouring in from every side. I had just time to show myself and take a photograph, when a howling multitude came rushing down to where I stood near my boat on the shore. Amid a shower of missiles I unscrewed my camera, with the still undeveloped photograph inside, took the apparatus under my arm, and presenting my iron-pointed tripod to the rapidly approaching foe, backed into the river and scrambled on board the boat. Chao-chow-fu bridge is not unlike the one at Foochow, which spans the river Min. It is built of stone and contains a great many arches, or rather square spaces for the passage of boats beneath. On each side of the causeway above, a row of houses has been erected, and these project beyond the parapets and overhang the stream for as much as three-fourths of their entire depth. There seems, indeed, to be no part of each house, except the brick wall in front, which rests upon the bridge; while as to the fabric itself, it is held up by a series of long poles, which abut upon the projections of the buttresses below, and thus serve to support the dwelling like the under-props of a bracket. This was what one would call a break-neck sort of architecture, and yet the great market of the town is held on this bridge, and there we find the dwelling-houses and shops of the merchants. There they trade and there they sleep, calmly awaiting the hour which shall drop them and their frail tenements into a muddy grave. But they had other means still to ensure safety both for property and life. Suspended between each archway hang two slender wooden frames, and these barriers the householders piously let down at night to deter malignant spirits from passing beneath their dwellings—a device, I need hardly say, universally successful.

Chao-chow-fu is open to foreign trade, and on one or two occasions the attempt has been made to establish a British Consulate in the town; but it has always been a failure. Turbulent mobs continually stone foreigners, and during the time of my visit the Vice-consul was the only European in the place. He, when I told him how I had been attacked by the rabble, said quietly, "You are no worse off than your neighbours; it is just what every white man must expect at the hands of the lawless ruffians of the town." So I was not sorry when I turned my back upon this part of Kwang-tung, and descended once more to Swatow. Every year sees an increase in the number of emigrants who leave this part of China to work on the plantations in Siam, Cochin China, or the Straits, and we may be sure that the price of labour in China is at a very low ebb, when we find that wages, running from two to four dollars a month, are all the inducement held out to allure the coolies from their homes; and that such a sum as this even is, by the toiling poor, esteemed sufficient to enable them to save money to invest in a farm on their return to their native land. It was up into this region that Juilin sent a military mandarin with a force of 2,000 men. This officer, at the time of my visit, was known in the district as Chao-Yang. His task was approaching completion and there was consequently more of peace and prosperity in the country than had been its lot for many previous years. Fang-Yao, for that was the mandarin's inharmonious designation, pursued a rough and ready sort of system in the conduct of his operations for putting matters to rights. Thus, at the village of Go-swa, near Double Island, he seized a man named Kwin-Kwong, well known to foreigners, and required him to surrender 200 of the chief rebels of his village. Kwin-Kwong produced 100, many of them, poor wretches, innocent substitutes for the true offenders. Under pressure and threats a few more victims were ultimately given up, and the whole were then beheaded, Kwin-Kwong's own skull being tossed into the pile to swell the number of the sufferers. It must have been bloody work; more than 1,000 are said to have been decapitated during Fang-Yao's memorable march.

Swaboi, one of the most powerful villages in the province, stands about two miles distant from Swatow, and for many years has monopolised the right to supply coolies to that town.

Several years ago, seventeen other villages combined against Swaboi, and resolved by force, if necessary, to put a stop to its monopoly of labour. The war lasted four years, and terminated in favour of Swaboi. At such times the villagers practise the most heartless cruelties on each other, burying their enemies, for example, while still alive, and head downwards, in graves prepared with quicklime and earth. It was, indeed, in this district that I gathered a notion of the inhuman treatment of idiots practised in some parts of China. I myself have seen an idiot exposed outside a village in a wooden cage, and there left for the passers-by to feed him, or better still to starve and die.

I afterwards went a second time to see this being that looked more brute than man, but he had died in his cage.

Amoy is the next open port in our northern route; and though situated in the province of Fukien, its geological features resemble those of Swatow. Thus the same decomposing hills crowned with huge granite bare boulders, are to be seen at the entrance of the harbour; and one of these boulders which faces the port, has some passages connected with the local history of the place engraven in huge characters upon its stony sides. Several of them rear their grey heads to a great height out of the water, or above the shore close by, and these the natives look up to with reverence and awe, as objects intimately connected with the Feng-shui, or good luck of the port. But in such a place as this it is but seldom that good luck waits upon the lower and most superstitious classes. The Amoy men make good soldiers, so at least it is said; they certainly fought well for their independence, and were the last to yield to the Tartar invaders, and those upon whom the conquerors seemed to have pressed most heavily. To this day they wear the turban which they assumed to hide the tonsure and queue imposed on them by the conquerors. The dialect here is so different from that spoken in Canton as to lead my boys to imagine that they were once more out of China and in some foreign realm. But a glimpse of the town quickly reassured them. There they fell in with men from their own province, and with odours and appearances so unmistakably Chinese that there was no getting over the fact; and they soon acknowledged that this indeed could still be no other than their own Chinese land. At Amoy, as in Swatow and most other Chinese seaport towns, the houses in the native quarter are huddled together like a crowd of sight-seers, all eager to stand in the front row along the water's

Buddhist Temple, Amoy.

edge. Many of these dwellings are in a sad state of decay and dilapidation; and the long, dark, narrow street which runs the length of the settlement is paved with cross flags of stone so worn and loose that they rest for the most part in treacherous pits of mud; and thus, if a foot be placed hastily on the rocking flag, a shower of most offensive dirt is splashed up over one's clothes. Every second shop reeks with a smell of roasting fat and onions. Mangy dogs and lean pigs yelp and grunt as we disturb their occupations: these are the sanitary authorities of the locality and to them the duty falls to clear up the refuse and garbage. Nor were these the only inconveniences; on nearly every occasion when I waded my way along the uninviting thoroughfares, I found it blocked at some point by a strolling band of players, hired to perform in public by one of the more liberal-spirited tradesmen. The approach to the foreign merchants' establishments can hardly be accounted better than the miserable Chinese alley which I have just described; but the offices themselves, when the difficulty of reaching them is overcome, are found to be venerable structures, filled with all sorts of produce beneath, and showing all the evidences of business above.

The trade of this port has grown, and is likely to continue growing, just in proportion as the rich island of Formosa opposite is developed, and its tea, sugar and other products increase. The late transfer of Formosa to the Japanese will alter the conditions of trade, although the Japanese may find it profitable to ship produce to the nearest markets on the Chinese mainland. The import trade and the distribution of foreign goods inland, is pretty effectually choked off by the illegal system of transit duties levied at the various stations, and regulated chiefly by the need or avarice of the local officials at the various points

7

along the route. There is also a grievous charge called Lekin, originally imposed as a war tax on foreign goods, and never since withdrawn. The American Consul, in writing on the subject, said: "At Swatow the local taxes levied on imports remain unchanged; that is to say, about one-fortieth of what they are in Amoy;" and he goes on to observe "that natives can still bring foreign goods overland from Swatow to the Amoy districts, and sell them at a cheaper rate than if they were imported and sold direct in Amoy." [1] This Lekin tax was instituted to defray the expenses either of the Taiping rebellion or of the "small knife" rebellion, or both. The "small knife" rebellion of 1853 was a serious affair for Amoy. The rebel chief, or ringleader, of this dagger society was said to be a Singapore Chinaman of the name of Tan-keng-chin. The outbreak was, in fact, a development of one of the secret societies that have been a source of continual trouble to all the countries into which Chinese labour has flowed.

In 1864, a few months after Nankin fell into the hands of the Imperialists, and when the cause of Tien-Wang or Heavenly King was all but crushed, the last remnant of his followers made a final effort and captured Chang-chow-fu, a city which stands in the same relationship to Amoy as Chao-chow-fu to Swatow. The place was eventually retaken by the Imperialists after a protracted struggle; and this barbarous war was then closed, amid scenes of cold-blooded massacre as inhuman as any that have stained the annals of the Taiping revolt, whose overthrow was brought about by foreign intervention, and by one or two powerful decisive blows dealt at the strongholds of the rebel towns. Alas! these successes were but too frequently followed

[1] Report on Amoy and the Island of Formosa, by A. W. Le Gendre.

AMOY NATIVES.

PRIMITIVE SOLDIER.

up by indiscriminate slaughter, for those are the means by which a weak government seeks to strike terror into the hearts of the people.

Occurrences such as that which I am now about to describe were accordingly by no means rare. The fight was ended and the fruits of the victory were reckoned up. It was reported to the conqueror that there were 254 heads and 231 queues and ears of people supposed to be rebels; at any rate, they were heads and ears and queues, and these the Imperialist troops had to lay at the feet of the authorities. It is astonishing how some of these mutilated wretches survived. Thus I myself saw a man who reported that his head had been nearly severed from his body, but who succeeded in reaching Amoy. There were certainly marks of a severe wound on the neck, similar to those described by Mr. Hughes in the "China Review" for June 1875. I have also seen a man enjoying good health who had both ears chopped off and part of the scalp carried away. Mr. Hughes again tells us, in another paper, that female infanticide is perhaps worse in this part of the Fukien province than in any other quarter of the Empire, and this corroborates the conclusion I myself had come to from enquiries I made on the spot. Mr. Hughes one day met a stout well-to-do-looking man of the coolie class, carrying two neat and clean round baskets, slung on a pole which he bore across his shoulder. "Hearing the cry of a child, I stopped him, when I found that he had two infants in each basket;" and it is recorded that this crafty old speculator in innocents was on his way to sell his living burden at the Foundling Hospital, where he would receive 100 cash, or about fivepence, for a female child, and as much as three pounds for a boy.

This Foundling Hospital was organised by a native merchant

whom I had the pleasure of meeting, and it is a lamentable fact that the prospect of receiving fivepence will tempt a mother to part with her babe.

The Amoy Hospital is, however, conducted on rather more liberal principles than that in Canton; for if any one wishes to obtain a child, he may get one here free of charge, provided that he can deposit suitable credentials as to his own respectability. One of the resident Christian missionaries informed me that he felt convinced that 25 per cent of the female children of Amoy were destroyed at birth. The natives themselves make no secret of this crime, and I saw one old woman who confessed to having made away with three of her daughters in succession. They excuse their misdeeds on the ground of extreme poverty, and they certainly are poor and wretched to a degree I had no conception of before I visited their abodes. The district around is naturally barren and unproductive, and plundering raids of rebel and Imperial troops crippled the energies of the needy inhabitants. War, it is true, has thinned the population, but not to such an extent as materially to affect its density.

An able-bodied man can here earn only fivepence a day, and skilled workmen, of whom there are many, are paid about eightpence per diem. There is a great trade carried on in one quarter of the town, or rather in a suburb, in the collection and preparation of manure, which is afterwards sold to the farmers to fertilise their poor lands. The people who deal in this commodity dwell on the edge of the foul pits into which filth of all sorts is thrown, and for the use of the hovels in which they reside many of them pay about fivepence a month in rent. Close to this spot is a hill on which the poor are buried. There is no lack of recent graves, but all such are covered with lime, mixed with fragments of glass and pottery, in order to keep pigs and dogs from digging up the bodies. How the people subsist here it is hard to say! Judging from the multitude of graves they must die in great numbers, and who can wonder at it, in an atmosphere that smells so putrid. I looked into one or two of the dwellings; they were single-roomed huts reared above the naked sod. Often they contained no furniture at all, and their ragged lean occupants were filthy in the extreme; and yet numerous children were to be seen running about, pitching pebbles into the pools, or chasing the pigs and pariah dogs to prevent them from eating up the only article of trade in the locality.

There was another hill not far off, and commanding a view of the harbour. On this I found a row of glazed earthen pots, each containing a skeleton; one had been broken and the bones lay scattered over the face of the rock, while a number of children were playing catch-ball with the skull. What mean these dishonoured relics, over which some Ezekiel might prophesy, lamenting the degradation of his people? These are the remains deposited here to await interment—a ceremony which can only be properly accomplished by attending to the times and places which the professors of Feng-shui may prescribe. But alas! too many of these unsepulchred skeletons will never know any resting-place more hallowed than the pots in which they were originally stored. There they crumble, unfriended and forgotten, for their surviving kinsmen are perhaps themselves cut off from the land, or else too poor to pay the expenses of the for ever deferred burial rites. Now, then, my readers can appreciate the true motives of a Chinaman, who, as I have already said, will devote his earnings to the purchase of a coffin, funeral raiment and a burial site in anticipation, many years before his death.

My sketch of Amoy has thus far been a dark one, and yet the true picture is not without some glances of light striking down even into the lowest quarters of the town. Thus, in one of my many perambulations I came to a very narrow and very dark lane, where I found the humble tenants of the houses engaged in what, to me, was quite a new industry. Men, women and children were all busily occupied in the manufacture of most beautiful artificial flowers, from a pith obtained in Formosa, from the same plant (*Aralia papyrifera*) as that out of which the so-called rice-paper is made. I entered shop after shop, and everywhere found thousands of flowers spread out on trays, and each one so lifelike that it might almost be mistaken for nature herself. But tiny hands were at work here too, and roses, lilies, azaleas and camelias grew up with wonderful celerity beneath them. The workshops are the dwellings, the offices and the warehouses of each firm, or family; and the workers within are so closely packed that strangers not unfrequently must watch the process, or make a purchase, by taking up a position outside. I bought a great many of these flowers from a man in a very mean shop indeed. He was extremely poor, and he asked me for an advance of money, offering to furnish security if I wished. I lent him a few dollars without troubling him for securities; and though I knew nothing about him, he carried out the transaction with the most scrupulous honesty.

There are many wealthy Chinese merchants in Amoy, who live in good style and in superior houses on the hills above and beyond the town. On those hills, too, we may find temples and monastic establishments, built in the most romantic situations among great granite boulders which tower in some places many hundred feet above the plain. Thus from the rock on which the "White Stag" monastery stands one obtains a commanding view

●f the town, harbour and island of Ku-lang-su. It is on Ku-
lang-su that European settlers chiefly reside; and there the
houses environed with parks and gardens, are second to none
in China. Some Christian missions also are established in
the same quarter, and not unfittingly, for there is a wide
opening for mission labour in a field so benighted and so woe-
stricken as Amoy.

From Amoy I crossed over by steamer to Formosa; but
before I left the harbour I had time to pull off to the steam-
ship "Yesso," and take a hurried leave of an esteemed friend
broken down in health, and then homeward bound. I never
saw him again, for he died before reaching home. I had a
pleasant companion in Dr. Maxwell, the medical missionary of
Tai-wan-fu, in Formosa, and from him I heard some interesting
accounts of the savages on this strange island. Leaving the
harbour at 5 p.m., we passed the Pescadore group of islands at
daybreak next morning. The wind all the while blew strongly
from the north, forcing me to forego my dinner, and to confine
myself a prisoner in my berth until I was summoned on deck
to see land. It was a grateful sight, but how the sea was
rolling! and the land—alas! the only thing that struck me about
it was that it must be a very long way off. Having once gained
my sea legs, I had one or two hours' leisure to scrutinise the
coast and the inland mountain ranges, which lost themselves in
the clouds above. A narrow rocky inlet was pointed out to me
as the only harbour accessible in this quarter; and it was
abreast of this spot, some two miles from shore, that the
steamer came to her moorings. Here I found myself keenly
interested in the experiences of a Malay on board, who informed
me that vessels were constantly being wrecked along this shore,
and that their crews were invariably eaten to a man by the

bloodthirsty savages, who perpetually scoured the beach in search of prey. He had probably heard of the wreck of the schooner "Macto" in 1859, and how the crew were massacred on this very beach by the natives; or else he may have been referring to the murder at a later date, of a number of American castaways by the aborigines further south. It is to punish outrages of this sort that a Japanese army was despatched to Formosa, in retaliation for some particular barbarities which chance to have been practised upon a Japanese crew; so say the Japanese. I predicted in my previous work the probability of coming difficulties between Japan and China.

We are told by the "Pall Mall Gazette" that when the Japanese fleet anchored off Formosa, and before a single soldier landed, a Chinese corvette and a gunboat steamed into sight, with guns run out, men at quarters and everything prepared for action. Between them these two vessels as they assure us, might have sunk the whole Japanese squadron; but after some palaver the Chinese men-of-war quietly steamed off again, and the Japanese troops were landed. It is possible that this visit of the Japanese to Formosa and their finding it a land greatly to be desired and full of undeveloped resources, had some influence in their eventually securing the island for themselves.

Before we disembark and proceed on our journey inland, it may be as well to give the reader some general notion of the island and its position. Isla Formosa, or the Beautiful Island, as the Portuguese named it, lies at the distance of about one hundred miles off the mainland. In time the Chinese crossed over and planted a settlement on the island, driving the savages high up into the almost inaccessible mountains. The island runs nearly north and south, its length is about 250 miles, and it is about 84 miles broad across its widest part. Down its

Mountain Gorge, Island of Formosa.

centre a rocky spine of lofty mountains stretches longitudinally nearly from sea to sea, with peaks, in some places, about fourteen thousand feet high. The Chinese occupy only the western half of the island and a small portion at its northern extremity, while the whole of the mountainous region to the east is held by independent tribes of aborigines. Before it was ceded to Japan the island was ruled over by a Taotai resident at Tai-wan-fu, and appointed by the Central Government. The Taotai of Formosa was the only officer of the same rank in the Empire who enjoyed the privilege of direct appeal to the throne. The population is about three millions, viz., two and a half millions Chinese and half a million aborigines. Naturalists suppose that Formosa was originally joined to the mainland; and what confirms them in this view is the great similarity of its flora and fauna to that of the nearest provinces of China. But let us land and see for ourselves.

CHAPTER VII.

FORMOSA.

Takow Harbour, Formosa—La-mah-kai—Difficulties of Navigation—Tai-
wan-fu—The Taotai—His Yamen—How to cancel a State Debt—The
Dutch in 1661—Sylvan Lanes—Medical Missions—A Journey to the
Interior—Old Watercourses—Broken Land—Hak-ka Settlers—Poah-
be—Pepohoan Village—Baksa Valley—The name "Isla Formosa"—A
long March—The Central Mountains—Bamboo Bridges—"Pau-ah-liau"
Village—The Physician at work—Ka-san-po Village—A Wine-feast—
Interior of a Hut—Pepohoan Dwellings—A Savage Dance—Savage
Hunting-grounds—La-lung Village—Return Journey.

A CHINESE pilot, named Opium, came off to the steamer and
brought her to a secure anchorage about a mile from shore.
There was a pretty heavy sea on at this time, rendering it
dangerous, even in a surf-boat, to make for the mouth of the
harbour; so Dr. Maxwell and I determined to go ashore with
Opium, trusting to his local knowledge to land us safely some-
where along the coast. This pilot was a cool, imperturbable
seaman, a daring specimen, who had been out in all weathers
and who was said to have earned his singular cognomen of
Opium from his notoriety as a smuggler of that valuable drug.

It is truly wonderful how in California the genius of the Chinese race has been times without number equal to the task of carrying on an untaxed opium traffic, and that too under a system of police surveillance that only falls short of submitting the Chinaman and his effects to a process of sublimation, which would leave the hidden juices of the narcotic behind. Nevertheless, their dodges have been detected one by one; a layer of opium glued in between the polished sides of a trunk will never reach shore, nor pass unnoticed though wrought into the well-made soles of a silken boot, or stitched into the skirts of a padded robe. But now we are on the top of the breakers, plunging as if the boat were going bow-foremost to the bottom. Opium is looking calmly on the while, with a countenance at once soothing and reassuring. We soon roll over the last billow and are swept into a small haven amid the rocks. These rocks are of igneous formation, and look like molten metal suddenly chilled while in a state of violent ebullition. We land, and scramble over a multitude of cell-like cavities with edges as hard as flint and sharp as splintered glass. Many of these cavities have the hollows filled up with a little sandy soil, in which luxuriant shrubs and a sort of dwarf date-palm grow. The wet sand along the beach was of a deep black hue.

As we made our way through the native town of Takow, I was much struck with the tropical appearance of the place, and with the shady palms, which reminded us of the villages in the Malayan Archipelago. But evidently neither Mohammedans nor Malays dwelt there, for huge porkers roamed free about the settlement, or kept watch around the cabin doors. At length we reached the Mission Station, and met with a cordial welcome. Here the Rev. Mr. Ritchie gave me some notion of the lawless state which prevailed in this portion of the island.

One day, when on a mission-trip inland, he fell in with the deputy magistrate (Chinese) of the Tung-shan district, returning to his "Yamen" from a place called La-ma-kai, with a troop of armed retainers at his heels. Passing this official and proceeding on to La-ma-kai, my friend there met a band of ruffians carrying spears, daggers and fire-arms; and behind them followed an old woman, who besought the marauders to return her son's matchlock, which one of them had just stolen from her house. The first question asked of Mr. Ritchie when he reached the Chinaman's hut where he proposed to sleep, was whether these armed men had been seen, as they were a band of highway robbers that had been plundering the neighbouring settlements. The magistrate, it appeared, had been despatched by his superior officer to seize on a rich relative of one of the bandits, and to hold him as a hostage; but the crafty knaves had been fore-warned of the threatened surprise, most probably by one of the servants in the mandarin's train, and had forthwith met their enemy with so overwhelming a force as to compel him to an undignified and speedy retreat. A wholesome dread of Europeans, inspired by the vigorous action of Lieutenant Gordon at Tai-wan-fu, saved my friend from falling an easy prey into the hands of the gang.

Two or three of the European firms at Amoy have branch establishments in Takow, or had at the time I speak of; and behind these foreign houses there rises a hill more than 1,000 feet high and commonly known as Apes' Hill, from the large apes, its only inhabitants, which may be seen in great numbers about the crags. From this hill I obtained a commanding view of Takow harbour, and the observations which I made here, as well as closer inspections carried out from other points, led me to the conclusion that in the hands of a civilised foreign power, a portion of the soft sandy lagoon, which is gradually invading and narrowing the available anchorage of the harbour, might soon be added to the now limited accommodation for shipping; while the bar at the mouth of the port might no less easily be removed. As the case now stands, with wind and tide favourable, a barque drawing twelve feet of water can find her way through the rocky entrance. Rapid physical changes have taken place within a recent period on this western side of Formosa, as I shall be able to demonstrate conclusively when we get to a point further north. It struck me, however, that the natural formation of the harbour of Takow belongs to a modern date. Thus, when the Dutch occupied the island, a considerable river existed at the southern extremity, and the channel, now nearly dry, is still known as "Ang-mang-kang," or estuary of the red-haired race. The combined action of the sea silting up debris on the one side, and of the river on the other, together with the growth of a crescent-shaped coral reef, has formed a natural barrier several miles in extent, now covered with a belt of most luxuriant tropical trees. This bar is joined at its northern extremity by a ridge of igneous rocks; and it is in this ridge that the break or flaw occurs which forms the mouth of the harbour. Much of the six or seven miles enclosed by this natural wall, consists of a shallow lagoon with a bottom of extremely soft mud. It is only towards the northern end that a depth of water is obtained sufficient for ships trading to the island.

Owing to the disturbed state of the country I deferred my visit to the aboriginal tribes of the south, and went with Dr. Maxwell to see Tai-wan-fu, the capital, twenty-five miles further north on the coast. Starting at daylight in the "Formosa," we reached the outer roads at 8 o'clock. It is singular to observe

that there is now no harbour at Tai-wan-fu. We could descry
the old fort Zelandia, erected there by the Dutch in 1633,
about two and a half miles from where we lay, and surrounded
by water so shallow as to render any nearer approach impossible; and yet in the Dutch accounts of Formosa it is stated
that Zelandia was an island where a spacious haven was formed;
and further, that on April 30th, 1661, Koksinga's fleet
appeared before Tai-wan-fu, ran into the spacious haven between Zelandia and Provincia, separated by a distance of more
than three miles; and the haven in which the Chinese invader
anchored his fleet is now a dry arid plain, crossed by a high
road, and having a canal cut through it, communicating with
the old port of Tai-wan-fu. A small portion of the plain is
flooded at high tide; while off the fort the water is now so
shallow that vessels have to anchor, as we did, two miles out
to sea. Neither is it an easy or safe business to cross these
vast shallows, at least when the sea is rough; and if there is
a strong south-west monsoon blowing, it cannot be done at
all. As for ourselves, we went ashore in a catamaran, a sort
of raft made of poles of the largest species of bamboo. These
poles are bent by fire so as to impart a hollow shape to the
raft, and are lashed together with ratan. A strong wooden
block, made fast to the centre of this surf-boat, supports the
mast, which carries a large mat sail. There is not a nail used
in the whole contrivance, and the most curious feature about
the strange vessel is the accommodation provided for passengers.
This is nothing more than a spacious tub. I thought it possible
at first that these were the boats of the local washerwomen;
but, so far as washing is concerned, the natives of Formosa
confine themselves to washing their customers occasionally
ashore in the tub and mangling them on the beach—a very

simple process, for the tub is in no way fixed to the raft, so that a heavy sea would, and does frequently, send it adrift. The tub into which we descended would hold four persons, and when we squatted down inside it we could just see over the top. Not feeling very comfortable, we came out and sat on the bare raft, to which we had at times to cling, *manibus pedibusque*, as the waves broke over us.

Tai-wan-fu, the capital of Formosa, is a fortified city of 70,000 inhabitants. The walls enclose a space of about five miles, planted to a great extent with fields and gardens, and still showing traces of the ancient Dutch occupation, in the ruins of Fort Provincia and in the extensive parks shaded with fine old trees or groves of tall bamboo. The suburbs are intersected by a multitude of green lanes, which run between walls of cactus interspersed with the brilliant flowers of the wild fuchsia and clusters of major convolvulus, or else shaded by bamboo hedges, which form a pointed archway above the path. The inhabitants of this part of the island are chiefly natives of the Fukian province, and the Hak-kas already described. These between them are daily carrying arts and agriculture further into the territory claimed by the aboriginal tribes.

Armed with an official introduction I paid a visit to the "Taotai" (or governor) of Tai-wan (Formosa). Waiting in my chair outside his yamen while my card—a red one, the size of a large sheet of note-paper—was sent in, I found myself surrounded by the idle crowd that is always certain to collect about a stranger in China—whence the gazers came, and whither they would go, would be difficult to tell—and all sorts of conjectures being thrown out as to the nature of my business. A little naked boy, with a face full of perfectly untutored innocent curiosity, ventured a trifle too near, so I leaned slightly forward and frowned at him. Bursting into a fit of screaming terror he fled from the yamen, while the mob looked grave, and wondered what devilry I could have practised on the child. Soon an officer appeared, and behind him followed a train of yamen attendants, who wore the usual conical hats with red feathers that suggested the idea of flames burning through the top of an extinguisher. Thus escorted, I was ushered into the yamen. Passing through the hall of justice, I noticed various instruments of torture, the substitutes for our sacred oath, to extract truth from a witness, or confession from the lips of a prisoner. Here I met a more venerable official, dressed in a long silk robe, a stiff girdle and heavily-soled satin boots. By him I was conducted through a court and along a series of corridors, and finally presented to the Taotai, with infinitely greater official ceremony and pomposity than when I was intro- duced to Prince Kung, or Li-hung-Chang. Indeed it seems to me the Chinese are not exempt from the peculiarity which makes small officials everywhere self-important, and fearfully exacting in all matters touching their personal dignity. The private quarters of the Taotai and his retainers were prettily laid out, the open courts being shaded with palms and decked with flowers in vases, besides shrubs, ferns and creepers; and the whole interior was surrounded with saloons or pavilions. Into one of these last I was led, and there presented to a full- faced pleasant-looking Chinaman, who, to my surprise, held out his hand, and addressing me in perfect English, said, "Good morning, Mr. Thomson, I am glad to see you here; when did you come over?" I recognised the speaker after a time, as a man whom I had met in Hongkong as a comprador, or a schroff, in a bank. He told me he was the nephew of the Taotai, and I have a strong suspicion that that functionary

himself had at one time been engaged in trade, and that he had by purchase obtained this post, out of which, if report spoke true, he was making a very good thing. After partaking of tea and fruit, my friend, whose mind was evidently imbued with the notion that I had come to the place on some secret mission, tried all he could to gain exact information as to my intentions. I told him plainly that my purpose was to go into the heart of the island to see the aborigines. He wanted to know why I should take the trouble to trudge so far on foot, through a region where no proper roads existed, merely to see the place, with the chance perhaps of being killed. " Depend upon it," he assured me, " you will never get near them; you will be shot with poisoned arrows, or lose yourself in the forest paths. But come and see the Taotai." This gentleman was rather a good-looking man, of middle age, and said to be remarkable for his administrative ability. At any rate, although apparently affected with suspicions as to my design in visiting the aborigines, he showed me some kindness, and in return for a portrait which I took for him, he sent me a box of tea and some dried lichees. The tea unfortunately spoiled before I reached Hongkong, but the lichees were very good.

A curious incident occurred in this town during the rule of the preceding Taotai. When the fort of Anping had been stormed by Lieut. Gordon and his party, the military mandarin in command of the troops at Anping, was supposed in some measure to have failed in his duty. To this charge was added an accusation of treason; for it was known that he had saluted Mr. Gibson, the late British Consul, with three guns, when that functionary left for Amoy. This unworthy commander, then, was dining one night with the prefect, when a message was sent from the Taotai, directing the Prefect to detain his military

8

guest until morning. At daybreak a second messenger arrived, who brought instructions for the Prefect to repair with his prisoner to the Taotai's yamen, and forthwith, as the business was urgent. When they reached the yamen, a servant came out to say that the Taotai would not receive the military mandarin, and ordered him to prepare for instant death. The unhappy man insisted on an interview, and with his men forced his way into the yamen, where he demanded an appeal to the Emperor. The Taotai informed him that the edict had been received from Peking, had him stripped of his official clothes, hurried off and put to death on the spot. In another such instance of summary vengeance a wealthy mandarin, who had aided the Government with loans of money, determined, as he saw no probability of repayment, to withhold an undue proportion of the local taxes. It is a very common course of procedure in the interest of the Imperial Government to wait until the official has amassed sufficient wealth by illegal exactions, then to trump up a case against him, squeeze his property and condemn him to death. Shortly after the mandarin had taken this step, an official was despatched by the Government to inquire into the matter. The district governor hereupon invited the defaulter to a quiet dinner to meet the governor-general's emissary, and during the course of a convivial evening the host and his friend between them so managed to outrage the feelings of the guest, that a quarrel finally ensued. Then the "yamen runners" were called in, the expostulating guest was cut down, and this was the new way in which an old state debt was paid.

A large tract of land outside Tai-wan-fu is known as the execution-ground, and this spot I visited in company with Dr. Maxwell. I tried to make a picture out of it, but there was nothing to lend grace to the scene; for the plain here is a per-

fectly flat one, whence the grand old trees of Tai-wan may be
seen crowding away into the background, as if they shrunk from
rooting themselves in unhallowed earth. Hardly a shrub relieves
the monotony of this gloomy place of death; and yet with
what a fearful interest it must have been gazed on by that
band of Europeans, 160 in number, who were led out there to
execution one morning in August 1842! The mob of the city
followed behind them with yells of exultation, but before the
terrible massacre had closed, their savage laughter was changed
into panic terror, for the sky became overcast and a dire storm
burst upon the scene. The water-courses were filled with impetuous torrents that flooded the land, sweeping trees, houses and
produce before its swollen streams, while the cries of perishing
people were drowned in the fierce tumult of the tempest. Thus,
say the thoughtful and superstitious natives, God wiped out the
bloody stain from the ground. It is alleged that about 2,000
persons perished on that eventful day. A tragic history attaches
to Tai-wan-fu, apart both from the incident which I have just
related, and the storming of Anping fort, more recently still —
an event too full of details to permit description here.

In olden times the city was the scene of the fierce struggle
which ended in the expulsion of the Dutch from Formosa in
1661, after a nearly twelve months' siege. Koksinga, who drove
the doughty Hollanders from this beautiful island, must have
been a bold adventurer. He was a sort of Chinese sea-king,
levying black-mail from all the surrounding islands. China now-
a-days needs just such an admiral to command her new steam
fleet. With resources so great at his command, he might have
taught the ambitious inhabitants of the small kingdom of Japan
that their safest policy is to keep their troops at home. When I
took my rambles through the sylvan lanes of Tai-wan-fu, no feature

so much struck me as their perfect repose; not a sign or sound
recalled the fearful conflicts which they too often witnessed.
The languid air was filled with no noise more warlike than the
hum of insects, the creak of produce-laden carts on their way
to market, or the merry prattle of children at play. Alas! the
quiet glades of Formosa may soon be stirred once more with
the din of a vital struggle for supremacy, between two races
who for the first time will confront each other with modern
weapons in their hands. The conflict when it takes place will
without doubt be severe and its issue may lead to important
results in opening up the vast continent of China. This forecast has been verified by the result of the late war, and China
has been found, as I supposed, with her beggarly troops, her
boasted navy, unable to cope with her much despised neighbour.
Her increased army and modern navy afforded an opportunity,
too tempting for the time-honoured and systematic plunder of
the mandarins. The existence of an army proved an illusion;
the ships of the navy were simply targets for the Japanese
cruisers; while the Chinese shells were filled with sand as a
harmless and economical substitute for gunpowder or other explosive material having a certain market value.

I determined to make an excursion into the interior, and to
visit the outlying mission-stations, where my friend hoped, if
possible, to open up new ground among the mountain savages.
Accordingly on Monday, April 11th, we left Tai-wan-fu for the
village of Poah-be, and were carried in native sedans ten miles
across the plain. I hired a number of coolies to convey my
instruments, as I had determined to photograph the objects of
interest which we might fall in with *en route*. The plain, a
highly cultivated one, was dotted with Chinese farms, and with
hamlets overshadowed by groves of bamboo ; the chief products

here were rice, sweet potatoes, earth-nuts and sugar-cane. Many
of the women were out at work in the fields; most of them
had the compressed feet so much in vogue among the females
of the Fukien province, and hence they seemed to limp about
uneasily over the furrows. They generally wore pretty dresses
of white calico, edged with pale blue. As for the men, they
were bronzed and fat, and they had a lazy, loutish appearance,
seemingly leaving the women to do the bulk of the field-work.
There were children to be seen too, but their attire consisted
simply of a small charm hung on a string around the neck. As at
Tai-wan-fu, we passed along some beautiful sylvan lanes, shaded
by areca-palms and bamboos, and leading to the settlements
which were truly enchanting when viewed from a distance, but
less attractive and thoroughly Chinese on a closer inspection.
The near approach to one of these hamlets was always known
by the conflicting odours of garlic and manure, mingled with the
fragrance of some sweet-smelling flowers of which the Chinese
are very fond, and which quite overpower the soft perfume of
the white wild-rose that grows in profusion in the hedges. In
the wild flowers which bloom hereabouts we discover the delicate hues of our more temperate climes, blending charmingly
with the vivid primary colours of the tropical flora. It was pleasant, too, to listen to the songs of the field lark, a bird common
to certain districts of the mainland both in the north and south
of China, and, so far as I can recollect, to some parts of Siam.

Halting at the first range of hills, we send back the chairs
and await the arrival of my boy Ahong and the coolies, who
were far in the rear. Ahong, unaccustomed to walking, was
already foot-sore. Against my advice he had put on straw
sandals, and so blistered the soles of his feet that the remaining
eight miles of our journey tried him severely. The road, if our

route could be dignified by such a name, was a broken track over dry hills, constantly interrupted by blocks of hard clay and by pitfalls six or eight feet deep. But these were trifles to what lay before us. Slowly we progressed, now wending our tortuous way along the verge of a clay chasm more than 200 feet deep, now diving down into the recesses of a huge clay pit, where the flat surface was so heated with the sun that it almost blistered the hands when we touched its bare walls. The soil became the more broken the further we progressed inland; the pits, too, grew wider and deeper. At the bottom of some of these we actually found cultivated fields, and traces of the mountain torrents that force a subterraneous passage during the wet season through the soft formation beneath, and thus effect the drainage of the central range of mountains, while at the same time they render farming in this hill region an enterprise full of peril. For the squatter tills the treacherous ground, and is liable to find his fields and his dwelling swept away by the sudden subsidence of the soil. But the Hak-kas, who cultivate this shifting clay, are prepared for such emergencies, and are quite accustomed to a hasty change of abode, cheerfully resuming their agricultural labours wherever they may happen to settle. At times, indeed, the sudden disappearance of their whole property may lead to very desirable results. They emigrate to a healthier or more settled neighbourhood, perhaps, or else to one where the trees and debris brought down by the torrents will furnish them with fuel during the winter months. I need hardly say that the Imperial Government has not seen fit to send a geographer to lay down a map of this ever-changing region; and it will be a matter of difficulty, I should think, for the farmer, at the end of each wet season, to find out exactly where he and his neighbours have settled. Poah-be was reached by about 4 p.m. This place is the first settlement of a tribe of aborigines whom the Chinese call "Pepohoan," or "foreigners of the plain." These people have a lively and warm recollection of their Dutch masters. They still cherish traditions of their kind-hearted, red-haired brothers, and for this reason they receive foreigners with a cordial welcome. Once, in the times of the Dutch, they lived down in those fertile plains which we had just been crossing; but they have long ago been driven back out of the richer land by the advance of the ruthless Chinese. Higher up, in the mountain fastnesses, their hardy kinsmen have held their own, defying all the forces of the Imperial conqueror.

The natives came out in great numbers to meet and welcome the Doctor, whom they had not seen for a considerable time. They were a fine, simple-looking race and had a frank sincerity of manner which was refreshing after a long experience of the cunning Chinese. These Pepohoans had acquired the Chinese arts of husbandry and house-building. Their buildings were even superior to those of the Chinese squatters, and the people themselves were better dressed. It struck me, as I have noticed elsewhere, that they resembled the Laotians of Siam both in features and costume, while their old language bore undoubted traces of Malayan origin. [1]

I visited several of the houses at Poah-be and found them clean, well-arranged and comfortable. Their mode of construction is as follows:—A bamboo framework is first set up; this is then covered with a lathing or rather wattle-work of reeds or split bamboo, and the whole is afterwards plastered over with the clay that abounds in the neighbourhood, and finished when dry with an outer coating of the white lime made out of

[1] See Appendix.

the limestone rock which is plentiful in these hills. The dwellings usually form three sides of a square; but I will describe the interior accommodation in more detail further on in my narrative. Only two articles in any of the Pepohoan settlements bore tokens of ingenuity and mechanical skill; these were the butts of their matchlocks and a native rat-trap, which was very curious indeed. The rat is esteemed a great luxury among the mountaineers—so great that the invention of this trap must have been a most important event in the history of their race.

Friday, April 11.—We left Poah-be at 7 a.m. to-day to walk to Baksa, twelve miles off. It was a beautiful morning, and the scenery gradually became so interesting as to warrant the belief that we had now got clear of the broken shifting lands through which our yesterday's journey had extended. By about ten o'clock the heat became intense, and Ahong was fairly knocked up. We had to reduce our pace, too, on account of his sorely blistered feet, so that it was twelve o'clock before we reached Baksa valley. Here again the people came out to welcome us, shouting "Peng-gan," "Peace be with you," while many a horny hand was stretched out from its toil to grasp the doctor's as we entered the village, or rather as we passed through the lanes, and beneath the palms that shaded the scattered dwellings in this Pepohoan paradise. I could now understand what the Portuguese meant when they named the island Formosa; and yet what we saw here was but the foreshadowing of the wilder grandeur of the mountain scenery inland. A crescent of limestone hills sweeps round Baksa valley, presenting in many places a bare rocky front in striking contrast to the foliage which luxuriates elsewhere. Perhaps the bamboos where the most remarkable feature in the scene, for these plants here attain exceptional proportions and are, some of them, more than 100 feet high. In the history of Tai-wan it is stated that there are thirteen varieties of bamboos (a species of grass) known in Formosa, one being reported to attain to the enormous girth of two feet. [1] I will here give a brief account of the many uses to which the bamboo is applied—a plant which figures extensively in the social economy of the people throughout the length and breadth of China. Were every other means of support withdrawn except rice and bamboo, these two plants would, I believe, supply the necessaries for clothing, habitation and food; indeed the bamboo alone, as I propose to show, would bear the lion's share of the burden. No tending is needed for this hardy-natured plant, nor is it dainty in the choice of its locality; and although it probably reaches its highest state of perfection in the rich valleys of Formosa, yet it grows with nearly equal vigour on the thin soil of rocky hill-sides. It is first used to hedge the dwelling around with an almost impenetrable barrier of prickly stems, and to cast a cool shade over the abodes with its lofty pale-green plumes. The houses themselves may be constructed entirely of its stems and thatched with its dry leaves. Within, the couches and chairs are made of bamboo, and so is the table, except its deal top; so, too, are the water-cans, the drinking jugs and the rice-measures. Hanging from the roof are a number of prickly bamboo stems, supporting dried pork and such like provisions, and warding off rats with their *chevaux de frise*. In one corner we may see the proprietor's waterproof coat and hat, each made out of the leaves of the plant, which overlap like the plumage of a bird. The agricultural implements are, many of them, made of hard bamboo stems, and, indeed, the fishing-net, the baskets of divers shapes, the

[1] Chinese Notes and Queries, ii. 135.

paper and the pens (never absent from the humblest Chinese abodes), the wine-cups, the water ladles, the chop-sticks and, finally, the tobacco-pipes are all of bamboo. The man who dwells there is feasting on the tender shoots of the plant; and if you ask him, he will tell you that his earliest impressions came to him through the basket-work of his bamboo cradle, and that his latest hope will be to lie beneath some bamboo brake, on a cool hill-side. The plant is also extensively used in the sacred offices of the Buddhist temples. The most ancient Buddhist classics were cut on strips of bamboo; the divination-sticks and the case which contains them are manufactured out of its stem; while the courts outside the temple are fanned and sheltered by its nodding plumes. There are a variety of different sorts of paper made from the bamboo, but the kind which struck me as showing a new property in the fibre of the plant was that commonly used by the Fukien gold-beaters in the production of gold-leaf, thus occupying the place of the parchment employed for the same purpose in Europe. Fans and flutes are also made of bamboo, and even the looms on which the Chinese weave their silken fabrics are chiefly made out of the plant. Indeed, it is impossible to estimate its value to the Chinese. This much, however, I may unhesitatingly affirm, that so multifarious are the duties which the bamboo is made to discharge, and so wide-spread are the benefits which it confers upon the Chinese, as to render it above all others the most useful plant in the Empire.

We spent the night at the Baksa mission-station and left early next morning to walk to Ka-san-po, a distance of twenty-six miles. The first hill we got to after quitting Baksa gave us some faint notion of the journey now before us. We had to climb a rocky ridge, where the soil had been completely broken away on either side; and thus along the sharp edge we made our way upwards to the summit of the hill. It was with no feelings of ease that I kept looking back upon our baggage-bearers (six strong Pepohoans from Baksa), who, had they slipped would have been precipitated several hundred feet on whatever side they chanced to fall. At last we reached the summit safely, and were rewarded with a view of a splendid valley surrounded by a circle of hills, while the central mountain ranges of the island could be descried towering heavenwards in the distance beyond. The little settlement of Kamana could just be made out at the eastern extremity of a long glen. Resting for a short time in a Pepohoan hut, where the people were glad to see us and where we had a refreshing draught of spring water, we then pushed on to Kamana, and were there met by a sturdy old native helper named Tong, a man of good Chinese education, who had formerly held a post in a yamen. He was a fine-looking fellow, and had suffered a good deal of persecution for having embraced the Christian faith. At about one o'clock, under the guidance of Tong, we left this station and commenced another toilsome ascent, beneath a blazing sun and without a breath of wind to temper the intense heat. At length, after surmounting the first range, we fell in with a buffalo herd, and found an old man living in a rude shed in the centre of a parched wilderness. He received us kindly and gladly shared with us his supply of water, which he held in a bamboo tube. Our arrival evidently afforded him great pleasure, and he was anxious we should remain for a smoke and a chat. Off again to climb another hill, or rather to scramble up deep fissures in one, over a broken stratum of clay and slate. Once on the top we flung ourselves down beneath the scant shade of some shrubs in a rocky cleft, at the same time dislodging from the

roots and stones numerous tribes of centipedes, each about as
long as one's finger and of a rich chocolate colour, with bright
yellow feet. These centipedes inflict a severe sting, but we
were too much exhausted to get out of their way, and fortunately they got out of ours. A steep descent on the other side
of this ridge brought us to our next halting-place, where a
brook was reported to exist; a channel indeed was there, but
the waters had dried up long ago. Here while at breakfast our
crowning trouble overtook us. One of the bearers incautiously
broke off the green stem of a plant, which in return for the
outrage sent forth a perfectly putrid odour. It was some time
before we discovered the cause of the nuisance, for the Pepohoan nose seemed to account it a luxury rather then otherwise.
This plant is known to them as the "foul" shrub, and is one
which the Chinese ought to prize dearly, for its very breath
might be sufficient to fertilise a whole region.

We were now on one of the spurs that lie at the foot of the
central range, and could enjoy a splendid view of a valley that
stretched out in front of us, half cultivated and half in its pristine grandeur; while the mountain sierras rose up pile behind
pile, Mount Morrisson lifting its deep blue peak on high above
them all. A river flowed far down beneath our feet, and we
could hear the distant boom of its waters, as they rushed onward
through dark ravines and over a rocky mountain bed. This
river was now at its smallest, but was still a broad stream, and
was spanned by a number of bamboo bridges, if such these
rude structures might be called. Far away, at the northern end
of the valley, the village of Pau-ah-liau could be descried peeping out amid a mass of foliage; and high above this settlement rose mountains wrapped in the gloom of primeval forests,
the haunts of wild beasts and savage men. These mountain

tribes just referred to, exact a heavy black-mail from their more civilised kinsmen in the valleys below; and not content with this, they will at times swoop down in troops of sixty or seventy to waylay travelling parties, whom they plunder and put to death, or else make a raid on some village in their vicinity.

We had now reached the banks of the stream, and had to cross it to gain the village; but the bridge here, which possessed the great merit—from an engineering point of view—of extreme simplicity, was about the most crazy, break-neck contrivance it has ever been my lot to see. The whole structure consisted of one or two poles of bamboo, stretched from bank to bank some twelve feet above the deep river. These elegant structures are the common property of the natives, and suffice for the purposes of trade and intercommunication in this region. They are understood to be rebuilt, or kept in repair, by the man who happens to break them, should he survive the accident, or by the next comer should he not. Providence has supplied a bountiful stock of raw material for their construction, in the surrounding vale and along the river's bank. There we may see the boulders for new piers, and ratans growing in the thickets, wherewith, if need be, to bind the cross-poles to the piers, and there are bamboos everywhere.

About half a mile from Pau-ah-liau we passed beneath the spreading branches of the "Png-chieu" tree, as the natives term it, whose roots spread along the ground in curious writhings and contortions, now forming an inviting chair, now a couch on which one might pass the hot nights with comfort; or elsewhere a small shrine connected with the fetishism of the village. These spirit-shrines were encountered at the roots of many of the finest trees, and consisted commonly of one basement stone and four other slabs, together forming three sides and a roof. Within, in the centre, was a tiny stone altar on which the offerings reposed. Our path was along a pleasant shady road, on the margin of a stream that had been made use of for irrigation. On our left hand was a hedge adorned with numerous wild flowers — fuchsias, roses, guavas, wild mint and convolvulus — besides a profusion of wild raspberry-bushes that had lately been laden with fruit, as sweet as our own English raspberries, if we may judge from what little still remained. Again we had to cross a bamboo bridge, and thence to follow a foot-road by the edge of the ricefields, where the young blades rose in vivid green above the water, just high enough to break up the reflection of the mountains on its glassy surface. We now entered the village of Pau-ah-liau, and made straight for the house of an aged blind Pepohoan, named Sin-chun. We were followed into his enclosure by troops of savage-looking women and children, the latter, some of them ten years old, without a rag to hide their youthful proportions. Here the men, women and children were all provided with bamboo tobacco-pipes, of which they made vigorous and unceasing use. I had not long to wait before a haggard old dame came up to where I stood and offered me her pipe for a smoke. When I accepted the courtesy, she went on to ask for my cigar, from which she took one or two hearty pulls, and then her face disappeared in a compound series of wrinkles, denoting delight at the unusual piquancy of the weed. After this the cigar was passed from mouth to mouth through the crowd, and carefully returned to me when they had all had a pull. The villagers were, most of them, tall and well-formed, with large brown eyes, kindling at times with a savage lustre that told of a free untamed spirit, born amid the wild grandeur and solitude of these mountain lands.

The women wear a profusion of dark brown or black hair, combed straight back from the forehead, and caught up and folded in behind the head. Then the long tresses are twisted into a sort of cable, into which a strip of red cloth is entwined, and the whole is then brought over the left ear, passed like a diadem across the brows and firmly fixed up at the back of the head. The effect of this simple head-dress is very striking, and contrasts well with the rich olive skin of its wearer.

The Chinese say the women are extremely barbarous, because even the finest of them never paint. Time appears to deal · hardly with them as they advance in years; toil and exposure rob them quickly of the attractions of their youth, but yet their hair is dressed neatly and carefully to the last, and they fight a stubborn battle against the encroaching hands of fate.

The men now came trooping home in greater numbers from the fields, tall erect fellows, wearing an air of perfect goodwill, frankness and honesty. In spite of their horny hands and poor clothing, there was a manly grace in their demeanour and a perfect gentleness, a heartiness, and a simple hospitality which it was truly touching to observe. In these respects there was a marked difference between the different villages. Thus, where the Pepohoans had come into closer contact with the Chinese, they were better dressed, but less friendly than in those villages where we encountered the aborigines alone. Sin-chun invited us into his cabin, and there I lay down on a mat to rest, and soon fell fast asleep. I awoke again with a start as a gust of fetid air passed across the apartment. These natives, I must tell you, have a way of salting their turnips and placing them in a jar of water, where they are kept till they decompose, after which they eat them as a relish to their rice.

It was now 3 p.m., and we were still six miles from Kasanpo.
Pursuing our way by the river-side, we arrived at that village
by five o'clock, and proceeded to the house of one Ah-toan, an
old man with whom the doctor was acquainted. Ah-toan was
not at home, but he soon appeared, driving his cattle before
him into the pen. He, too, was very pleased to see us, and
quickly made an apartment ready, in which we deposited
our things. On the verandah behind his dwelling a narrow
space had been screened off for bathing, and of this convenience
we at once took advantage. Our arrival was the signal for
the villagers to crowd in and have a look at us, but I could
not make out why the male portion of the community appeared
to treat our visit as a highly humorous incident, and why they
had lost the erect and dignified bearing peculiar to their race.
One old savage more than six feet high, got hold of my pith
hat, turned it round, and finally burst into a broad grin. I
noticed, too, that he had abandoned all control over his facial
muscles, and though he evidently meant to be civil, that he
could not bring back the normal expression of sober gravity
to his countenance; his features, in spite of him, would dissolve
into a grin. At last I smelt sam-shu, and it transpired that the
villagers had been thatching a neighbour's house, and, as is
customary, had been entertained at a wine-feast. The Pepohoans
distil a very strong spirit from the sweet potato, which they
cultivate as a staple food like rice.

I will now endeavour to describe our bedroom. The Pepohoan
huts are infested with rats, and the chamber we occupied did
not escape their forays. This apartment measured about eight
feet each way, one half of which area was taken up by a
platform of bamboo raised about eighteen inches above the hard
clay floor. This platform formed our bed, and the only other

articles of furniture to be seen within, were two billets of wood which served the purpose of pillows. By way of a lamp we had a small cup of oil, in which floated a few shreds of burning pith, and by this flickering light I could see that the clay walls were blackened and the rafters glazed with sooty smoke. In a corner above my head were a bundle of green tobacco, one or two spears, a bow, a heap of arrows, a primitive match-lock, and lastly,—an object which I had not hitherto noticed—a huge bin of unhusked rice at the side of the bed. I fain hoped that there the rats might find occupation during the night more profitable than worrying our slumbers.

Ahong informed me, in strict confidence, that the dexterity of the savages hereabouts in the use of the bow and poisoned arrows was no less wonderful than the cool way in which they boiled and ate their tender-hearted but tough-limbed Chinese foes. He besought me not to venture much further into the mountains, as the hill-men never show themselves when they attack, but discharge their arrows high into the air, with such unerring precision that, as they fall, they pierce the skulls of their victims and cause instant death.

We did not sleep much, as we found that rats were by no means the only vermin we had to entertain, and once or twice I woke up to find the rats making short tracks across my body for the rice-bin. Next morning we started for Lalung, about eleven miles distant, through some of the grandest scenery I have ever beheld. Old Atuan furnished us with an armed guide—a good-looking young fellow named "Teng-Tsai." The path was an unsafe one, leading as it did through the lower hunting-grounds belonging to tribes of savages higher up in the hills. Teng-Tsai called a friend who joined our party with his matchlock, and both carried small priming-flasks of

9

staghorn, suspended round their necks with strings of glass beads. They had also cord fusees coiled on bamboo rollers or bracelets, round their left arms. These cords will keep alight for twenty-four hours, and when kindled the burning end is attached to forceps, which bring the light down into the powder-pan, when the trigger is pulled. All the savages hereabouts use English powder for priming, when they can get it supplied them by the Chinese. As soon as our guides lost sight of the village, they lighted their fusees and enjoined us to keep to-gether and make our way in silence. For the first half of our journey we were marching along the bed of a stream, but at length we ascended a narrow defile where mighty rocks towered high above our heads, arched over in places by great forest-trees, or giant ferns. A clear rill leapt from ledge to ledge, where with its glassy surface it mirrored the bright reflection of the ferns as they flung their fronds from the rock to form a frame around the pool. Here we halted awhile to admire the loveliness of the mountain gorges, and to obtain a photo-graph of the scene. An armed party of six friendly Pepohoans came upon us as we were enjoying a bath and a swim in the clear pool. They were out on a fishing excursion; and one old fellow was cleverly shooting his fish with an arrow, while the others were hunting for crabs among the rocks, twisting off their legs and devouring them shell and all, alive. The younger members of the party caught fish by beating the water with a bamboo rod and thus stupifying their prey. A tedious climb over a mountain path that wound its way through the forest, brought us at last to a change of scene.

Here the trees, many of them, were of gigantic proportions, their great lateral branches striking out at a considerable altitude like the yards of a ship, from which hung a multitude of the

bare stems of parasite plants, like cables and rigging flying
adrift before the breeze. We noted a number of fine specimens
of the camphor-tree, the largest about four feet in diameter,
and rising to a great height, straight as an arrow, with a slight
taper and devoid of branches, till it reached the free air above.
Besides there were interminable ratan plants, and in a comparatively open space we fell in with a splendid lily of great size
and in full flower, the entire plant standing about twelve feet
from the root. Orchids, too, were there in abundance, filling
the air with their perfume on every side. From the summit of
this hill we got a view of the central mountain chain. A
Pepohoan here joined our party; he had travelled over the
mountains from the other side of the island, and was now
homeward bound. From him we learnt the existence of a fine
harbour on the eastern shore, and he added that the tribes
granted him a free pass over their territory on the payment of
three bullocks. It was about four o'clock when we entered
Lalung; this village stands on the banks of a broad river, now
reduced to narrow dimensions and to be seen winding along
some half mile from its proper banks, which rose about sixty
feet above the dry channel of the stream. But during the rains,
we were assured that the river swells to such a volume that
it fills up this entire bed. This is evidently one of the great
arteries of the drainage of the central mountains; and if we take
into account the great altitude of those mountains, and the
force of the torrents which make their way over the narrow
plain, carrying with them annually, immense quantities of debris
that the sea continually throws back and deposits along the
western shore, we shall get some insight into the way in which
land is being built up and redeemed from the ocean on the
west, independently of the volcanic action still at work in cer-

tain quarters of the island. Thus we may account for the disappearance of the Taiwan harbour within the brief period of 200 years, as well as for the formation of Takow harbour further south. The formation of a great coral-reef breakwater must also be taken into account. Perhaps no example can be found anywhere better than in Formosa, of the power of water to transform the physical aspect of a country. In many places on that island no settled water-courses exist; and thus the torrents in the impetus of their headlong rush down the mountain steeps, attack weak positions in the rocks and soils and form new passages for themselves.

On leaving the mountain top our course lay for an hour through the dry bed of a stream, cut through a black rock stratum, where we discovered traces of shale and coal. On reaching a small stream we found Mrs. Hong, who told us that her husband would put us up at the village. This lady was accompanied by a party of young savages who carried tackle for fishing. Lalung village is only separated from the territory of the most purely savage aborigines by the stream which I have just described, and its inhabitants number about 1,000 souls. Hong we found from home, but he soon returned and informed us that Boon, his eldest son, had lately lost his wife and was off to his savage kinsmen in the mountains to secure another bride. He was expected to return that night, and would be accompanied by an escort from his partner's tribe. Here, in these Pepohoan villages, I found the only instance I encountered of Chinamen employing middle-men or brokers to deal with natives of the country. It seems that Pepohoans are very often used as go-betweens in the barter trade between the mountaineers and the Chinese; for the latter, though they are great and patient traders, yet as a rule possess but little of the bold spirit of adventure, and entertain a wholesome dread of these highlanders. They are not without good grounds for their fears; for in one village at least, a missionary, who lately repaired thither, found the men adorning their huts with skulls of their Chinese foes, and the report goes that they are cannibals too. Strangely enough the weapons and ammunition used by the hill tribes to destroy wild animals and Chinamen are supplied by the Chinese themselves.

Family ties between the wild hill-tribes and the Pepohoans are kept up by constant intermarriage. * The wedding ceremony is a simple one. The father of the lady merely takes his daughter by the hand and passes her over to her lord, and then there is a drinking-revel to conclude the rites. In the old Dutch accounts of the people it is said that the offer of a present by a suitor and its acceptance by the lady, entitles the giver to be esteemed the legal husband, according to the rule "Nuptias non concubitus sed concensus facit"; and the marriage tie is with equal facility dissolved. Indeed it would almost seem as if the "Free Lovers" of America had borrowed their creed of inconstancy and their fickle practices from the unchivalrous Formosan tribes.

Hong, having at length appeared, gave us a cordial welcome to his house, insisting on the sacrifice of a pig for the more perfect accomplishment of hospitable rites. The porker was therefore slaughtered before the door and in the presence of a pack of half-starved hunting-dogs that fought savagely over the drops of blood. My boy Ahong set it down as his solemn belief that these people could not, after all, be classed as utter

* See for further information, *Natives of the West Coast of Formosa*, translated from an old Dutch work, by Rev. W. Lobschied.

barbarians, for they clearly understood the use of roast hog. At this place I collected a number of old Pepohoan words which appear in the vocabularies in the Appendix.

Next morning we resumed our journey under the guidance of Goona, the youngest son of our host. Goona was a pure young savage, full of laughter and frolic, wearing a crown of ferns on his head and little else by way of clothing. We were now descending a narrow path to the dry bed of the river, when our progress was arrested by a yellowish snake about seven feet long, which shot out his head across our track. I struck him over the neck with a heavy bamboo staff which I had in my hand. On this the reptile rolled down the bank, and when we had completed the descent we found him again, lodged beneath a boulder. Aided by one or two natives I managed to topple the mass over, and then our enemy made another dart forward,—I dealt him another blow and despatched him. I should have carried him off, but he was too big to be easily disposed of, so I left him to be devoured by the Pepohoans, who are said to be fond of snakes. I was anxious to cross the river, but was urged not to do so, as two men had been killed by a hostile tribe about a month before, just opposite where we stood.

I obtained some good types of the aboriginal tribes in this quarter, and managed also to photograph the scenery. About two o'clock we set out again to walk to Lakoli, which lay some twelve miles off. At one place we crossed a small stream of strongly alkaline water, and here, on the banks, some alkali, soda or potash, had crystallised in such quantities as to resemble a recent fall of snow. The banks of the main stream now towered more than 200 feet above the dry bed, and alternating strata of clay and boulders could be distinctly seen. Before us

Right bank of Lakoli river, Formosa.

we had a panorama of surpassing grandeur. The grandeur of this region during the wet season must baffle description. Then a thousand cataracts veiled in vapour and illumined with rainbow hues, leap from the mountain sides, roaring and tumbling in their downward course to the broad river.

Before us, as in a peaceful vale, we could see the settlement of Lakoli—a few rude dwellings, and a patch of tilled land, amid a jungle wilderness. In the fast-failing light we could just make out its hedges and areca-palms, its mango and langan trees; but ere long the darkness closed in around, and left us groping our way forwards at the outskirt of the hamlet. We could hear the sounds of rude music, laughter and dancing; but there was no one to be seen until we fell in with the hut of one "Kim-Siang." Here we met but a cool reception. The old man was laid up with the effects of rheumatism and opium-smoking, and we found a slave girl fanning him in an adjoining hut. His son, a fellow over six feet high, stood in front of the doorway of the cabin, and beside him was his wife, a woman from a friendly mountain tribe. Outside this abode hung festoons of deer-skulls and boar-heads that had been taken in the chase. When the father had finished his opium-pipe, he consented to allow us to occupy an outer shed for the night.

Anxious to procure food, and a vessel in which to boil down my nitrate-of-silver bath to dryness (photographers familiar with the wet collodion process will know what is meant by the bath having struck work and obstinately refusing to produce a picture), I made my way by torchlight to the hut of one "La-liat," an Amoy man, engaged here in barter traffic with the hill-tribes. We found little or no evidence of any goods in La-liat's abode; there was a table on the clay floor, and a taper flickering feebly in a cup of oil above it, and here, in this cheerless dwelling, a boisterous party had gathered themselves together and were engaged in smoking and drinking. Our entrance was but little noticed and less appreciated; they had nothing we wanted, not even a civil word. A drunken old woman staggered up with a teapot containing sam-shu, and offered to sell us the vessel, when she had first carefully exhausted its contents. Meanwhile La-liat, who had been sleeping on a sort of counter, woke up, recognised my friend and agreed to trade. Strange to relate, in grateful remembrance of his former acquaintance with the Doctor, he supplied us with a dozen eggs and a brown jar, and then positively refused to accept payment. He also showed us raw camphor, skins, horns, boars' tusks, ratan and other wares which he had obtained from a party of savages who had come down from their hunting-grounds to Lakoli the day before. In return for these goods he had supplied them with beads, turkey-red cloth, knives and gunpowder.

Our armed guide slept on a mat in the hut beside us, while Ahong, my servant, and I were engaged till about 2 a.m., boiling down my bath in the Chinese pot. It was a tedious job. First Ahong slept as we sat before the fire; then I slept; then we both slept, and the fire went low and had to be tended. I complained of my boy's sleeping and immediately dozed off myself, and so on until the whole liquid was evaporated. Once the alcoholic fumes in passing off caught fire; then I heard a terrible shriek and started up to find the scared face of a savage old woman glaring close to mine. She must have been placed there to watch us, and she vanished instantly into the darkness whence she had appeared. Ahong, disturbed in his sleep, caught sight of the apparition and declared that it was the—

well, never mind what! But he did not rest quite so comfortably after that incident. I am not prepared myself to say what
the old witch could have been, or how she vanished. She
certainly looked haggard, hideous and unearthly, and her flight,
too, was sudden and noiseless. Four hours' rest and we were
up again by daylight and ready for the road. After the night's
doctoring, my nitrate-of-silver bath gave every satisfaction;
only the water which I used to dilute it, was so extremely alkaline that I had to employ a goodly supply of Chinese vinegar
to turn it—slightly, to the acid side.

As I must quit Formosa with this chapter, it will be necessary
to summarise my experiences from this point and to condense
my narrative within narrower limits. On the summit of the
first range, on our homeward route, above Lakoli, in place of
setting up my instrument to photograph, I felt I would much
rather have lain down and slept,—but there was no time for
that, as we had by the route we followed, between twenty and
thirty miles to walk before night, and a day's work of photographing to overtake besides. My friend was not feeling well;
he had, however, promised to be at Baksa next day to conduct
the service in the chapel there, so we pushed on. At the foot
of another range, on the brink of a clear, cool stream, I secured
two more photographs, and waited for a short time to admire
a sedgy pool and to bathe our feet in its cool water. The
remainder of the day's journey was almost an uninterrupted
toil over hill and dale.

At noon we halted at a small village, in front of a hut where
an old woman was selling fruit. Here a large party of Pepohoans—in clothing that might have been decent had it covered their nakedness—assembled to see us eat. We came
upon a large sheet of water at the place where we next halted,

and there we swam about for some time. It was probably an imprudent thing, but it refreshed us for the moment. A few hours after this my friend became very ill, and had to lie down beneath the shade of some shrubs, in a place where there was not a drop of clear water to be procured for miles around. At his request I gave him a dose of quinine and iron, and after an hour's rest we resumed our march. I took a picture of one of the deep dry clay-pits of this region, and had to proceed ten miles farther on before I could get a drop of water to wash the plate and finish the negative. It turned out one of my finest pictures, nevertheless. On the hill above Baksa we halted at a hut and were there regaled with a cup of pure honey. Descending the ridge which I described at starting, my foot slipped, but fortunately I saved myself from the fearful fall by clinging to the sharp edges of the rock, cutting my hands badly in the accident.

But I must now quit this island, remarkable no less for its beauty than for the hospitality of its simple inhabitants. I afterwards travelled overland to Takow, for the purpose of visiting the haunts of the savages farther south, but they were at war with the Chinese, and their territory could not be entered with safety.

CHAPTER VIII.

FOOCHOW AND THE RIVER MIN.

THE island kingdom of Japan is to all appearance destined to
afford an unparalleled example of progress. She has indeed
preferred, to quote Professor Tyndall's words, "Commotion
before stagnation, the leap of the torrent before the stillness
of the swamp;" and we have just seen, in Formosa, how such
leaping torrents in their impetuous courses cut out new channels
in the mountain sides, spread fertility over the plains below,
and even reclaim the land from the barren domain of the ocean
with the debris which they sweep down.

There is vigorous life and hope and high promise for the
future in the busy movement that is carrying Japan from darkness into civilisation and light; and the impetus, if we mistake
not, which she is gathering in her onward course will clear away
mighty obstacles and check stagnation and decay in other
quarters as well as her own.

"The invasion of Formosa by Japanese troops was a fact full of deep significance, and more righteous grounds for such aggressive action it would be impossible for any government to possess. Scores of Japanese sailors, wrecked from time to time upon the Formosan coasts, have there been plundered and murdered by the savage tribes; and as these barbarities were perpetrated on Chinese soil, redress was applied for at Peking. The members of the Imperial Cabinet, in a moment of weakness—moments of not infrequent occurrence in Chinese history—appear to have conceded the right for the Japanese to proceed to Formosa and seek redress for themselves. It would be extremely interesting to know what share the aborigines of Formosa have really taken in the cold-blooded massacres of castaways that have been reported from the island. It seems pretty clear that it was the Kalee tribes who put the crew of the "Rover" to death; at the same time it is equally certain that the murder of the captain and sailors of the "Macto" was perpetrated by Chinese villagers at Takow. If we are thus to believe that pure motives of humanity gave rise to this invasion of Formosa by the Japanese, it would be only just to award to the Mikado and his ministers the highest meed of praise; but perhaps it ought to be borne in mind that the Japanese have not yet forgotten their ancient feuds against China, and still fall somewhat short of that almost unattainable pitch of national virtue, which would induce them to enter upon costly expeditions to redress outrages committed upon native crews. However the matter ends, its results will as I should anticipate, be advantageous. China may get off by paying the cost of the expedition—a proceeding which, while it humbled her national vanity, might stir her up to imitate and rival Japan, so as, if possible, to outstrip her in the march of progress, from the sheer necessity of self-preservation; and I have no hesitation in saying that China, petrified and stagnant as she is, and has been for so many centuries, yet contains within herself all the material elements that will one day win her a proud pre-eminence among the nations of the earth. Truth even now is busily at work loosening the earth about the ancient foundation of classical lore and superstition on which her venerable wall of fossil institutions is reared; and that wall, ere long, will be lowered stone by stone, or overthrown with some violent shock, till a way has been opened across it for the purer institutions of progressive government. Should war be the alternative, it will probably only hasten the work of regeneration." This is a fairly accurate forecast which I made some years ago, of the position which China has taken as a fighting power, shown in the result of the late Chino-Japanese war. It is extremely doubtful if the lesson taught by the issue of the conflict will lead to the introduction of any serious measures of reform. Since the date of the Japanese raid on Formosa the Chinese have practically done nothing to strengthen their position and secure themselves against the attack of even a third-rate power.

I will now take leave of the island of Formosa and cross again to the mainland of China, where, in the province of Fukien, I gathered some information relating to the supposed progress made by the Chinese in the arts of natural defence and the construction of implements of war.

The river Min, flowing through the heart of the Fu-kien province, is one of the main outlets for the drainage of the mountainous region where the celebrated Bohea hills stand, and is also the channel down which the produce of one of the richest tea districts in China is conveyed for exportation. The stream, however, although a broad one, is not navigable for large vessels beyond the town of Shui-Kow, which stands on its left bank, at the foot of dangerous rapids, one hundred miles from the coast. The entrance to the Min by the south channel is nearly opposite to a group of islands known as the "White Dogs." There are, however, two other channels now in use; the most northerly between Sharp Peak Island and the mainland, and only available for vessels of light draught; while the middle channel to the south of the Sharp Peak, has a breadth of about three-quarters of a mile, and is nearly three fathoms deep at low tide. The south channel is not quite so roomy, nor yet so direct, except for vessels trading south. A lighthouse built on the "White Dogs" proves of great advantage to the port. The Kin-pai and Min-Ngan passes, through which the anchorage is gained, recalled the approaches to the Pearl river.

The harbour is about thirty miles from the mouth of the river, and is wide enough to contain the entire merchant fleet of China. This spot is called "Pagoda Anchorage," and takes that name from a small island crowned with an old pagoda, which forms a conspicuous object in the landscape. But for this purely Chinese edifice, one might readily suppose oneself transported suddenly to a scene on the river Clyde. There stand the houses of a small foreign settlement, and yonder are a dock, tall chimneys and rows of workshops, whence the clang of steam-hammers and the hum of engines may be heard. Here, in fact, is the Foochow Arsenal, on a piece of level ground redeemed from an old swamp, and looking in the distance like an English manufacturing village. This was destroyed by the French in 1884, and has since been reconstituted. A French mission under the direction of M. Doyère has just been intrusted with its reorganisation. But side by side with the residences on the hill, there is a crescent-shaped stone shrine of imposing proportions, designed to correct the Feng-shui, which has been seriously disturbed by the construction of an arsenal after a foreign type.

This arsenal, like all the others on Chinese soil, was raised simply because the authorities deemed it expedient to remodel their military equipments with all possible speed, and then Feng-shui, or the Geomantic luck of the locality, was treated with but scant consideration. Feng-shui, indeed, had to yield to the stern necessity of the times, and was relegated to this very humble station on the hill-side. By steps like this the fanatic dread of the common people will readily be overcome; for they account their scholarly mandarins much better judges of Feng-shui and its influences than they themselves can pretend to be. But let us visit the Chinese foreign arsenal. The first building we enter when we land, reminds us, by its lofty roof and general appearance, of a plain English railway-station. It is constructed of brick on a solid granite foundation, and is enclosed by a wall, which is also of granite and which rises about five feet above the floor. Passing in through a spacious doorway we make our way along an iron avenue, lined on both sides with smiths' forges, whose blast is supplied by steam. The engine which ministers to these forges has a driving-wheel of colossal proportions, and may also be seen quickening a row of steam-hammers, with forces mighty enough to forge a shaft for the biggest steamer afloat, or so delicate as to straighten a pin. Strange as it may appear, these giant tools when first seen working, produced but little impression on their Chinese spectators. The next workshop we visit is as spacious as the preceding one, and contains the half-formed skeleton of a mammoth engine for rolling out sheet-iron and steel armour-plating for iron-clad ships. An iron driving-wheel, eighteen feet in diameter, is to be seen there, propped up in position. We next cross a broad paved court having a line of railway along one of its sides, used in conveying materials to the different workshops which run parallel to the rails and face the river. In these shops practical engineering and shipbuilding in its various branches are being carried on; and in one there is a sort of school, where mechanical drawing and modelling are taught by French masters. These instructors, all of them, remarked to me on the wonderful aptitude displayed by the Chinese in picking up a knowledge of the various mechanical appliances employed in the arsenal. Many of the men who are there working at the steam-lathes and guiding the planing-machines, had two or three months before been ordinary field labourers. In one apartment a powerful machine is punching rivet-holes in boiler-plates. In another department we found men at work, making wooden patterns for iron castings; and others constructing models of steam-engines, to be used in educating the pupils of this training-school. There are indeed many admirable specimens of complicated work carried out solely from drawings; the whole betokening an advanced degree of skill and knowledge on the part of the workmen. All these results have been achieved under the guidance of European foremen. For my own · part, from what I have seen in these arsenals, I firmly believe that when the Chinese find it convenient to throw off their grossly superstitious notions regarding foreign inventions and appliances, they will excel in all that pertains to the exact sciences, and in their practical application to the construction of machinery. The mandarins connected with the arsenal look with pardonable vanity at the steam gun-boats that have been built under their own eyes, and sent into commission

NATIVE HERBALIST.

NATIVES—FUKIEN PROVINCE.

from their own naval and shipbuilding yards. A gunboat had been launched from the patent slip a few days previous to our visit, and the sister vessel was already on the stocks.

Proceeding on board the former, we are received by the Chinese captain and his lieutenant, with great courtesy, and conducted all over the ship. This a nautical friend present pronounced to be an honest, solid, masterly piece of work throughout. The woodwork of the cabin is simply varnished, and relieved with narrow gold mouldings. The officers' cabin and mess-room are finished in the same unpretending and yet not inelegant style; and in the sailors' quarters we notice that each seaman is supplied with a strong teak bunker to hold his effects and to serve him also instead of a couch or chair. This gun-vessel carries one huge Armstrong gun on her upper deck, and is to be fitted with the same weapons throughout. Her armament, therefore, will render her a formidable enemy to pirates, though not perhaps of much service in a combat with any European power.

Our next visit is to a vessel in commission lying off the arsenal, and manned throughout, from captain to cabin-boy, by an entirely Chinese crew. Stepping on deck from the gangway, we are saluted in military style by a Ningpo marine, who informs us in tolerable English that we shall find the captain in his cabin. The dress of this marine is admirable, consisting of a black turban, blue blouse, pantaloons with red stripe, and a pair of neat and strongly made native shoes. A well-kept belt fastens in the blouse at the waist and supports also a cartouche-box and side-arms. An officer of marines next welcomes us on board, and says, "S'pose you likee my can show you my drill pidjin," an offer which we gladly accept. "My hab got two squab, one too muchee new, other olo, can saby drill pidjin."

He means to say that he has two squads, one well trained and
the other raw recruits. It wants still fifteen minutes to drill
time, so, at the captain's request, we will take a peep into
his cabin.

In most respects this resembles that of some English gunboats;
but on a small table, supported by graceful brackets, we note
a strange assortment of foreign nautical instruments spread
around a small idol. This idol was the only visible token of
native superstition, and was used in conjunction with the baro-
meter and thermometer to avoid coming storms, or to
find out lucky days for sailing. Having partaken of wine with
our hospitable entertainer, we next return to the upper deck to
see the marines at drill. The bugleman sounds to quarters, and
the men, with Enfield rifles in their hands, fall, or rather tumble
into position, six or eight at a time. Then one more dilatory
than his fellows, pops his head out of a hatchway, in order to
satisfy himself that his company could not be dispensed with,
scrambles on deck as he drags himself into his blouse and pantaloons, and fixes his belt as he falls in. Some, too, have mis-
placed their rifles, but all have now fairly got into line, and all
appear orderly enough, until one unlucky fellow, feeling perhaps
a sudden twinge of itch, drops his weapon to have a scratch.
A comrade politely leaves the ranks to clear his throat over
the side; and so the drill proceeds, its forms seemingly well
understood by most of the men, but its object, so far as we
could judge, almost entirely ignored. Thus there is a marked
absence of the discipline we always associate with naval or
military training.

The opticians make ships' compasses, portions of sextants
and the brass work of other nautical instruments. How they
acquired these arts it is difficult to make out, as their foreign

FOOCHOW FEMALE.

CHINESE SEAMSTRESS.

teacher confessed to his complete ignorance of their language. P. Giguel was the chief director of this establishment.

The Viceroy Tso, under whose auspices the arsenal was built, is also deserving of some credit, although he was not the first to see the need for a change in the construction of the warlike implements of his nation. The monthly expenditure of the whole establishment was reported at about £17,000. It appears that the authorities discharged the foreign employés, though what may have been their reason for this step, which happened just before the Japanese invaded Formosa, it is impossible for me to say, and as may be supposed, the step has proved far from beneficial.

Foochow city, one of the great tea marts of China, stands about seven miles above the arsenal and the harbour where the vessels load tea. Of all the open ports this is perhaps the most picturesque, and its stone bridge of "ten thousand ages" proves that the Chinese, had they so chosen, might have left monuments behind them more worthy of their civilisation and prowess than their great unwieldy wall monuments, which would have shed a gleam of truth across the obscure pages of their bygone history. This bridge was erected, it is said, about 900 years ago, and displays no pretensions to ornamentation except in its stone balustrade. It is indeed evident that its builders had convenience and durability alone in view; and the masses of solid granite then employed, still but little injured by the lapse of time, bear high testimony, in their colossal proportions, to the skill of the ancient engineers who raised them up out of the water and placed them in position on the stone piers above. The bridge is fully a quarter of a mile in length, and the granite blocks which stretch from pier to pier are, some of them, forty feet long.

The foreign settlement is separated from Foochow city by the great bridge, and by a small island which here rises in the middle of the stream. The site was formerly that of an old Chinese burial-ground, and abundant disputes arose in consequence when plots had to be purchased for the erection of houses, the natives being loath to see the dwellings of living "foreign devils" erected over the resting-places of their own hallowed dead. But money, which exercises as potent an influence here as elsewhere, procured a solution of the difficulties; even the spirits of the departed were to be consoled by timely offerings at their shrines; and so now, on these hills, the dust of the long-forgotten dead is trodden under foot by the hated foreign intruder, and mingles with the roses with which his garden is adorned. Even the tombs have, some of them, been turned to account. Living occupants have entered into joint tenancy with the silent inhabitants who repose beneath, and pigs or poultry may be seen enjoying the cool shade and shelter which the ample granite gravestone supplies. But I need not give any detailed description of the foreign residences at Foochow.

This notice of the graves in the foreigners' quarter may be supplemented by some account of the living tenants to be met with in a city of the dead close by; but before proceeding to describe the condition of these wretched beings, it may be as well to give the reader a notion of the condition of the poor in Foochow. In China the beggar pursues his calling unmolested, and has even won for himself a protection and quasi-recognition at the hands of the civic authorities. The fact is that the charitable institutions of the country cannot cope with a tenth part of the misery and destitution that prevails in populous localities. No poor law is known, and the only plan

Chinese Tomb.

adopted to palliate the evil is to tolerate begging in public, and to place the lazzaroni under the local jurisdiction of a responsible chief. In Foochow the city is divided into wards, and within the limits of each ward a head-man is appointed, able to trace his descent from a line of illustrious beggar chiefs, who, like himself, exercised the right to keep the members of their order under their own management and control. During my stay in Foochow I was introduced to one of these beggar kings; he was an inveterate opium-smoker, and consequently in reduced circumstances. I afterwards visited the house of another head-man. His eldest son received me at the entrance and conducted me into a guest's chamber; and while I was seated there two ladies dressed in silks passed the door of the apartment in order to steal a glimpse at its inmate. These were the chief and second wives of this Lord of the Lazzaroni, who was himself unfortunately absent on business. I afterwards secured his photograph.

Beggar chieftains of this kind have it in their power to make an agreement with the business men of the streets in their respective wards, under which they levy a kind of fluctuating poor-rate for the maintenance of themselves and their subjects. A composition thus entered into exempts the streets or shops whereon the chief has placed his mark, from the harassing raids of his tattered troops. Woe betide the shopman who has the courage to refuse his dole to these beggars! The most loathsome and pertinacious specimens of the naked tribe will be despatched to beset his shop. Thus, while walking along one of the best streets of the city, I myself saw a revolting, diseased and filthy object carried on the shoulders of another member of the fraternity, who marched into a shop and deposited his burden on the polished counter, where the tradesman was serving customers with ornaments for shrines and food for the gods. The bearer, with cool audacity, proceeded to light his pipe and smoke until he had been paid to remove the cripple. A still worse case was narrated to me by an eye-witness. A silk-mercer had refused to contribute his black-mail, and accordingly received a domiciliary visit from a representative of the chief. This intruder had smeared his bare body with mud, and carried a bowl slung with cords and filled with foul water to the very brim. Having taken up his stand in the shop, he commenced to swing this bowl round his head, without indeed spilling a drop of its contents, yet so that, had anyone attempted to arrest his arm, the water would have been distributed in a filthy shower over the silks piled upon the counter and shelves.

But there is still another and a worse class of beggars —outlaws who own allegiance to no prince or power on earth— and these were the men whom I visited and found dwelling in the charnel-houses in a city of the dead. Many of the little huts in this dismal spot were built with brick and roofed with tiles. They contained coffins and bodies placed there to await the favourable hour for interment, when the rites of Fengshui might be duly performed, and the remains laid to rest in some well-situated site where neither wind nor wave would disturb their sacred dust. But poverty, death, distress, or indeed a variety of causes, not infrequently intervene to prevent the surviving relatives from ever choosing this happy site and bringing the final ceremonies to a consummation; and thus the coffins lie forgotten and moulder into dust, and the tombs are invaded by the poor outcasts, who there seek shelter from the cold and rain, creeping gladly to slumber into the dark corners of a sepulchre, and then most happy when they most imitate the dead. On my first visit to this place I recollect being

Open Altar of Heaven, Foochow.

attracted to an ominous-looking tomb by hearing some one moan there. It was growing dark and I may have, perhaps, felt a little superstitious as I peeped in and beheld what seemed to be an old man clad in rags too scant to cover his frame. He was fanning a fire made up of withered branches, but he was not the only tenant; there was a coffin too, looming out from the darkness within, and I almost fancied he was the ghost of its owner. But no! there was no mistaking the moan of suffering humanity. The cold wind was chilling his thin blood and racking his joints with pain. Administering some temporary relief and passing on to a tomb where I could hear sounds of mirth, I found four inmates inside, the members of a firm of beggars. I visited them again next morning and came upon the group at breakfast. The head-man—a lusty, half-naked lout— was standing in front of the entrance, enjoying a post-prandial pipe, and he offered me a smoke with the air of a Chinese gentleman. After this he invited me in to inspect the interior, where his partners were busily engrossed with chopsticks and bowls of reeking scraps collected on the previous day. They were chatting noisily, too, forgetful of their cares and of the coffins that surrounded them. One, the jester of the party, was seated astride a coffin, cracking his jokes over the skull of its occupant.

While at Foochow, after visiting the beggars, I thought I might as well see what the detectives are like. These men are commonly known as the "Ma-qui" or "Swift as horses," and are attached to the yamens of the local authorities, receiving a small stipend out of the Government supplies, but obtaining the bulk of their earnings from persons who seek to recover stolen goods, or even from the thieves themselves.

The Ma-qui is supposed to know personally all the professional robbers of his district; and one wishing to recover his property from the thieves must make a liberal offer to the Ma-qui, at least one half the value of the articles lost; failing this, it is probable that he will never hear of his goods again. But transactions of this kind are generally effected through the Ma-qui, who simply acts as a broker, and takes his heavy percentage from both sides. Should the thieves refuse to yield up the property at the price he offers, they run the risk of being imprisoned and tortured. I photographed a thief who had just escaped from gaol; he had been an unprofitable burglar, a bad constituent of the Ma-qui, and was accordingly triced up by the thumbs until the cords had worn the flesh away, and left nothing but the bare bones exposed. It was told of this detective, who might more appropriately be called the chief of the thieves, that he, one day, fell in with an old thief whom he had known and profited by in former times, but who was now respectably clad and striving to lead an honest life. ' He at once had the man conveyed to prison, and there, in order to impress upon him the danger to which he exposed himself in falling into honest ways, suspended him by the thumbs, stripped off his clothes, and discharged him with one arm put out of joint, When a thief is not in the profession and cannot be discovered, the Ma-qui is liable to be whipped. He then whips his subordinates, and they in turn whip the thieves. Should this plan fail, it is reported that the police have been whipped and that the stolen property cannot be found.

A word about leprosy and the leper villages of the Chinese. This disease—not an uncommon one in China—may be seen in a variety of its loathsome forms in the public streets of almost every city. This disease, however, is not held to be infectious by many Asiatics, as well as by a number of European

SZECHUAN HERMIT.

LEPERS.

physicians, who have had to prescribe for the sufferers, and, for my own part, I am inclined to adopt their view. It has also been proved that the malady, although to a certain extent hereditary, will at last die out of a family. Thus, in the Canton leper village there are direct descendants of lepers, now alive, who are entirely free from the disease; and in the leper settlement at Foochow I was informed that the inhabitants were permitted to marry and rear families; and the statement was evidently true, for we found there many parents surrounded by children, some of whom, though they had reached maturity, were still free from the fearful blight that had fallen on the wretched community around.

The village to which I allude is a walled enclosure, standing about a mile beyond the east gate of the city; I set out with the Rev. Mr. Mahood to pay a visit to this asylum. It was now about four in the afternoon; a drizzling rain had already set in and a sudden darkness overcast the heavens as we entered the gate of the village. The dreariness of the weather and the gloominess of the gathering clouds overhead, intensified the wretchedness of the scene; and we were soon surrounded by a crowd of men, women and children, some too loathsome to bear description, and all clamouring for alms to buy food to sustain their miserable lives; nor did their importunity cease until the governor of the place, himself a leper, came out to keep his subjects in order. It would appear that the original idea of the institution, like the majority of native institutions in China, had been lost sight of, and that it is now made as much the means by which the officials extort money from wealthy lepers, as of conferring a boon upon the community by keeping the lepers shut up and cut off from contact with the outer world. The poor among them, who are unable to pay

for their own maintenance, are allowed a nominal annual sum
by government, sufficient to support them probably one month
out of twelve, and for the rest they are daily sent adrift into
the public highways, and I believe, as in the case of ordinary
beggars, certain shops and streets may unite together and
purchase freedom from their most objectionable visits. This
little settlement numbered something over 300 souls, and had
once contained a theatre for the amusement of its inhabitants,
but that edifice had long fallen into decay.

The streets of Foochow are so similar to the streets of all
the other cities of Southern China as to require no description
here. Foochow, too, has its parade-grounds, its yamens, its
temples and its pagodas; all of great importance to the citizens
themselves, and of comparatively little interest to the stranger
from outside, unless to one who wishes to make himself acquainted with an endless variety of dry details as to religion,
Feng-shui, or local jurisdiction; none of which subjects could
possibly be digested into a volume of such dimensions as mine.
I will therefore only remark as I quit the town, that the visitor
must not fail to observe the oysters—oysters which are not
only very good, but very remarkable too in their way. It may
be said that a bamboo rod is not the "native climb" of that
highly-prized shell-fish; and yet, in the main thoroughfares at
Foochow, one finds an endless array of fish-stalls where oysters
are served out to passing customers, and these oysters are grown
in clusters on bamboo rods, stuck into the beds at the proper
season, pulled up again when mature, and brought in this fashion
to market.

There are a number of trades which are peculiar to this city,
and among the most interesting is that of the lamp-maker. One
lamp, of a very pretty though fragile kind, is made up of thin

rods of glass, set so closely together as almost to imitate basketwork. The light shines through these rods with a very effective lustre; and though no lamps of the sort, so far as I know, have yet been introduced into this country, they would form very attractive novelties at a garden fête.

There are many charming resorts in the vicinity of Foochow; but to my mind "Fang-Kuang-Yen-tien-chuan," better known as the "Yuan-fu" monastery, is the most fascinating of them all. It was my good fortune to visit that retreat as the guest of a foreign merchant, who made up a party for a cruise on the Yuan-fu branch of the river Min. Intense cold with drifting sleet made the prospect ahead unpromising. The bold mountains known to the natives as the "Wu-hu" or "five tiger" range, were wrapped in a thin veil of mist; but it was nearly mid-day before the last shred of vapour had withdrawn from the rugged overhanging crag, which has been called the "Lover's Leap." The mountains rise to a considerable altitude about this part of the river, and terminate in bold rocky cliffs; but beneath, wherever an available patch of soil is to be found, it has been terraced and cultivated up to the very face of the rocks. Two days were spent amid a ceaseless diversity of grand river and mountain scenery; and on the third morning, at a short distance above the first rapid, we landed to make the journey to Yuan-fu monastery. My friends had brought their sedans and bearers with them; as for me, I hired one at the nearest village, my dog, as was his custom, at once scrambling inside, and stowing himself comfortably beneath the seat. The chair being intended for mountain use, was so small that I had to sit in a cramped and awkward position. At one spot there is a flight of 400 steps (I had the curiosity to count them as our progress was slow), and this brought us to the entrance of the ravine overlooked by the monastery, which was also perhaps the most romantic bit of scenery to be encountered there. Above these steps the path winds beneath a forest, and around a rich undergrowth of ferns and flowering shrubs, and finally seems suddenly to terminate in a cave. This cave in reality forms the passage through which the dell is approached. A small idol stood at the foot of the rocks, on the right of the entrance, and there was incense burning before its shrine. As we ascended a narrow path cut in the face of the rocks, we obtained a full view of the monastery. There it stood with its broad eaves, carved roofs and ornamental balustrades, propped up on the face of a precipice 200 feet in height, and resting above this awful abyss on nothing more durable than a slender-looking framework of wooden beams.

There were only three monks in residence here; one a mere boy, the second an able-bodied youth, and lastly the abbot, who was old, infirm and blind. I was accommodated with an apartment commanding a good view of the valley far beneath, and built out of thin pine planks, plastered over with lime. Inside this chamber were a pine table, a pine chair and a pine bed, and on the latter the same unyielding wooden pillow which forms its usual cheap and durable appurtenance. As for the bedstead itself, it was a kind of square chocolate-coloured well of wood; and in this unluxurious contrivance I had to pass the nights, which were here extremely cold. My coolies slept in the apartment beneath, packed together like sardines, to keep themselves warm. Every evening at about sunset, my friends, dressed in their yellow canonicals went up into the temple to pray. The fervour of a long-winded prayer was much impaired in my eyes when I found that it was meaningless mummery to the young devotee who chanted it. On one of the altars I saw

Yuen-fu Monastery, Fukien Province.

an image known as the "Laughing Buddha," the god of longevity; and before this jovial-looking idol a joss-stick timepiece had been set up. This timepiece consists of a series of thin fire-sticks, placed parallel to each other over a flat clay bed contained in a box of bronze. Each stick will burn for twelve hours, and a fresh one is ignited when the one already burning is about to expire. Thus the time of day or night might be ascertained at a glance. This fire, like the vestal fires of Rome, so the old monk assured me, had been smouldering uninterruptedly for untold years before he came to the place.

"Ku-Shan," or "Drum Mountain," stands about seven miles below Foochow, and forms part of a range that rises abruptly out of the level, cultivated plain. The mountain enjoys a wide celebrity, as the great "Ku-Shan" monastery is built in a valley near its summit, on a site said in ancient times to have been the haunt of poisonous snakes or dragons, able to diffuse pestilence, raise up storms, or blight the harvest crops. One Ling-chiau, a sage, was entreated to put a stop to these ravages; so the good man, repairing to the pool in which the evil serpents dwelt, recited a ritual called the Hua-yen treatise, before which, like wise serpents, they took instant flight. It must indeed have been a powerful composition, for not even deadly snakes would risk a second recital, and the Emperor, hearing of the miracle, erected the Hua-yen monastery on the spot, in the year 784.

The establishment, though repeatedly destroyed, has been constantly rebuilt on its original foundations, receiving considerable additions from time to time, until at the present day it accommodates 200 monks. The ascent from the plain is a steep and tedious one, but many picturesque views of the surrounding country are to be obtained *en route*, and we reach the monastery itself at length, through a grove of ancient pine-trees, 2,500 feet above the level of the sea. Inside the main entrance sit four colossal images of the protectors of the Buddhist faith. Ku-Shan monastery, like almost all such edifices in China, is made up of three great detached buildings, set one behind the other, in a spacious paved courtyard; and opening inwards from the walls which surround this enclosure, we may see the apartments of the monks. At this shrine a number of relics of Buddha are shown, and it is said that they annually draw crowds of weary pilgrims from afar. Sacred animals too are maintained in the grounds, and if there be any member of the brute creation that has shown more than usual instinct, it will find a welcome reception here.

The "Three Holy Ones," the chief images of every Buddhist temple, were here as conspicuous as usual in the central shrine; each figure being in this instance more than thirty feet in height, and rising up behind the customary altar bespread with candelabra and votive offerings of various sorts.

I remained three days in this place, and occupied some of my leisure in visiting the rooms of the priests, one among them more frequently than the rest. Having mounted the ladder by which access to this chamber was to be gained, we entered a bare apartment, lit by a small window above and furnished with a deal table and a chair. Within I was always certain to find some member of the order improving himself by sitting like an image, meditating on the precepts of his sect, and at long intervals tolling a bell suspended in a tower above. Then again, some distance from the central temple, in one of the many beautiful avenues on the mountain-side, was a water-bell, that could be heard tolling there night and day: Against the foot of one of the rocks a small hut had been constructed. One

THE MORNING BELL—YUEN-FU MONASTERY.

OPIUM SMOKING.

day I ventured within . it and found a Buddhist image, set up on a stony ledge inside. I was thinking it was about the finest thing of the sort I had seen for some time, when the head moved forward, the limbs unbent, and the idol descended from its perch—"Venus incessu patuit Deus?" No, I can hardly venture to affirm so much of this bald-headed, yellow-robed god. "Tsing, tsing, sir, good morning; what side you come?" was his greeting, as he lighted on the ground. Less awe-stricken than might perhaps have been expected, I returned the enquiry, and asked: "What side you come?" to which his response was quickly vouchsafed: "Long time my got this side." This, then, was the hermit, of whom report had said so much. It turned out that he had been an Amoy trader, and after years of strife with the world, had come to end his days and repent him of his sins within this mossy dell.

The nearest tea-plantations in this province are in the Paeling Hills, about fifteen miles north of Foochow. These I visited in company, as the guest of two of my Foochow friends. We put up at a small temple on one of the farms, and made a three days' stay in the locality. Here some foreigners who had visited the district before us, had imparted a very limited and confused acquaintance with the English tongue to the priest who presided at the shrine. It therefore startled us when we approached the edifice, to be met by this ragged follower of Buddha, evidently proud to parade his knowledge of our language, with the salutation: "Good morning, can do I you bet I" Can do what, we enquired; but alas I our friend's vocabulary was limited to this single phrase.

The farms are usually small, seldom exceeding a few acres in size, and are rented by the poor from capitalists who pay the land tax. To these landowners the tenants undertake to dispose of their crops at a certain stipulated price. Thus the men who grow that tea which is a source of so much wealth to China, very rarely possess any capital at all themselves; and like millions of their labouring fellow-countrymen, they can earn but a hard-won sustenance out of the luxury which they thus produce. At the proper season—that is usually in the beginning of April—the first picking of the leaves takes place. These leaves, when gathered, are partially dried in the sun, and then offered for sale in baskets, at a kind of fair, at which all the neighbourhood attends. The native buyers from the foreign ports—usually Cantonese—here enter upon a keen competition, and buy up as much as they can of the leaves. In the end the lots bought from a variety of these small farms are mixed together by the purchaser, and then subjected to the firing already described, up-country, in houses hired specially for that purpose.

Thousands of poor women and children are next employed in picking out stems and stalks; after which the leaves are winnowed, the cured portion is carried away, and the uncured left behind to be subjected again to the fire. When the firing process is completed, the tea is sifted, and separated into two or three different parcels, or "chops" as they are called, the quality of each parcel varying with the quantity prepared at a time. Thus the first and highest "chops" consist of the smallest and best-twisted leaves; the second is somewhat inferior; while the third is made of the stalks, dust and siftings. This last, which is perfectly innocuous and wholesome, is used in this country to mix with better sorts of teas and thus to produce the cheap good teas of commerce.

These parcels or chops are next packed into chests of about 90 lbs., half-chests of 40 or 45 lbs., and boxes of 21 lbs.,

lined each of them with lead, and thus forwarded to the open
ports for sale. Most of the Bohea teas are brought down to
Foochow by the river Min—a voyage, as we shall presently see,
requiring no ordinary nerve and skill. The cargoes, as a rule,
begin to arrive at about the end of April; but at the
time I speak the market, for two or three seasons past, had
not been opened till some time in June. The year before the
mandarins gave native dealers credit for the duties on the leaf,
and thus aided them to hold back their teas until scarcity
should force the market into rates highly favourable to China.
The Europeans do not seem to succeed in banding together,
like the Chinese, to secure the tea crop on profitable terms.
The probable advantage to be gained by being first in the market
presents a temptation too great for the impetuous foreign
merchant to resist. But although the Chinese sellers enjoy
many facilities, such as borrowing money from the Foreign
banks in Foochow against the " chops " which they hold, they have
to pay high rates of interest, and the up-country competition
among themselves too, is strong; so that they are not unfamiliar
with losses—and heavy ones too sometimes.

But now let us proceed up country and gather some notion
of the difficulties which beset the transit of this precious herb.
I made an excursion for 200 miles up the Min, as far as
Yen-ping city, in the company of Mr. Justice Doolittle, whose
valuable book on the "Social Life of the Chinese " is the result
of years of painstaking labour and careful observation among the
people of this district. Armed with the requisite passports, we
started for Shui-kow, at mid-day on December 2, in a yacht
kindly placed at my disposal by one of the English merchants
at Foochow.

Boating on a Chinese river and with a Chinese crew is

11

always a trying experience to the temper of a European, except where the men have been bound by contract to perform their work for a fixed price and within a given period of time. If this precaution has been neglected the notion takes possession of the boatmen that foreigners are by nature wealthy, and that as a duty to themselves—who are always, both by birth and by necessity, extremely poor—they must take the most of the rare opportunity which good fortune has cast in their way. Inspired by such considerations as these, the men set themselves to enjoy a good deal more than their usual scanty leisure, a good deal more food, a longer spell of the opium-pipe and deeper drains out of the sam-shu flask. Hence in one's diary such jottings as the following by no means infrequently recur: "The men have been amusing themselves all day long, running the boat on to sandbanks and eating rice." "Tracking-line entangled again with that of another boat; two crews quarrelling for half an hour, another half-hour spent in apologies, and a third in disentangling the lines."

Sunday we spent quietly at a place called Teuk-kai, or Bamboo Crags. Here I had a walk ashore with my boy Ahong, and stopped for awhile to rest on a green mossy bank, whence our boat could dimly be made out through a sheet of mist that rose above the river, like the steam from a cauldron's mouth. We next passed over a lovely bit of country, through olive and orange plantations, where the trees bent down beneath their fruit, and the air seemed laden with perpetual fragrance. In one orchard we fell in with a watchman ensconced in a snug little straw hut, containing a bamboo table, a tea-pot, two chairs and a fine cat and kittens. The old man had been watching the place, he said, for more than half a century; he showed us the way to the farm, conducting us through fields of sugar-cane to

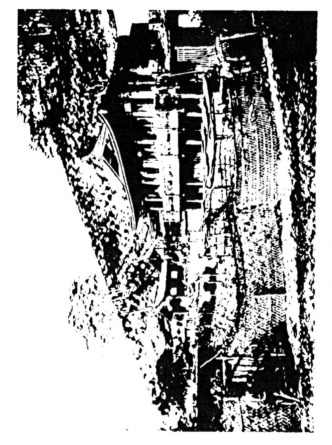

Up country Farm, Fukien Province.

the group of picturesque well-built brick houses of which the settlement was composed. When we had left this place and had sat down on a hill-side to talk over old times and former scenes of travel, Ahong confessed to me, among other matters, that he had no particular religious views at all. He had at one time been a Christian in Singapore, but had got bullied out of his change of faith by his friends. In a general way he thought it a good thing to have plenty of pork while alive; then to be laid in a comfortable coffin and buried in a dry place, and hereafter to have one's spirit fed and clothed continuously by surviving sons.

Next day we reached Shui-kow and found it built on the slopes of the hills, on the left bank of the river. This town was unlike any which I had seen on the plains. There was something new in its piles of buildings towering story above story, and in its picturesque situation; and here, too, I found that a water system had been elaborated out of a complex series of bamboo pipes and gutters, which passed from house to house, and brought constant supplies of water from a spring more than a mile away, in the hills. At Shui-kow I hired a "rapid-boat" to take us on to Yen-ping-fu. Our captain was Cheng-Show, or rather his wife, a lady who had a great deal to say both for him and herself too. Thus, when we ascended the first rapid, there was Mrs. Cheng to be seen well to the fore; at one moment nursing her baby, at another the child had been tossed into a basket, and the mother was fending her boat with a long pole from destruction on the rocks. Then to her brat again, or to cooking, cleaning, or husband-baiting; to each and every pursuit she was found equal, as fancy prompted or necessity compelled. Ours was a small boat, like all the others, carrying a high bridge and a rudder in the shape of a long oar, which swung on a pivot aft. This oar was nearly as long as the boat itself, and its effect when used was to make the vessel turn at once in its own length. The craft is built entirely of pine, is as strong as it is light, and admirably adapted in every respect for the navigation of the perilous rapids which begin to show themselves about half a mile above Shui-kow. We anchored for the night close to a military station, if two or three shanties and the half-dozen miserable-looking soldiers armed with match-locks, who occupied them, could be honoured with so dignified a name.

Next morning, as usual, there was a thick fog upon the river. This prevented our seeing more than two or three feet around the boat, and put a stop to all traffic till within an hour of noon. Our halting-place that evening was the village of Ching-ku-kwan; and there Mr. Doolittle and myself went ashore to inspect a Snake Temple. There was no image of the snake to be seen in this shrine; but the tablet of the snake king was there, set up for worship in a holy place, and we learned that during the seventh month a living snake becomes the object of adoration. Next day Mrs. Cheng and her husband had a little conjugal disagreement. As for Captain Cheng, he sat meekly smoking his pipe, a true example of marital equanimity, waiting till the storm should be over-past. Half an hour later his wife was working away as busily as ever. Each night the boat is arched over, waggon-fashion, with a telescopic arrangement of bamboo matting, forty feet long, ten feet wide and four feet high, which covers the entire deck. My friend and I occupied a small space at the bow. Ahong, the cook and fourteen boatmen were stretched out amid-ships, a small space at the stern being curtained off for the captain and his spouse. The representatives of three generations of the Cheng family are to

Rapids near Yen-Ping City, River Min.

be found living on board the craft. First the grandfather. He does almost nothing except smoke; and his pipe, a bamboo-cane with a knob at the end of it, he cherishes with wonderful affection. On his head is a relic of antiquity as venerable as himself—the tattered framework of a greasy-looking felt hat; while as for his thickly-padded jacket, it is reported that he removes that garment from his person about once a week, in order to destroy the small colonists that disturb his repose. For upwards of half a century he had been learning to swallow the smoke of his pipe, but with only partial success. Once or twice I fancied that he had fairly choked himself, and was about to expire; but he came to himself again by-and-by, and was seen puffing more vigorously than before.

As soon as the roofs were drawn over for the night, smoking commenced—the entire crew, Mrs. Cheng and all setting to work in business-like fashion; and as there was no outlet for the fumes, the atmosphere can be imagined much more easily than it could be endured. On the following day we passed a newly-wrecked boat, which had struck a sunken rock and then gone down. We also encountered a second boat dashing down the same rapid with a fatal way on her. She was bearing straight for the breakers, away from the main channel; the helmsman could not alter her course, and so she too struck and settled down, but not before the crew had had time to scramble out on the rocks and make the wreck fast with a cable. At one little village where we went ashore, a number of small-footed women were washing clothes in the stream. At our approach they fled with startling celerity, scaling the rocks and finding foothold where only cloven-hoofed goats might have been supposed to make their way.

On Sunday we reached Yen-ping, in time for service at the

Methodist Mission Chapel in that place, which stands on a hill and faces the main stream at a point where it is fed by two nearly equal tributaries, the one flowing from the Bohea Hills and the other from a source further to the south-east. The town contains a population of about thirty thousand souls, and does a considerable trade in paper, lackered ware, baskets and tea. The. foot of the hill was encircled by a high wall, from within which rose an inclined plane of roofs, broken here and there by groves of trees and temples, but still almost appearing one solid slope of tiled steps, over which an Alpine tourist might scramble to the outermost wall above, whose top could be seen in a faint line sweeping round the heights that closed in the city from behind. Beyond this hill, which looked as if it had been made for the town that covers it, a high range of mountains rose up in a deep purple belt, like a great protecting barrier.

The Mission House in the main thoroughfare was a miserable place enough, and we learnt that no one would let a decent house to Christians. The native missionary when we entered the chapel was conducting the morning service in the midst of an attentive congregation. He resided here with his family, and looked happy and contented; although, as I have said, his abode was a poor one, built and partitioned off with bamboo-laths and plaster, so thin that one could have pushed one's fingers through the walls; while the roof was festooned with cobwebs and admitted more daylight and air than was either necessary or agreeable. The interior beneath, however, wore a clean and even cheerful look. The back of this dwelling, like many others, was perched upon the city wall; and there was a path running beneath the fortifications, along which I picked my way with caution, and yet narrowly escaped being tripped up by a herd of pigs, as they rushed to banquet upon some filthy refuse dropping down from a house above. Yen-ping was a Chinese city, and yet one could breathe pure mountain air on its upper wall, and encounter some very pretty sights. On one occasion, when taking a view from a steep hill on the other side of the river, and while making my way up to a level space, I slipped my footing and caught hold of some grass that stood twelve or fifteen feet high there. The blades of this grass are furnished with an array of sharp teeth, that ripped my hands up like a saw; but at the same time it saved me a rapid descent of about two hundred feet, and a final plunge of a clear hundred more into the river below. Near this place, in a small village, we found the two widows and family of a deceased mandarin, sending a complete retinue to the spirit of their departed lord. A pile of huge paper models of houses and furniture, boats and sedans, ladies-in-waiting and gentlemen-pages were brought down to the banks of the river and there burned before the wailing widows. These effigies are supposed to be transformed by fire into the spiritual reality of the things which they represent. Many of the articles were covered with tin-foil, and when the sacrifice was over a seedy-looking trader bought the ashes, that he might sift them and secure the tin that had refused to put on an ethereal shape.

Many of the men hereabouts appeared deformed, but the deformity was due to the small charcoal furnaces which they carried concealed beneath the dress, and used to keep their bodies warm. As there are no fire-places in the houses, these portable furnaces prove very convenient substitutes. At first, when I saw so many humps about, I supposed that some special disease must be common in the place, or else that the sufferers had gathered themselves together from different parts of the empire to test the efficacy of some curative spring, like those hot wells near Foochow, where I have seen crowds of feeble and infirm folk bathing in the healing vapours. But the little copper furnaces encased in basket-work supplied a less melancholy explanation of the mystery.

When I watched the coolness, pluck and daring with which these poor river navigators will shoot the rapids of the river Min, risking their lives in every voyage—in a country where there are no insurances, except such as the guilds may chance to afford, and where no higher reward is to be gained than a hand-to-mouth subsistence on the most wretched fare—I began to get a truer insight into the manly and hardy qualities latent in this misgoverned Chinese race. In some of these watery steeps the channel winds and writhes from right to left, and forms acute angles among the rocks at every two or three boats' lengths. Once, when we descended, our frail craft tearing down these bends at a fearful speed, I thought for a moment that our fate was sealed, for it seemed impossible that the helmsman could ever bring the vessel round in time to clear a huge rock which rose up right ahead. There he stood on the bridge, calm and erect, with an iron grasp on the long rudder, impassive until we were just plunging on to the rock; and then, as I prepared to leap for life, he threw his whole weight on to the oar, and brought the boat round with a sweep that cleared the danger by the breadth of a hair. Thus we shot onwards, down! down! down! like a feather tossed to and fro by the caprice of the irresistible waves. As we passed down stream we saw a great number of men fishing with cormorants. These fishermen poled themselves about on bamboo-rafts, and on each raft was a basket and two or three cormorants, trained to dive and bring up fish for their owners. As I intended to take some pictures on the way down to Foochow, my friend, who was pressed for time, determined to find his way home in a native

FISHING WITH CORMORANTS.

KNIFE GRINDER.

passenger-boat that was about to leave Shui-kow. So after dinner I accompanied him on board, not without a last vain effort, as he was but in feeble health, to persuade him to complete the voyage in the yacht or house-boat in which we had come. A Chinese passenger-boat makes a pretty swift trip, and may be very suitable for natives, but it does not quite come up to our European notions of comfort. Thus the steerage accommodation consists of a long low cabin, in which one can scarcely kneel upright; and within this narrow space we found about fifty persons stowed away. Many were pedlars, carrying their wares along with them for sale; and the air of this packing-box was strongly tainted with garlic, tobacco, sam-shu, opium and a variety of other Chinese perfumes, which issued from the mass of humanity that writhed and tumbled about in fruitless efforts to discover places for repose. When they were a little settled, we had literally to grope our way over a reeking platform of half-naked limbs and bodies, and amid a torrent of cursing and abuse, in order to reach the state cabin, where my stout friend, after sundry efforts, succeeded in depositing himself at last. This cabin measured about four feet by three. The door was shut, and there he was in a sort of locker with one or two openings to admit the air, or rather the stench and din of the unwashed, noisy crowd in the steerage. So we parted to meet again and recount our adventures in Foochow.

CHAPTER IX.

THE opening of the Suez Canal wrought as great a change
in the China trade as in the commerce of the Malayan
Archipelago; and nowhere is this change more marked than in
the carrying traffic from port to port along the coasts of China.
Old lumbering junks, lorchas and even square-rigged sailing ships
have given place to the splendidly equipped steamers of the
local companies that ply regularly between the different stations
from Hongkong to Newchang; and then innumerable vessels,
owned, not a few of them, by private firms, as well as by
native and European companies, frequently find lucrative employment when the tea and silk seasons have not yet begun, either
in running between the treaty ports, or in making short voyages
to the rice-markets of Indo-China.

It was my good fortune to make a coasting trip to Shanghai

in a fine steamer belonging to a private line, engaged in the
tea trade during the greater portion of the year, but at that
time making a cruise northward till the Hankow tea-market
should be open. As we neared Shanghai the glass indicated
either that a typhoon was approaching, or else that we were
just upon its verge. The latter conclusion was a true one. It
turned out that we had followed in the wake of a hurricane,
and thus our experience afforded a good example of the limited area to which the circles of these typhoons are frequently
confined. We had encountered nothing save calms and light
winds throughout our passage; and yet when we entered Shanghai
river we found many ships disabled, some of them swept clear
to the deck—masts, spars and rigging having all gone over the
side. Here we had to wait twelve hours till a licensed pilot came
on board; and when that individual did at last make his
appearance, he gravely remarked that he was only a fifteen-foot
man, but that he could make it all right with another pilot of
superior depth to take us up. What he meant to convey to
us was that his license only allowed him to pilot vessels drawing
fifteen feet. An unfortunate accident occurred as we were
steaming up the Wong-poo to the wharf at Shanghai. The
Chinese have a superstitious belief that bad luck will attend
their voyage, if they fail at starting to cross the bows of a
vessel as she sails across their track; and so, as we steamed on,
we perceived a native trading-boat making frantic efforts with
sails and sculls to pass under our bows. The whistle was plied,
but in vain. On they pulled to their own certain destruction.
The engines could not be backed amid such a crowd of shipping,
and I was gazing helplessly over our bulwarks when we came
crashing through the timbers of the fated craft. There was a
yell of despair, and the wreck was next seen drifting down

the stream. A number of the crew had been projected by the shock some distance into the water; others clung to their property until it was submerged; but fortunately none of them perished, as a number of boats had seen the incident and had put off to their assistance at once.

Shanghai has always been able to hold its own as the great Chinese emporium of foreign trade. It was therefore with feelings of profound interest that I for the first time beheld the splendid foreign settlement that stands there on the banks of the Wong-poo, at a spot which about sixty years ago was a mere swamp dotted with a few fisher huts, and inhabited by a miserable semi-aquatic sort of Chinese population. In 1831 Dr. Gutzlaff, who visited the place for the first time in a junk, describes it as the centre of a great native trade, and tells us that from this port, "more than a thousand small vessels go up to the north several times annually, exporting silk and other Kiangnan manufactures," and besides, that an extensive traffic was carried on by Fukien men with the Indian Archipelago. But we may venture much further back in the history of the town. Several centuries ago, even before the Wong-poo river became a navigable stream at all, there was a great mart established in this locality on the banks of the present Soo-chow Creek, twenty-five miles distant from the harbour in which we have just anchored.* The topographical history of the district is full of records telling of the physical changes to which the vast alluvial plain where Shanghai stands has from time to time been subjected. Streams have been silted up, new channels have spontaneously opened; and yet, amid constant difficulties and never-ceasing alterations, the ever-important trade of the place has been maintained within

* See the *Shanghai Hein Chi.*

ART DEALERS.

CHINESE COSTER.

the same narrow area, where the annual floods of the Yang-tsze-kiang deposit their alluvium on the margin of the ocean and raise up new land out of its bed.

The political as well as the commercial and physical history of this region is no less full of interest. In process of time the old Wu-sung-kiang became unnavigable; and during the thirteenth century, a settlement was founded on the present site of Shanghai, to which trade was rapidly transferred by the closing of the old waterway: finally, in A. D. 1544, the settlement was converted into a walled city, as a defence against the repeated attacks of the Japanese. These Japanese raids, which date from A. D. 1361, when the Ming dynasty had just come to the throne, were not confined to this quarter, but distributed generally over the maritime provinces in the north. The Japanese, time after time, proved more than a match for their less warlike foes; but the latter always managed, in the long run, to prevent the daring invaders from obtaining a permanent foothold upon their coveted shores. These Chinese successes were sometimes secured by intrigue and diplomacy, or by fair promises and bribes; the slow-moving ponderosities of Chinese warfare being only resorted to when all else had failed. To illustrate these two methods of repelling an invading force, I will relate the following story. In 1543 when the Japanese had spoiled and laid waste no small extent of the country around Shanghai, the Chinese seeing that they were too feeble to fight against their enemies with success, had recourse to intrigue. Accordingly, the Governor-General of the province invited the Japanese leaders, Thsu-hai, Cheng-tung, Ma-yeh, and Wang-chen to come over to the side of the Chinese; promising them the rewards of high rank and untold treasure, if such valiant leaders would but join the Imperial standard. Tempted

by the offer, they presented themselves to arrange conditions,
and were forthwith seized, despatched to Peking and there put
to an ignominious death. On another occasion it is reported
that the Japanese came down upon their enemy with a fleet of
300 vessels; and after carrying all before them, and plundering
to their hearts' content, they departed laden with their spoil;
the Chinese troops pursuing them valiantly out of the country
and making an imposing hostile demonstration on the shore as
they unfurled the sails of their ships.

As to the settlement itself, those of my readers who have
not visited China will feel interested in a brief description of
its appearance. The approach by the river almost looks like
that of any busy prosperous European seaport. There one
finds ships of all nations; and, anchored in mid-channel, or
making their way to their moorings, a long line of ocean
steamers; while steam-launches, bearing mails and despatches,
dart in and out among the crowd of native craft that are seen
around. Advancing further up the river, we pass rows of store-
houses, foundries, dockyards and sheds. Next to these the
substantial buildings on the American concession; and then a
full view opens before us of the public garden and the imposing array of European offices which front the river on the
English concession ground. What surprised me most about this
settlement was the absence of anything temporary or unfinished
in the style of its buildings, such as might remind one that the
place was, after all, nothing more than a trading depôt, planted
on hostile and inhospitable shores, and sustained in its position
in spite of the envy which its appearance excited among the
rulers of the land. What pangs of regret and remorse ought
to be awakened among these proud unenlightened men, when,
in their moments, if any, of honest reflection, they cast their eyes

upon this "Model Settlement," and perceive that a handful of outer barbarians have, within the space of sixty years, done more with the little quagmire that was grudgingly allotted to them, than they themselves, with their highest efforts, have achieved anywhere in their own wide Empire during all the untold centuries of its fame. As I have said already, there is a finish about the whole settlement, a splendour and sumptuousness about its buildings, its wide roads and breathing spaces, its spacious wharves and elegant warehouses, that stand as a solemn rebuke to the niggardliness and grinding despotism which within the adjoining native city have penned thousands of struggling beings in the most temporary abodes; there to carry on a ceaseless strife for existence, breathing the fetid air of narrow polluted alleys, exposed to the constant risk of fearful conflagration and the grim horrors of pestilence or famine.

Su-kwang-ki, or "Paul Su," celebrated as the pupil of Matthew Ricci, the great Jesuit missionary of the sixteenth century, appears to have been a man who mourned over the condition of his country. He was a native of Shanghai, a scholar of great renown ; and he not only aided Ricci in his translation of a number of the books of Euclid, but left behind him many valuable original works; notably one on agriculture, which is still highly prized. But although admitted by the Emperor Kia-tsing and his successor to be man of singular ability and foresight, his wise counsels were disregarded, and he himself was repeatedly treated with suspicion, due to the intrigues of jealous rivals. Accordingly his counsel was set aside, and his measures for the preservation and defence of the last Chinese dynasty were systematically neglected. But to this day he occupies a shrine in one of the temples of Shanghai, and there his fellow-townsmen pay him reverent worship as a sort of divinely-inspired sage.

Most of my readers are aware that in spite of a host of troubles (not the least of which was the Taiping rebellion, or rather, I believe, the attack upon the city by the short-sword or dagger rebels) Shanghai has continued to advance steadily, and has always maintained its position as the greatest emporium of China. It must be at the same time borne in mind that this commercial success is, in some measure at least, attributable to the European customs' administration which was inaugurated at this city in 1843, and which now extends its ramifications to all the open ports of the Empire.

Some of my readers will naturally inquire whence the labour came which transformed this dismal swamp into what I have just described, and built houses there fit for any capital of Europe and superior to some of the edifices that adorn our own greatest ports. One might think that structures such as these must have been reared by skilled workmen from Europe; but a very short residence in Shanghai suffices to undeceive us. Then we mark the avidity with which native builders, carpenters and mechanics of every sort compete with each other to win the remunerative employment which those buildings afford, and the facility with which they pick up the extended knowledge needful to enable them to carry out their contracts and to impart to their work that elegance and perfection which the cultivated tastes of the foreign architect demand. But it is not to these buildings alone that we must look to discover the hidden resources of Chinese toil. Visit the dockyards and foundries, and there too watch the Chinese craftsmen—the shipwrights, engineers, carpenters, painters and decorators, busily at work under European foremen, who bear the highest testimony to the capabilities of their men. Pass on next to the Kiang-nan arsenal, outside the city walls, and there you will find perhaps the highest development of Chinese technical industry, in the manufacture of rifles and field-guns and the construction of ships of war. It is computed that in 1898 there will be established at this port eighteen or twenty Chinese, Japanese and European cotton mills, equipped with the best and most modern appliances throughout. There are native mills already in operation, and in 1895 capital to the extent of 38,000 taels was subscribed by foreign joint-stock companies, for the erection of four spinning and weaving mills. It will be gathered from this, and the cheap efficient labour available for the industry, that the Chinese are beginning to supply their own markets with a certain class of cotton goods, and that ere long a large export trade will be created in cotton fabrics suitable for commerce all over Eastern Asia. The native cotton is of short staple, and the thread spun only suitable for weaving the coarser fabrics of native wear.

The native walled city of Shanghai stands to the south of the foreign settlement, and is separated from it by the French concession ground, and by a canal which here sweeps round and forms with Soo-chow Creek and the river a water boundary for the entire English ground. The latter, on its western side, supports a Chinese population of over 50,000 souls; but inside the walls of the Chinese city, in an area measuring little over a mile long by three-fourths of a mile in breadth, and in a densely crowded suburb on the water's edge close by, about 130,000 inhabitants reside.

Like all other Chinese towns, Shanghai has its tutelary deity, upon whom the Emperor, as brother of the Sun, has conferred an honorary title. This guardian of the fortunes of Shanghai stands in the "Cheng-hwang-Miau" or "Temple of the City God," in the northern quarter of the town; and though he and his shrine have from time to time been rudely overthrown, both,

after each disaster, have been reverently restored; and now he
may be seen looking out upon wide pleasure-grounds—in a more
or less dilapidated state, it is true—but still now and again
regaled with theatrical performances, and leading, for an idol, a
not altogether unenjoyable life.   In the same spot are two drum-
towers, superintended by a number of inferior deities, and used
more especially to spread the alarm of fire, or to notify the
approach of a foe.   Then there is the Confucian temple; besides
a host of other Buddhist and Taoist sacred edifices, occupying
the best spaces of ground within a city where the miserable
population have too often scarcely breathing space.

Our route now lies away among the azalea-clad mountains in
the province of Che-kiang.   But before re-embarking we must
have a parting glance at the streets of the "Model Settlement."

There are no cabs; but the residents, many of them, possess
private carriages.   The substitute for the cab here is the wheel-
barrow and Japanese jinricksha—very undignified sort of convey-
ances, but nevertheless comfortable enough when one has once
grown accustomed to their use.   Ahong procured me two of these
wheelbarrows from the nearest stand, and thus, with my two
boys, my baggage and "Spot," I set out for the Ningpo steamer.
There is not much risk of accidents in a steady-going vehicle
such as this.   The coolie who propels it is neither skittish nor
given to shying, and the pace he puts on is never dangerous.

The Portuguese were established on the river Yang at the
beginning of the sixteenth century, and were finally massacred
by the natives in revenge for their barbarous conduct, according
to the Chinese account.   These Portuguese were said about that
time to have joined with the Japanese in several of their raids
on the maritime provinces of China; and it will be remembered that, some fifty-six years ago, there was another massacre

of Portuguese and Manilla men at this very same town. They were then in some way implicated in the piracies of daily occurrence in the China Sea at that time, and the general feeling was that the retribution was not altogether undeserved. Another disaster befel Ningpo in 1861, when it fell into the the hands of the Taipings; remaining in their possession for about six months, when it was retaken for the Imperialists by the English and French war vessels, and since that time, like many other Chinese cities, has been labouring on peacefully in an effort to regain what it lost at the hands of the rebels and the Imperial troops.

It was daylight when we steamed up the Yang river; and the harsh outlines of the islands and of Chin-hai promontory close by, were mellowed in the morning light. A great fleet of fishing-boats bound seaward contributed to enliven the scene; and there were Fukien timber-junks, too, laden till they looked like floating wood-yards, and labouring their way up stream. One feature full of novelty was the endless array of ice-houses lining the banks of the river for miles and presenting the appearance of an encampment of troops. These ice-houses, or ice-pits, are thatched over with straw, and the ice is used to preserve fresh fish during the summer months.

There is a small foreign community on the banks of the Yang of different nationalities, including the missionary body. The native city is a walled enclosure, somewhat larger than that at Shanghai, and with nearly double its population; but as for the foreign trade of the place, it has never been very important, in spite of the proximity of Hang-chow-fu, the capital of the province, which the great Venetian, when he passed through it, described as an Eastern Paradise.

Among the chief attractions of Ningpo are the Fukien guild-

hall, the " Tien-how-kung, " as it is called, or " Temple of the Queen
of Heaven"; one of the finest buildings of the kind in China.
Indeed it is only the temples, the yamens and the houses of
the rich—the latter, outside the official ranks, few and far between when one considers the vastness of the population—that
possess any noteworthy architectural features in the country.
The comfortable, elegant and tasteful abodes of the middle classes,
which adorn the suburbs round our cities at home, are conspicuous by their absence in the " Flowery Land. "   In this town
I met the remnant of that " ever-victorious army " which achieved
so many triumphs.   Now, "after much turmoil, " these warriors
rest from their labours, and form the Ningpo city guard, a small
compact body of native troops under two English officers, well
drilled, well cared for and well paid.   This, I fear, is more than
can be said of a large portion of the Chinese forces under arms.
At any rate they are not all well, and but few of them regularly paid. Notwithstanding this the condition of the Chinese
soldiers is perhaps better than it has been in former years; and I
believe that, were the Imperial Government obliged to make an
effort, they might turn out an army better equipped than is
generally supposed; although at the same time any force the Chinese
might thus muster would be wofully deficient in the discipline,
organisation and science, required in coping with the machine-
like masses that are placed upon the modern battle-fields of
Europe. These are the impressions I gathered from actual observation of bodies of men encamped and under review in China.
I think that a Chinaman who has received an English education
of a not very high-class sort, might try to put a letter together
in pure English with just about as much success as his government, with the knowledge they at present possess of the science
of modern warfare, to send a thoroughly efficient army to face

foreign troops. I cannot indeed march a regiment of Chinese
before my reader for review, but of their shortcomings in European literary composition I will give an actual sample. An
Englishman had occasion to send a note to his doctor's native
assistant, and here, in facsimile, is the reply:

"Dear Sir,—I not know this things. Dr. — no came Thursday.
More better you ask he supose you what Fashtion thing can
tell me know I can send to you.

"Yours truly,

"HANG SIN."

Now in the foregoing we have a very fine specimen of the
sort of results achieved by Chinamen who flatter themselves
that they can write English. There are a tardily increasing number of well-educated natives to whom this remark does not apply.
They have learnt the letters, and something of the syntax and
grammar, but not enough to be of value to them; and so it
is with the Chinese soldier of to-day. He possesses occasionally
the right weapons, but he lacks the knowledge essential to
make use of them effectively, and the perfect discipline which
alone can unite him to his fellows on the field, as an important
unit in a compact and well-organised mass.

On April 4th I left Ningpo for Snowy Valley, in a native
boat which I hired to take me up stream to Kong-kai. It was
close on midnight when we started from Ningpo wharf, and we
hoped to reach Kong-kai village by about 9 or 10 a. m. next
day. In the end we reached Kong-kai within the allotted time.
My party consisted of my two China boys, and four Ningpo
coolies engaged to transport my baggage to the hills. Our path
lay across fields of bean and rape, now in full bloom and exhal-
ing a delightful fragrance, which contrasted strikingly with the
morning whiffs from the manure-bestrewed fields, which com-

monly salute the wanderer in China. Everything hereabouts
shone with freshness and beauty, and it was evident that we
must have landed in a real paradise of cultivation.

There lay the village in front of us, nestling cosily amid the
trees! And as we marched along I pictured to myself a quiet,
rustic hamlet, such as we encounter in our English counties.
But notwithstanding the natural beauty of the situation, Kong-kai
was disappointing. No perfume of rose or honeysuckle greeted
us as we approached, no rustic cots, no healthy, blooming
children, not even the fondly-expected sturdy villager were among
what was to be seen here.

At this place we procured mountain-chairs for an eighteen
miles' journey to the monastery of Tien-tang. The chair-bearers
looked worn and feeble, but as I walked a good deal they were
not over-fatigued. One or two of the hamlets which we passed
on the road were much more attractive than Kong-kai; and indeed
the people seemed to improve in condition the further we
advanced inland. Near the hills the women and children adorn
their raven tresses with the bright flower of the azalea—a plant
found in great profusion in the highlands of the locality. The
halting-places were little wayside temples, and in one of these
I met two old women, the priestesses of the shrine. Most haggard, ill-favoured crones were they, and it was with grave fore-
bodings that I allowed them to prepare my repast.

The bearers rested as often as they possibly could, and spent
their money and their leisure in gambling among themselves
or with wayside hawkers. Some of the small temples hereabouts
differed from any which I had seen in China, having their outer
porches adorned with two or three well-modelled life-size figures
in the costume which appeared to be that of the ancient lictors
of the Ming dynasty. But the idols within were invariably the

WAYSIDE GAMBLING.

same, the ordinary Triad of the Buddhist mythology. Each shady nook about these shrines was the resort and at times the sleeping-place of wayfarers; and there too vendors of fruit and other provisions had set up their stalls, ready either to sell the traveller his daily food, or to gamble with him for it, if he preferred that plan. The wandering minstrel and the story-teller were not absent from the scene, beguiling the mid-day repast with quaint ballads or with some tale from the stores which the folklore of the country has to supply. At one of these halting-places, while the coolies were tossing dice with an aged hawker, a Chinese pedlar laid down his burden for a rest. He had been carrying two baskets slung on a pole, and from these there issued such an incessant pattering and ceaseless chirping, that my curiosity induced me to open one of them and have a look inside. There I found about a hundred fluffy little ducklings, all of an age, flapping their rudimentary wings and opening their capacious mouths, clamorous for food. They were of our friend's own hatching and but one or two days old. Hatching poultry by artificial heat has reached great perfection in China.

The plain which we were crossing was dotted with little grave-mounds crowned with shrubs. And here and there a farm-house could be seen peeping out amid the groves, or a haystack clinging round the trunk of a tree and propped six feet clear above the ground.

The ascent to the monastery of the "Snowy Crevice" afforded a succession of the finest views to be met with in the province of Cheh-kiang. The azaleas, for which this place is celebrated, were now in full bloom, mantling the hills and valleys with rosy hues, and throwing out their blossoms in clusters of surprising brilliancy against the deep green foliage which bound the edges of the path. The mountains themselves were tossed

in wild disorder, swelling into richly-wooded knolls, or rising
in cliffs and beetling crags. As the day declined the hills
seemed to melt and merge into the fiery clouds; deep shadows
shot across the path, swallowing up the woody chasms and
warning us that night was near at hand. Darkness had already
set in before we arrived at our destination. "Spot", my dog,
had proceeded on, and his appearance had brought out a
venerable bonze, who, almost without question, suspended the
evening reckoning of his sins on his rosary, and lit us to our
quarters in a large block of buildings behind. The apartment
assigned to us was a plastered, white-washed chamber built out
of pine wood, and containing a magnificent hardwood bed. After
intimating that foreign wine was much better than any of his
country's liquors, our old guide took his leave. We were not long,
however, in finding our way to the kitchen for ourselves, and
there the boys kindled a fire, while I smoked with the monks.

The monastery of the "Snowy Crevice" reposes far from the
haunts of men and the tumult of cities, in a broad, fertile
valley, part of the imperial patrimony upon which its members
subsist. It has of course a miraculous history, and, like many
similar establishments, is popularly supposed to be extremely
ancient. One of the stories connected with the place is that,
in 1264 A.D., the Emperor Li-tang dreamed a dream about the
temple, and named it accordingly "The famous Hall of Dreams."
This formed one of the most important events in its annals,
for the dream was followed by substantial gifts. There is
another legend which tells us of an anchorite, and of an Emperor
who essayed in vain to slay the Holy Man. At last the
monarch fell down and worshipped the priest, for he had never
before come across a being whom he could not slay. This
Emperor was distinguished for his wise rule, and had just put

a million of the common sort of his subjects to death; but he was, at that time, athirst for some victim of rarer eminence and sanctity than any of those whom he had already brought to their end. He died at last a pious priest, and left some suitable gifts behind him. Something like this is not unknown even at the present time. There are monks, I am told, in those places, who have passed their lives in crime, and who find it expedient to retire to these choice retreats (making them places of refuge, like the temples of the ancient Jews and Greeks) to die pleasantly chanting "Omita-Foh!"

Such holy ones, rescued from the grasp of justice and the jaws of the pit, take good care, nevertheless, to live as long as they can. Some Buddhists are doubtless sincere, if judged by the laws of their own faith; and many of them, whom I came across, I found hospitable and kind to strangers. They seldom failed, however, to let me know if the presents I chanced to give them were not quite equal to those which other visitors had bestowed.

Early next morning a mute and aged monk conducted me to view the "Thousand-fathom Precipice." A heavy cloud was hanging like a pall over the scene as I followed the guide along a mountain path. At length we reached a summit that stood out bold and clear, though still wet with vapoury rain; and there, in a small rest-house, perched upon one of the rocks, we sat down to listen to the roar of the fall and the foaming torrent beneath. The monk next led me to where, clinging to a tree, I could lean over the edge of the precipice and get a look right down into the abyss; but there was nothing to be made out save a sea of mist, through which the deafening roar of the waters could be heard as they leapt from rock to rock in their descent to the valley more than 1,000 feet below. The sun gradually shone out, and by its aid we descended to the foot of the fall through a steep shady path, and secured some pictures of the scenery. The cataract takes a leap of about 500 feet and then gushes downwards over the cliffs and edges like the graceful folds of a bridal veil; while the variously coloured rocks are covered with ferns and flowering shrubs.

It was interesting to watch the monks at their refections; and this we contrived to do without being noticed ourselves. We found them as a rule particular in observing those rules of Buddhism, by which the external semblance of cleanliness is enforced. * The following are some of the laws which regulate diet:—

"The dinner of a priest consists of seven measures of rice mixed with flour, the tenth of a cubit of pastry, and nearly the same weight of bread. To eat more is cupidity, to eat less is parsimony; to eat vegetables of any kind besides these dishes is not permitted."

The last injunction is by no means commonly followed in China:—

"Then the priest shall offer to the good and bad spirits, and repeat five prayers. He must not speak about his dinner, nor steal food like a dog, nor scratch his head, nor breathe in his neighbour's face, nor speak with his mouth full, nor laugh, nor joke, nor smack in eating; and if he should happen to find an insect in his food he must conceal it so as not to create doubt in the minds of others."

There are a host of other very good rules laid down for his guidance; but their general tendency when observed is to make a monk's dinner a most solemn and most unsocial event. When we look through the Buddhist laws and precepts, we find them so minute and so wide-reaching, that they hedge the priest

* *Laws and Regulations of the Priesthood of Buddha, in China*. Trans. by C. F. Newmann.

completely around, shutting him out from the gratification of his most natural desires and rendering it indeed uncertain whether any perfectly devout and faithful Buddhists can possibly exist in China.

The return voyage to Ningpo and Shanghai I must pass by unrecorded, that I may hurry forward to describe my journey up the Yangtsze river to Sze-chuan.

Having dined with a literary friend in Shanghai, I returned to the hotel towards midnight and there found my boys with everything in readiness, and a gang of coolies waiting to bear our baggage on board the "Fusiyama," which was getting up steam for Hankow. It was a bitter night, and the scene was as dark and gloomy as the wind was cold. The lamps blinked and shivered as the blast swept by. The bund was deserted; only some stray woman would now and again emerge from the darkness, and then be swallowed up once more, like a sinful victim in the jaws of night. We soon passed on to the "Fusiyama," across the floating landing-stage alongside of which she was moored. She was a fine steamer, although by no means the finest among the S. S. N. Co's fleet.

Reserving what I may have to say about Nanking and the ports on the lower Yangtsze, I will transport the reader at once about 600 miles higher up—to Hankow, the furthest point on the Yangtsze river to which steam navigation had at that time been carried. Hankow holds an important position at the confluence of the rivers Han and Yangtsze. The ancient name of the Han river was the Mien, and its·course, as well as the point at which it joins the Yangtsze, have been subjected to frequent change. It was only in the last decade of the fifteenth century that the river created its present channel, and at the same time the advantageous site, to which Hankow owes no little portion of her prosperity. The early trade of the district was confined to Hanyang, a place described as a flourishing port at the remote period treated of in the "History of the Three States." Hanyang is now chiefly taken up with official residences, though its suburbs are still the resort of a considerable native trade.

Hankow flourished under the rule of the Mings, and does not seem to have suffered greatly during the disasters which attended their fall. It was then known as the great mart, in fact the commercial centre of the Empire, and was the resort of traders from the furthest north, and from the southernmost provinces Kiang-su and Yunan. Most of the provinces indeed were represented there by guilds, whose halls are still famous for their size and decoration. During Kien-loong's time the prosperity of Hankow continued to advance until the disastrous epoch of the Taiping rebellion. Then the decay was as rapid as the ruin was complete; and finally, in 1855, the whole city was burned to the ground.

After the Taipings had been expelled from Hupeh, Hankow rose once more out of its ashes, and in 1861 the final arrangements for a concession of land to the British Crown were carried into effect. The hoisting of the English colours was followed at once by a splendid settlement, erected on a very unfortunate site. The land was bought up in small lots at 2,500 taels each, and enormous sums were squandered before it was discovered that the spot chosen for a foreign settlement was exposed to constant inundations of the most destructive kind. Thus, in the year before my arrival, the flood, which is always looked forward to as the event of the season, bestowed its fertilising favours with no grudging hand; and indeed there was no foretelling to what height the waters, which had already swept away entire suburbs from the cities higher up stream,

HANKOW. 189

might deluge the vicinity of Hankow. Well, first of all, it rose slowly until it had submerged its banks; thence it made excursions along the outlying streets; crept up like a silent foe till it had breasted the fortifications; and finally made the captured settlement over to a sort of watery sack. The inhabitants retreated to their garret fastnesses, while pigs, poultry, and even cattle were sheltered in boats, or found refuge in the bedrooms on the upper floors. At any rate it was a convenience to "Paterfamilias" to have his milk-cow next door to his nursery, and chanticleer perched upon a friendly bedpost to screech the approach of day. But when the novelty of these domestic arrangements had worn off, and when the richly-papered walls began to weep through a lacework of fungus, and the limbs of the polished furniture to show symptoms of dissolution; when silken hangings grew mildewed and pale, and the boundary walls tottered and sunk with a dull splash into the red stream, the insecurity of the position pressed heavily upon the despondent inhabitants. The halls and staircases became docks and landing-stages where visitors might disembark, and a dining or drawing-room made a much better plunge-bath than one could have imagined. Bachelors, too, while they indulged in a morning swim, could call at the bank to enquire the rate of exchange, or dive to their breakfast beneath the doorway of some hospitable friend. At length the water reached its height; and then to the relief of all began slowly to recede. It is apprehended that but for a back wall (erected originally by the Chinese Government at a cost of £80,000, as a protection against organised raids from the banditti of the plain) which acted as a breakwater, the entire settlement might have been swept into the Yangtsze by the strong reflux currents from the Han.

The business at Hankow has never come near the anticipations

of the Europeans who flocked thither when the place was opened ;
but, nevertheless, as the centre of the districts which produce
the Congou teas, it must always secure a very important share
of foreign commerce. The total value of the trade in foreign
shipping was reported to be about 14,000,000 taels in 1871,
while in 1873 it appears to have fallen off; but this was owing
to a sort of commercial stagnation which has been felt all over
China. In 1895 it stood at 44,507,502 taels.

The Taotai of Hankow, Ti-ming-chih, who furnished me with
a passport for the upper Yangtsze, and whom I had twice the
pleasure of meeting, had been born in the province of Kiangsu,
and commenced his official career at the age of thirty, by an
appointment to a modest clerkship. From this his abilities
advanced him step by step, until he attained his present position,
where he earned a high reputation by his just, mild and intelligent rule.

Woochang city, on the opposite bank of the river presents
a picturesque appearance, due partly to the elevated ground on
which it stands and partly to its celebrated tower, which tradition
reports to have been first set up there 1,300 years ago. This
tower was overthrown by the followers of the "Heavenly King"
during the Taiping rebellion, and after an interval of about
fifteen years rebuilt and finished. It is quite unlike the ordinary
Chinese pagoda, and from its peculiar design runs no risk of
ever being mistaken for any other monument.

During the journey to the upper Yangtsze, which I now propose to describe, I had two American gentlemen for my companions. Two native boats were secured, and we engaged them
to carry us to Ichang. Into the smaller of these craft we stowed
the cook and servants, reserving the larger one for our baggage
and ourselves. Our boat was divided into three compartments

with well-carved bulkheads between. The fore-cabin was taken up by a boy to wait on us, and by our newly-appointed Chinese secretary—Chang. This secretary was a small compact man, full of Chinese lore and self-satisfied complacency. The "central state" room was our own, while Captain Wang and his wife found shelter in the after-cabin. Besides this there was an ample hold, which contained our baggage, our provisions and our crew.

We left Hankow about mid-day, but as there was no wind, we had to pole our way through thousands of native boats, and anchor for the night at Ta-tuen-shan, only ten miles above the town. A hard frost set in during the evening, and it seemed quite impossible to keep the intense cold out of our quarters. To make matters worse, the skipper and his spouse smoked stale tobacco half through the night, and the fumes came through the bulkhead and filled my sleeping-bunk. Next day we set to work with paper and paste to cure both evils by patching up every crevice and by fixing up a stove which had been lent us by friends for the voyage. These preparations were a source of disquietude to Mrs. Wang, who turned out to be a tartar more desperate even than the lady of the Min.

The boatmen were a miserably poor lot. They neither changed their clothes nor washed their bodies during the entire trip: and "Why should they?" said Chang the secretary; they could only change their garments with one another. They have but a single suit apiece, and that, too, some of them only loan for the winter months. Their clothes were padded with cotton and formed their habiliments by day and their bedding by night. Poor souls! how they crept together, and huddled into the hold! and what an odour arose from their retreat in the morning, for they had smoked themselves to sleep with tobacco, or those of them who could afford it, with opium. It was always a difficult matter to get them up and out on deck to face the cold. I confess I never cared to be the first to lift the hatch. But the voice of Mrs. Wang was equal to the occasion. She shook those sluggards from their rest with her strident tones; she stamped in her cabin and "slung slang" at them like the foulest missiles. At last, about seven o'clock, they might be seen unwillingly turning to and hauling up the anchor, not more slow-moving than themselves. As it happened, we had a fair wind and made a good day's run, but the iron stove seemed to be a failure, or at any rate our coal would not burn. It took us half a day of hard work to turn "Farmer's Bend," although one might easily walk across the neck of land which divides the two extremities of the curve, in a quarter of an hour. A canal cut across would be a great saving in the river navigation. We noticed many timber rafts from the Tung-Ting lake, looking like floating villages, and indeed they are neither more nor less than hamlets. Each on its substructure of timber supported two rows of huts, and in these dwelt the little colonies of Chinamen who had invested their time, labour and small capital in the trade. When the rafts reach Hankow, these huts are lifted off and placed on the river's bank; the owners residing inside them till all their wood has been disposed of. When steamers are seen thus far up the Yangtsze river (46 miles above Hankow) experienced pilots would be required, especially at this season when the water is at its lowest, and it might perhaps be necessary even, to survey the stream annually, for its channel tends constantly to shift. Steam navigation is now carried beyond—to Ichang, at the entrance to the Gorges of the upper Yangoge. At Paitsow, where we anchored for the night, we found men manufacturing bamboo cables. They had no rope-walks, but only high temporary-looking scaffoldings, with some men above

OUR NATIVE HOUSE BOAT—UPPER YANGTSZE.

and others below, making and twisting the thick strands.
Next morning the skipper's wife and the crew got through a
good deal of bad language between them before we made a
start. The conversation was a shrill-toned one, and alternated
between Mrs. Wang in her cabin at one end of the boat and
the crew in the hold at the other. The latter objected to turn
out until their captain was at his post. This difficulty the
gentle wife settled ultimately by kicking her husband out of bed
on to the deck, hurling torrents of abuse at his unhappy head
and supplementing those delicate attentions by a plentiful supply
of cooking utensils. Let the reader imagine himself afloat in
such a vessel as I have described, with such a crew, on a river
red like the soil through which it flows, and from half a mile
to a league in breadth; let him conceive himself ascending the
stream between low level monotonous clay walls; he will then
have a picture of our craft and our surroundings for many
days as we pursued our voyage up to the Gorges. We break-
fasted and dined, anchored and slept, surveying the river as
well as we could, and here and there marking out sundry sand-
banks and other barriers to commerce, formed since the one
and only chart of the river had been made.

We had chosen our opportunity well. There can be no
better time for examining the features of a river than when it
is at its lowest, and the Yangtsze was now running far below
its banks, which in summer are completely submerged. But
our careful soundings, our notes of bearings and our chart-
projecting need find no record here. Their very sameness grew
wearisome at last; but, as for our secretary, he would have
been quite willing to sail on until he had digested the whole
of the ancient classics, drinking our wine and smoking our
cheroots as frequently as they were offered. He had marvellous

13

raiment—Chang. A padded robe of classic cut, with sleeves reaching down to his knees, and a collar that stood up like a fortress, around his neck. When in a corner, seated at study, he looked like a huge bolster surmounted by a tiny cap. He would remain in this posture for hours, with his eyes closed, and audibly rehearsing whole books of classic lore; but he had also a good deal of accurate information about the country, and was extremely polite in his manner, and willing to make himself useful. It was a mistake having two boats; their unequal sailing powers caused grievous delay—delays which the servants and cook readily turned to account in explaining all sorts of shortcomings, and which contributed greatly to the leisure and enjoyment of the crews who were paid by the day. On the 23rd we passed the point where the Ta-Kiang — or great river—is joined by the stream from the Tung-Ting lake. At this place there were abundant evidences of considerable trade in the fleets of boats we continually passed. The river, in some of the long reaches hereabouts, would be dangerous for steam navigation, at any rate during the months when the banks are submerged. Hence suitable landmarks would have to be erected, as not a single tree, shrub, or knoll, can at such times be seen for many miles around. All the shoals at this (the winter) season are well defined, and, with the exception of two reefs of rocks which stand well clear of the water, consist of soft mud and sand, and occur just at bends, where anyone accustomed to river navigation would expect to find them. Wherever the current struck upon the clay, a good channel was almost invariably to be found.

On the 24th we ascended a small rapid which ran about five knots, and were detained by a snow-storm for about six hours. The little hamlets we passed, or anchored at, day after day, were temporary, miserable-looking settlements, conveying the idea of a thinly peopled country; and the inhabitants wore the poverty-stricken look only too common in other parts of China. We have walked over the country, and along the banks, for nearly half a day without encountering a single individual. At many places the river had undermined the banks, and these were falling in great blocks eight or ten feet wide; and there was one point where we noticed that the stream was cutting out the heart of an old settlement, for there were foundations of houses exposed, and many coffins protruding from the bank.

On the 27th we reached Shang-chai-wan, and remarked that the banks in front of an old pagoda there, had been carefully faced up with stones. Thus a useful sort of landmark was well protected from the inroads of the stream, while the houses were left to be swept away as the bank fell in.

This village indicated some slight degree of prosperity and presented a pretty winter's scene. There was no one astir, not a footprint stained the white mantle in which the soil was wrapt; only on one level patch the leaves of a winter crop shot up in rows, and formed a pale green pattern on a snowy ground. A little further on was the town of Shang-chai-wan, where our boys went ashore and spent half a day in a vain search for coal. Then the crew had to be hunted up all over the place, and one by one the men dropped in, each with as much sam-shu as he could hold inside him, or else stupified with opium. Capt. Wang we found in a filthy alley, enjoying the nectar of a grog-shop, amid a group of natives who were civil enough. Few of them had ever set eyes upon a genuine white man before, and all made numerous good-natured enquiries about our relations and our clothes; one old man even suggested that our faces and hands had only acquired a pale colour through the use of some wonderful cosmetic, and that our bodies were black. I bared my arm to refute this calumny, and its white skin was touched by many a rough finger, and awoke universal admiration. Not knowing exactly what our barbarous views of decency might be, we were kindly recommended by an unwashed, but polished member of the community not to gratify vulgar curiosity by stripping entirely, as we had already completely satisfied the more intelligent members of the crowd.

The reader can easily gather from such incidents as these what depraved notions some of the Chinese must entertain about ourselves and our customs. They always seem to feel that we have a great deal to learn; the merest coolie, if he be a kindly-disposed person, will readily place his knowledge at our service and put us in the way of picking up something of Chinese civilisation. I have in my possession one of the valuable works upon which this popular belief is fed. It is a sort of ethnological treatise, written down to the limited comprehension of facts and to the inordinate craving for fable which characterise the lower classes among this highly superstitious nation. The author gravely describes races of men, who, like ourselves, live on the outer edges of the world, that is outside the benign influence of Chinese rule. Some are very hairy men clothed with leaves; others hop about on one leg; while others again are adorned with the claws of birds. There is one very singular tribe indeed. These have only a single huge eye in the forehead, while the women carry a multitude of breasts. There are men too with big holes through their bodies above the region of the heart, so that they may be spitted like herrings, or carried about on poles; and lastly there is one community more gifted still, for they can fly through the air with wings.

It was at this place that our writer Chang, who said he was

suffering from cold, despatched one of the boatmen ashore to buy a bottle of sam-shu. The trust which he displayed in the integrity of the messenger was no less marvellous than touching. "I do not know how much there is here," said he, as he placed his purse in the boatman's hands; "but take what you require and put back the rest." Just before, however, I had noticed the crafty rogue carefully count the cash in this very purse, which, as it turned out, contained no more than exactly sufficient for the purchase.

On the 29th, when passing a customs' station, we were pursued and overtaken by a fiery official, who came on board, received a cigar and a glass of wine and went away greatly impressed with our respectability. We also sailed by a large cotton-junk lying wrecked on the bank, and a second one which had run aground where the water was deeper, and whose owners were now living in a mud hole, waiting till the river should rise high enough to float their craft.

At Shi-show-hien we bought a quantity of fish; among them was one described by Captain Blakiston, which carries a sword above its wide toothless mouth. This sword it is said to use for boring into the soft mud to dislodge the tiny fish, which thereupon rush for shelter down its dark capacious throat. The stomach of the specimen we purchased, contained one or two of these half-digested mud-fish. Its colour, from the spine half-way down to the belly, was dark blue or slate; the belly was white; the tail and fins were white and red. Length from point of sword to tip of tail, 4 feet 2 inches; length of sword, 14 inches.

Shi-show-hien was formerly held by the Taiping rebels. Here they built a fortress, whose ruins may still be seen. We were now within sight of the hill ranges in the province of Hunan, and on one hill close at hand stood a temple called the Ti-tai-shan,

which forms a striking land-mark for river navigation. The
changes which have taken place since our Admiralty chart was
laid down renders that map comparatively useless, both for this
and other parts of the river, at any rate when the waters are low.

Shasze stands on the left bank of the Yangtsze river, which
is here more than a mile and a half broad, with a deep roomy
channel; and we may gather from the crowd of native shipping
that lies anchored off the town or close to its fine stone
embankment, that we have reached an important centre of trade.
This embankment terminates at its upper end in a sort of bul-
wark, crowned with the finest pagoda to be found anywhere
along this river. Immense labour has been bestowed in fortifying
this site against the undermining influence of the current; and
the town is placed at such an angle on the stream, that the
action of the water always keeps a clear channel close to its
strong stone-retaining wall. Stone is freely used in this part of
the upper Yangtsze, and is readily obtainable in unlimited
supplies in the gorges above the town. At Shasze, landing-
stages for steamers might be made at almost any part of the
bank; while there are splendid sites for a foreign settlement
on the hills across the stream.

Coal abounds in Hunan and Szechuan, and yet we found it
difficult to procure. In the former province it is worked at
two places only—Tsang-yang-hien and Pa-tung-hien, and there
to an extremely limited degree; but in Szechuan there is a good
deal more coal-mining going on. The coal is of good quality,
in every way suitable for steam purposes—at least the samples
which we collected were excellent.

We arrived on February 3rd at the town of Kiang-kow.
Here the men struck work, as they wished to go ashore for
what they called rice, but which Chang interpreted as wine.

We offered to supply them with rice; but that they would not accept, demanding an advance of money and leave of absence to spend it. This we steadfastly refused to concede, and threatened to cut off their captain's pay unless he brought his men to terms. The mutineers next hauled in the sails and sat themselves down for a smoke; but in about an hour, seeing no prospect of our yielding, the skipper consulted his sweet spouse, and then forthwith ordered the men to turn to, under penalty of letting the wife of his bosom loose on them. This prospect produced such a powerful effect on the men that they instantly resumed their work.

We were now fairly entering the mountainous region, and quitting the great alluvial plain that stretches hundreds of miles southward to the sea. We could just see the "Mountains of the Seven Gates" towering in dark masses above the horizon, as the evening closed in upon us and we cast anchor for the night. Our skipper determined to serve us out for our obstinacy. He assured us that the place was infested with pirates, and that it would be necessary to keep an armed watch all night. Perhaps he feared his men, who were certainly a dare-devil-looking set.

We noticed men fishing with trained otters on this part of the river. There were a number of boats, and each boat was furnished with an otter tied to a cord. The animal was thrust into the water and remained there until it had secured a fish; then it was hauled up, and the fisherman, placing his foot upon its tail, stamped vigorously until it had dropped its finny prey. We passed two prosperous-looking little towns, Po-yang and Chi-kiang; and on the morning of February 5th were sailing beneath bold rocky bluffs backed by a chaos of fantastic mountain peaks. Here, on the highest pinnacle, a Buddhist monastery was perched, not far from the brink of the river. It was fronted by a precipice of 600 feet, and looked quite inaccessible at its altitude of more than 1,200 feet above the stream. But after all, to scale this stony height and to rear a shrine amid the clouds, although a wonderful achievement in its way, sinks into insignificance when compared with the task of self-subjection daily set before each inmate of the cloister, who, even in such a retreat as this, removed as far as it well can be from the haunts of men, finds the lusts of the flesh and the pride of life too strong to be effectually subdued. Many of the Buddhist monastic establishments in China, as we have already seen, are planted in most romantic and lovely spots; and in the one now before us we found no exception to the rule.

On the same day, at noon or a little after, we anchored at Ichang. This city is one of considerable commercial importance, and as it stands at the entrance of the Gorges, it is the highest point to which steam navigation can be carried until these rocky defiles, which extend for upwards of 100 miles beyond it, shall have been thoroughly surveyed, and some obstacles removed, which render the navigation there by far the most dangerous on the rivers of China. Ichang is now open to foreign trade, and is the present limit of steam navigation on the river. I must here refer the reader to the Imperial Maritime Customs' Reports for 1895, for information regarding the trade of Ichang. At present, foreign goods are distributed from this port through the surrounding provinces, while the rich plains of Hupeh, besides the usual cereal crops—beans, millet, rice and rape—produce yellow silk, tung-oil and opium; the latter in small quantities, although it is raised more plentifully in Szechuan and Yunnan.

The town of Ichang sweeps in a crescent-shape round a bend on the left bank of the river, and is divided into two halves by a canal. The one half occupies high land, while the other is on lower ground, and comprises a large suburb which suffered severely in the flood of 1870, but has since been rebuilt. In the afternoon we were the spectators of a naval review. Six small gun-boats, each mounting a six-pound gun at the bow, were drawn up in line and fired their cannon at irregular intervals. I say irregular, because some of the artillery refused to go off at all; and when the sham fight was all over, we could hear them discharging themselves during the night. The boats were small, and had each about forty rowers on board. When the review was over, the admiral landed and rode off on a gaily-caparisoned pony, followed by his retainers.

At Ichang we had to hire a large rapid-boat to make the ascent of the Gorges, and we left our sailing vessels to await our return. Before we started a cock was sacrificed to the river goddess; its blood and feathers were sprinkled on the bow, while a libation was poured upon the water. We had a crew of twenty-four men at the sweeps, who worked to the tune of a shrill piping song, or rather yell, and under their exertions it was not long before Ichang had been passed and the mouth of the first gorge was before us. Here the river narrows from half a mile to a few hundred yards across, and pours through the rocky defile with a velocity that makes it difficult to enter. The hills rose on each side from 500 to 2,500 feet in height, presenting two irregular stone walls to the river, each worn and furrowed with the floods of ages, and showing some well-defined water-markings 100 feet above the winter stream, up which we were now toiling on our way. The further we entered the gorges the more desolate and dark became the scene; the narrow barren defile presenting a striking contrast to the wide cultivated plains through which we had been making our way from the sea, for more then 1,000 miles.

The only inhabitants of this region appeared to be a few fishermen, who prosecuted their avocation among the rocks ; while their rude huts could be seen perched high in inaccessible-looking nooks and crannies among the mountains above. Huts, indeed, they could hardly be called; at least those of them which we visited were either natural caves, or holes scooped out beneath the sheltering rocks, and closed in with what resembled the front of an ordinary straw-thatched cottage.

These smoke-begrimed abodes called to my mind the ancient cave-dwellings which sheltered our forefathers at Wemyss Bay in Scotland. The interiors were dark and gloomy, the clay floors cold and covered with fishbones and refuse, while a dull light glimmering from a taper in a recess in the rocks, revealed at once the grim features of a small idol and the few and simple articles of furniture that made up the property of the inmates. A residence of this sort, with all it contains, might be fitted up at an original cost of probably one pound sterling; and yet it was in such places that we found the frugality and industry of the Chinese most conspicuously displayed; for out-side the caves, wherever there was a little soil on the face of the rocks, it had been scraped together and planted with vege-tables, which were made to contribute to the domestic economy of the inhabitants. This was indeed taking bread out of a stone! Further on we found a number of men engaged in quarrying the stone, and in forming river embankments. The stream in many places hereabouts had undermined the limestone formation of the rocks, so that the softer portions had been washed away, and a series of grotesque flint pillars were left, supporting the upper strata which towered above our heads in precipices of a thousand feet. In other places the rocks looked like the high walls and ramparts of a fortress, or the battle-

ments and towers of a citadel. The inhabitants of this sterile region must have a severe struggle for existence, but they are a hardy and independent race, scorning the mendicant tricks of their more abject fellow-countrymen in the plains. Thus I only fell in with a single beggar in these mountain passes. Our men slept on deck in the open air, and I was always afraid lest I should find some of them dead in the morning, for the cold was intense during the night. But they huddled themselves together beneath the awning of matting, and thus managed to keep the night air from freezing their blood. Near the upper end of the gorge the huts were of a better class ; the soil improved and small orchards came into sight, displaying a profusion of plum-blossoms even at this season of the year.

We were compelled to spend half a day at a place called Kwang-loong-Miau, that the crew might celebrate the Chinese New Year. The festival was conducted at the village shrine, which stood on a picturesque spot surrounded with pine and backed by a mountain 2,000 feet high. Chang had here a dispute with the boatmen, who, as he protested, had sullied his honourable name. He complained of their riotous, drunken conduct; but I soon found that our venerated interpreter was himself not without sin, and was indeed unable to stand erect. He suggested that the chief offenders ought to be taken before the nearest magistrate.

In truth they made a great uproar during the night, firing crackers, quarrelling, and gambling; but next morning they were once more ready for work, though some of them had sold a portion of what little they had in the shape of clothing, to give the new year a fair start, and looked all the more savage for the change. They soon got heated, as we had cleared the first gorge and were now ascending a rapid. It was the first, but by no means the least dangerous. The bulk of the men were on the bank, attached to a tracking line. Off they sped, yelling like fiends above the roar of the water; while the boy, to add to the din, lustily beat a gong, and the cook a small drum, for the purpose of stirring the men to put forth their full strength. At about the centre of the rapid there was a dead halt, as if the boat had stuck fast on a reef, though the trackers were straining to their utmost with hands and feet planted firmly on the rocks. The skipper stamped, danced and bellowed to his crew; and they, responding with a wild shout, a desperate tug and a strain, at last launched our boat into the smooth water above. The danger of this rapid consists not so much in its force as in the narrowness of the channel, and in the multitude of rocks, sunken as well as above the water, on which the boat, were the tracking line to part, would certainly drift, and there be dashed to pieces.

In the second, or Lukan Gorge, the mountains rise to a greater altitude, projecting in some places over the chasm as if to join and exclude the light from the already darkened river. There were numerous strange perpendicular markings in these rocks, like borings for the purpose of mining. These had apparently been made by a sort of natural sand-drill. Small hard pebbles imprisoned in the recesses of soft rock, with the aid of sand and water, have in time pierced these deep vertical shafts, and the attrition of the water on the face of the rocks has at last brought the tunnelled apertures to light.

At the next rapid, Shan-tow-pien, we noticed the wrecks of two Szechuan trading-boats, making in all nine which we had come across since we started from Ichang. It was snowing heavily as we made our way over the rocks to the village, which came down close to the water's edge; and towards dark we

found ourselves in front of a small cabin made out of the debris
of a wrecked boat.   The owner of the wreck, an aged man,
resided within, and had been residing there for some days past.
He looked cold and wretched, but he would have nothing to
say to us and haughtily rejected our proffered help.

We had now reached the great rapid of the Upper Yangtsze,
which occurs at the mouth of the Mitan Gorge.   Here, while I
was engaged in photographing the scene, I fell in with a mandarin, who asked many questions about my honourable name and
title, my country, my kinsmen, and as he had never set eyes
on a photographic instrument before, he wanted to see the result
of my work. When the picture was shown to him, he enquired
by what possible means a drawing could be so perfectly completed in so short a space of time; and then, without waiting
for an answer, and casting an anxious glance at me to make
sure I had neither horns, hoofs, nor tail visible, he hurried
off to the village, with the conviction that my art was an
uncanny one, and that my diabolical insignia were only craftily
concealed.

Accordingly, on taking my next view at the same village, I
was surrounded by a crowd of sullen spectators who, though
it was explained that I was only securing a picture, favoured me
with sundry tokens of their dread in the shape of sods and
stones. Chang tried his eloquence on the people, but with little
effect.   We packed up as quickly as possible and marched down
the bank to cross over to the other side, where my companions
were preparing for the ascent of the rapid.   No doubt these
villagers, some of them, had heard the popular fiction that
pictures such as mine were made out of the eyes of Chinese
babes.   I narrowly escaped a stroke from an oar as I took
refuge in a boat; but the blow was warded off with a force

that sent its author spinning headlong into the stream, from which he emerged below the rapid, a good deal shaken and bruised, but with no serious injury.

This rapid is one of the grandest spectacles in the whole panorama of the river. The water presents a smooth surface as it emerges from the pass; then suddenly seems to bend like a polished cylinder of glass; falls eight or ten feet, and finally curves upwards in a crest of foam as it surges away in wild tumult down the gorge. At this season sundry rocks enhance the peril of shooting the rapid. On our way down we persuaded Chang to come in the boat with us; but as the vessel plunged and groaned in an agony of straining timbers, he became perfectly sick with panic fear. It was indeed hardly to be wondered at. The pilot we employed at this time was a tall bony man with dark piercing eyes, a huge black moustache and a mouth full of protruding teeth. He and his assistant guided the boat to what seemed the worst part of the rapid, and then launched her into the raging waters broadside on. After the first plunge she swept round, bow foremost, tossing and writhing until I thought she would go to pieces and disappear. Meanwhile the pilot, flinging his arms on high, shouted and danced about the deck, conveying the notion that the craft was doomed, although in reality he was only guiding his men at the helm. But the boat, regardless of oaths, oars and rudder, sped forward with a fearful impetus, bearing right down for the rocks, dodged them at the last moment, and then darted into comparatively smooth water far below. The pilot's buffoonery is probably part of his game. It pays when at last he presents himself for his legitimate fee, and for the trifle extra which he expects for saving our lives at the risk of his own. That there is great danger in shooting this rapid may be gathered from a survey of the

wrecks that strew the shore, from the life-boats in constant
attendance, or from the fact that the Chinese unload their boats
at the head of the rapid, and have their cargo and themselves
transported overland to the smooth waters below.

This Tsing-tan rapid, then, is the greatest obstacle to the
steam navigation of the Upper Yangtsze. We had to hire fifty
trackers from the village to aid our men in hauling the boat up
the stream, which here ran about eight knots an hour; but I
see no reason why the kind of steamer Captain Blakiston has
suggested should not navigate this, and indeed any of the other
rapids on the river, the steam power to be capable of either
towing the vessel up, or retarding her swift and hazardous
descent. Were the river once opened to steam, daring and
scientific skill would be forthcoming to accomplish the end
in view.

The mountains of this gorge are on the same stupendous
scale as those of the Lukan passage below. On the 11th we
reached a small walled town called Kwei, with not a single craft
nor a human being near it to betoken trade of any kind. Here
we halted for the night, and in the morning visited some coal
mines at a place called Patung, where the limestone strata in
which the coal is formed, stand up in nearly perpendicular walls
against the edge of the river. Adits had been carried into the
face of the rock, but they were all of them on an exceedingly
small scale—simple burrowings without any depth. No shafts
were sunk, and no ventilation was attempted. Coal abounds,
and even with such rude appliances as the miners possess, is
turned out in considerable quantities; but the quality is not so
good as some we got further up the gorge. The miner when
at work, carries a lamp stuck in his cap, much the same as
those in use with us before Sir H. Davy's invention. The coal

was shunted from the mouth of the pit down a groove cut in the face of the cliffs, and when conveyed any distance is transported in kreels on the backs of women. There were several mining villages at this place; and there every household is employed entirely in the trade, the children making fuel by mixing the coal with water and clay, and then casting it in moulds into blocks which weigh one catty ($1\frac{1}{3}$ lb.) apiece. The miners who are occupied in this work earn about seven shillings a week, and their hours of labour are from seven o'clock in the morning to about 4 p.m.

Baron von Richthofen has assured us that there is plenty of coal in Hunan and Hupeh, and that the coal-field of Szechuan is also of enormous area. He adds that at the present rate of consumption the world could draw its supplies from Southern Shensi alone for over a thousand years; and yet, in the very places referred to, it is not uncommon to find the Chinese storing up wood and millet-stalks for their firing in winter, while coal in untold quantities lies ready for use beneath their feet. These vast coal-fields will constitute the basis of China's future greatness, when science shall have been called in to aid in the development of her enormous mineral wealth.

Wu-shan Gorge which we reached on the morning of the 18th, is more than twenty miles long, and we entered this great defile about ten o'clock. The river was perfectly placid; and the view at the mouth of the gorge was one of the finest we had hitherto encountered. The mountains rose in confused masses to a great altitude; the most distant peak at the extremity of the passage, resembling a cut sapphire, with snow-lines that sparkled in the sun like the gleams of light on the facets of a gem, while the cliffs and precipices gradually deepened in outline

until they reached the bold lights and shadows of the rocky foreground.

The officers of a gunboat stationed at the boundary which parts the provinces of Hupeh and Szechuan, warned us to beware of pirates, and they had good reason for so doing. We came to anchor at a place where the rocks, towering overhead, wrapped the scene in darkness; and it was nearly 10 p.m. when our skipper sent to say we had better have our arms ready, as pirates were prowling about. One boat had just passed noiselessly up alongside, and its occupants were talking in whispers. We hailed them, but they made no reply, so then we fired over their heads. Our fire was responded to by a flash and a report from some men on the bank not far off. After this we kept a watch all night, and at about two in the morning were all roused again to challenge a boat's crew that was noiselessly stealing down on our quarters. A second time we were forced to fire, and the sharp ping of the rifle-ball on the rocks had the effect of deterring further advances from our invisible foes. The disturbers of our repose must have been thoroughly acquainted with this part of the river, for even by day it is somewhat dark, and at night it is so utterly without light that no tradingboat would venture an inch from her rock-bound moorings. On another night in this gorge, I was summoned by my boy, who appeared in the cabin with a face of blank terror, and told me that he had just seen a group of luminous spirits that were haunting the pass. It was evident that something unusual had occurred, as I had never before seen the boy in such a state of clammy fear; so we followed him on to the deck, and looking up the precipice, about eight hundred feet above our heads, we then saw three lights on the face of the rock, performing a series of the most extraordinary evolutions. My old attendant

14

declared, the cold perspiration trickling down his face the while, that he could make out sylph-like forms waving the lights to warn wayfarers off the edge of the abyss:

> " This seraph band, each waved his hand,
>   It was a heavenly sight:
> They stood as signals to the land,
>   Each one a lovely light."

The true explanation of the phenomenon lay in the fact, perhaps, that in this very gorge there are hapless beings, convicts, immured in prison-cells cut in the face of the rocks, into which they are dropped by their gaolers above, and from which they can never hope to escape unless to seek destruction by a plunge into the river below. Here, too, we find inhabitants of a widely different stamp, a number of philosophic followers of Laou-tsoo, who pass their lives as hermits in these dark solitudes. In one cave we came across the remains of a Taouist philosopher of this sort; a recluse who expired, so it was said, at the ripe age of 200 years. Several of the boatmen averred that they knew him to have been more than a century old. His relics lay in the centre of the cave, covered over with a cairn of stones and sods, which had been thrown up by passing mountaineers.

February 15.—To-day we met with a disaster as we were ascending a rapid. The boat was caught by a blast of wind, and this, aided by a strong eddy, was just sending her over, when the skipper's mate, the most active youth on board, sprang forward and cut the tracking line. The trackers unexpectedly relieved of the great strain, were sent sprawling over the rocks; while as for the boat, she righted at once and then drifted down the rapid, till at last she settled on a spit of sand half a mile below the scene of the accident. So far the result

was satisfactory; but then we were on one side of the stream
and our crew on the other. As there was a village near at
hand, we at once repaired thither to engage a boat to convey
our men across; but not a soul would stir unless we paid them
beforehand nearly as much as would buy another village, such
as it was. We offered them what the boatmen considered a
fair hire, but this they stedfastly refused; until at last we jumped
into one of their boats, and threatened to use it ourselves.
Seeing this, they thought better of it, apologised and struck a
fair bargain. We came to, for that night, above the Wu-shan
Gorge. Before us, on the left bank, lay the walled town of
Wu-shan, surrounded by low hills and richly-tilled valleys; and
here we noticed the outlet of a small river that joins the
Yangtsze, and down which salt is brought in great quantities
from mines at a place called Ta-ning.

Opium, silk and tea are among the chief products of this
district, and it is also singularly rich in fruits of various sorts.
We bought the most delicious oranges I ever tasted in China,
for a shilling a hundred. Next day we made a strenuous
though futile effort to reach Kwei-chow-fu; but we could make
no headway in the face of a storm that swept in fearful blasts
down the gorge and filled the air with a fine blinding sand,
most irritating to the eyes. We therefore left Szechuan on the
16th, after having ascended a distance of over thirteen hundred
miles above Shanghai. The return voyage was comparatively
easy, and eighteen days after leaving Szechuan we again set
foot on the foreign settlement at Hankow. Here our friends
received us with a hearty welcome, and plied us with the most
minute enquiries as to the state of the river and the exact
appearance of the proposed new treaty-port at Ichang.

At Hankow I rejoined some of my oldest friends in China,

and it was not without a pang of sincere regret at parting from them that I stepped on board the steamer.

I stopped at Kiukiang on the downward trip, and spent two or three days in the settlement. The native city, although it holds an important position near the mouth of the Po-yung lake, and thus communicates with the network of canals and streams that form the trade routes into the vast green-tea fields of Kiangsi and Ngan-Hwei, has nevertheless failed to attain a high commercial position; nor has the foreign settlement either, done much yet towards monopolising the traffic of the richly productive districts by which it is surrounded. The city, which suffered a severe blow at the hands of the rebels who left it a ruined waste in 1861, had not, even at the time of my visit, regained its former prosperity.

Kiukiang will probably rise into much greater commercial importance when the Po-yung lake shall have been thrown open to steam navigation. One or two excursions which I made into the surrounding districts, enabled me to form a very favourable estimate of the fertility of the soil and the prosperity of the cultivators. The region, however, seemed thinly populated, and this fact alone is sufficient to account for the absence of the poverty and misery which fall to the lot of the toiling millions in many quarters of the land.

At a place called Tai-ping-kung, about ten miles inland from Kiukiang, I found the ruins of an ancient shrine, presenting most remarkable architectural features. All that remained of a once extensive edifice were two towers pierced with windows, which looked something like the pointed gothic apertures of a medieval European building. The walls of a small joss-house adjoining were built partly of finely sculptured stones; and the whole ruin, indeed, was unlike anything I had before seen in

China. It seemed more European than Chinese, and possibly
may point to Ricci's Jesuit mission to that part of the province in
1590. It is, however, said to have once been one of the greatest
Buddhist establishments in Cathay. On the way back from this
old shrine I passed over classic ground, where the rocks are inscribed with the praises of Chu-fu-tze, a celebrated Confucian
commentator and philosopher who lived in the twelfth century.

The next point at which I touched was Nanking, the ancient
capital of China, where there was no foreign settlement, nor
any port open for trade. It was dark when, with my boys and
baggage and two Chinese officers of the Governor-General's
household, I descended from the steamer "Hirado" into a native
boat, and landed on the muddy bank beneath the outer walls
of this famous city. We had to spend the night in a small
shed which had been provided for the convenience of passengers
making use of the river steamers. The place was crowded
with an orderly company of natives, who very kindly made room
for me to repose myself on a table; but it was in vain
that I courted sleep, for the air was obscured by clouds of
tobacco-smoke, and conversation was kept up with an incessant
clamour all night through. As it happened the talk was of the
deepest interest; Tseng-kuo-fan, the Chinese general who had
fought side by side with Li-hung-chang and Colonel Gordon in
the suppression of the Taiping rebellion, had just expired at
his palace in Nanking. Many present said that he had perished
by his own hand, or had succumbed to an overdose of gold-
leaf; whereas the truth was, as I afterwards discovered, that he
had died in a fit of apoplexy, the second with which he had
been attacked. His death was a great disappointment to me,
as my chief motive in visiting Nanking had been to see the
celebrated leader, and, if possible, obtain his likeness for my

larger work. I carried with me an introduction to him from Li-hung-chang the Governor-General of Pei-chil-li, and this note I duly presented to his son, who sent me a reply expressing the deep regret of the family that they should have missed the opportunity of obtaining a portrait. But a general officer subsequently remarked that after all it was perhaps as well for me that I not arrived in time to take the picture, as most assuredly the speaker himself, and others as well as he, would have accused me of causing the untimely death. It is a wide-spread Chinese belief, from which men of intelligence are by no means free, that in taking a photograph, a certain portion of the vital principle is extracted from the body of the sitter, and that thus his decease within a limited period is rendered an absolute certainty.

The reader will gather from this that I was frequently looked upon as a forerunner of death, as a sort of Nemesis in fact; and I have seen unfortunates, stricken with superstitious dread, fall down on bended knees and beseech me not to take their likeness or their life with the fatal lens of my camera. But all this might have occurred in our own country not many years ago, where a photograph would have been esteemed a work of the devil.

Tseng-kuo-fan was one of the foremost statesmen of his time. He was a member of the Grand Secretariat, and was created a noble of the second class after the expulsion of the rebels from Nanking. He was then at the zenith of his power, and it was even said that his wide-spread influence was dreaded by the court at Peking. In 1868 he became Governor-General of Pei-chil-li, and was removed from that office after the Tientsin massacre, and for the third time appointed Governor-General of the two Kiang.

The view of Nanking was a disappointing one. It is simply

a vast area enclosed within a high wall which makes a circuit of twenty-two miles, and is therefore the largest city in the kingdom. Near at hand are several heights crowned with temples, and such-like sacred buildings; while a number of yamens and religious edifices may be seen dotting the great open spaces where cultivation is carried on. But the city itself, as usual, is crowded into the narrowest limits, capable of supporting half a million struggling sons of Han. There were still many dreary acres of demolished streets with not a single occupant, but in other quarters the work of restoration was being actively carried on. This great "Southern Capital" must probably have been at one time what Le Comte stated, "a splendid city surrounded by walls, one within the other," the outermost, "sixteen long leagues round." Such may have been its condition some fourteen hundred years ago, when it first became the Imperial head-quarters, or perhaps even so late as the fourteenth century, when Hung-Woo, the first Ming Emperor, is reported to have restored it to its pristine glory. But the place had already fallen sadly off at the advent of the Tien-wang, who conferred upon it the honour of making it the capital of a Chinese dynasty once more. It was said to have been at the recommendation of a very humble follower, an old sailor, that the "Heavenly King," as he styled himself, decided on making Nanking the seat of his celestial government; but in other matters this self-made potentate was not so easily pursuaded. Why should he have been? He professed to believe implicitly that he was a second son of God, sent down to redeem China.

When the Imperialists were marshalling their forces around the great Ming tomb, and when his old soldiers and faithful adherents were starving in the streets, he gave orders that they should be fed on dew, and sing a new song till the hour of deliverance came. Calmly he sat within his palace, looking with disdain upon the gathering forces that ere long were to strike the fatal blow. The city had not yet fallen into the hands of his foes, when his faith and fortitude forsook him, and he ended his days by his own hand.

It is a tedious journey round the city moat to the southern gate. Many boats were to be met winding their way along this canal, or else drawn up into groups and forming little market-places every here and there. At one small bridge beneath which we passed, it was told me that there, after the fall of Nanking, the canal had been dammed up by rebel heads. Outside the southern gate there is a large suburb. Why it should have been planted there, when there is so much vacant space within the walls, is difficult to tell. Many of its dwellings are nothing more than rude huts, erected over ground strewn with the graves and bones of Taipings and Imperialists mingled together in kindred dust. Here, too, I found the old porcelain tower of Nanking (once one of the seven wonders of the world, but now levelled to the earth); and a number of small speculators driving a trade in its porcelain bricks. But most of the bricks of this tower and of the "Monastery of Gratitude" to which it belonged, were used in constructing the Nanking arsenal close by; and of the two edifices I should say that the latter, planted as it had been by Li-hung-chang, in the very heart of the "Central Flowery Land," will be held to be far the more wonderful structure of the two. Here, then, the old Buddhist tower and the monastery with its monotonous chants, have been replaced by a temple dedicated to the Chinese Vulcan and Mars, whose altars are furnaces, whose worshippers are melters of iron, and from whose shrines come the never-ceasing rattle of machinery and the reports of rifles that are being tested for service.

This arsenal, built as I have said, under the auspices of Li-hung-chang, was the first of its kind in China, and is conducted on the most advanced scientific principles under the superintendence of Dr. Macartney, now Sir H. Macartney. It is, indeed, a startling innovation on the old style of things. If the Chinese first taught us the use of guns (They are said to have employed them in 1232 at the siege of Khai-fung-fu), we are certainly repaying the obligation with interest by instructing them how our deadliest weapons are to be made. In this arsenal some hundreds of tons of guns and ammunition are manufactured every year, and I have no doubt its products have already proved of service in the suppression of the Mahometan outbreak in the provinces of Kiangsu and Shensi. Here the Chinese can turn out heavy guns for battery-trains, or field-artillery, howitzers, gatling-guns, torpedoes, rockets, shot, shell, cartridges and caps. The rocket factory stands on an open plot of ground some distance from the main building, and 'this place is appropriated to the filling of rockets and shells with their explosive contents. With respect to these arsenals and their high state of efficiency, I have one further remark to offer—and that is, that were the strict foreign management under which they ,have matured to be withdrawn, they could not be carried on so as to be of the slightest effectual service. Probably the same amount of money would be spent on their maintenance, but it would be subjected to a process of official filtration which would admit of nothing more than the purchase of inferior materials and the employment of underpaid labourers. An experiment of this sort was once tried, to humour an officer who boasted himself able to produce everything in the shape of modern warlike inventions as perfectly as any foreigner in the Empire. But the attempt was not repeated, as the shells he manufactured turned out much more

deadly projectiles in the hands of his own men than they could
ever have proved in the ranks of an enemy. They were badly
cast with coarse iron, and their dangerous imperfections were
filled up with black-leaded clay. So my humble opinion is that
before the Chinese can hope to take a position among the
civilised Powers of the world, they must acquire something of
simple honesty, and unlearn much of the science of deception
by which they study to enrich themselves, while making ready
to conquer their foes.

"Kin-Shan" or "Golden Island," "Silver Island," and the mouth
of the Grand Canal were the last objects of interest I saw on
the Yangtsze river. The Grand Canal may be set down as the
greatest public work of the race who wasted years of needless
labour in constructing the Great Wall to shut out the barbarous
hordes, who, after all, are masters of the Empire. But this
huge artificial waterway is now useless in many places, and
utterly broken down; although it might have proved of incalculable service in draining off the great waters of the Yellow River,
which have, from time to time, spread their desolating floods
over the vast productive plains of the interior.

CHAPTER X.

CHEFOO is a favourite watering-place for foreigners resident at
Peking or Shanghai, for there bracing air and sea-bathing may
be enjoyed during the hottest months of summer.

The beach on which the European hotel is built, skirts the
foot of a low range of grassy hills, and reminded me, in its
semicircular sweep and general aspect, of Brodic Bay in Arran,
on the west coast of Scotland. I have a lively recollection of
Chefoo Bay; of its stretch which at the time appeared interminable; and of the soft yielding sand over which, with a friend
remarkable alike for his good-nature, weight and agility, I had
to run from the steamer to forestall the other passengers and

secure the best apartment for an invalid lady from Shanghai.
The thermometer at the time was standing at about one hundred
degrees in the shade, so that after completing our task we were
in a condition to enjoy to the full the cool breeze that swept
through the verandah of the hotel. It was an unpretending but
charming retreat, and none the less so on account of the many
comforts which the enterprising proprietor had in store for
his guests.

Chefoo foreign settlement lies on the opposite side of the
bay, and is about the least inviting place of the kind on the
coast. But still we must not forget that it enjoys the honour
of standing on the ground of the most classic province in the
Empire, where the engineering labours of the celebrated Yu were
in part performed. Confucius, too, was a native of the Shan-tung
province, and so indeed was Mensius, his successor. While
Pythagoras was pursuing his philosophical researches at Crotona,
Confucius was compiling the classical lore that has since been
to China what the compass is to the mariner at sea. But this
ancient guide to national prosperity, social, political and religious,
when relied on by those who now-a-days control the helm of
the Empire, is as untrustworthy as the compass of a man-of-
war when the steersman makes no allowance for the influences
of the iron plates and steel guns with which science has surrounded his needle. And yet fain would the wisest Confucianists
of the "Central Flowery Land" still rivet their fond gaze on
their ancient books; fain would they guide their steps by the
rushlight of a dim science and philosophy, lit by sages of four
thousand years ago; and that though truth, like the sun in
noonday splendour, is shining on the nations around.

The foreign trade of Chefoo is small, though not unimpor-
tant. Whether it be that the natives affect more the simple

robes of their ancient sages than the less costly cotton fabrics of
Manchester, or whether the constantly recurring floods of the
Hwang-ho or Yellow River, have so impoverished the inland
districts as to materially damage trade, is a difficult point to
determine.

Since the Yellow River has changed its course and now flows
to the north of the Shan-tung mountains, a great portion of the
Grand Canal has been rendered useless. The change of course
to which I refer, took place in 1852, but in 1889 it again changed
and forced its way to the south where it joined the Yangtzse.
The Chinese, however, breaking away from their modern policy
of squandering money on armaments and defences, found scope
for their energy and perseverance in turning back to its northern
channel the waters of the Hwang-ho. This they eventually succeeded in doing by the aid of foreign appliances, a task which
may be fairly accounted a triumph of engineering skill. In many
places the banks had been carried away, and an eye-witness
has described the scene in the following words: *—"For dreariness and desolation no scene can exceed that which the Yellow
River here presents; everything natural and artificial is at the
mercy of the muddy dun-coloured waters, as they sweep on their
course towards the sea."

But we shall see as we pass through Pei-chil-li, how these
floods actually affect the people. Thus, while a considerable
extent of country suffers from the withdrawal of the great
river from its old channel, parts of Shan-tung and Pei-chil-li
come in for a superabundant share of its waters. Notwithstanding
this there are some portions of the former province which are
as productive as any soil in the world, and where the nature

* Journal of the Royal Geographical Society, vol. xl , p. 5.

of the climate is favourable to the culture of a wide range of products. These include millet, wheat, rice, tobacco and beans—the latter, in the shape of "bean-cake," forming a valuable article of exportation. Besides the foregoing a certain sort of dark-coloured silk fabric, known as "Pongee" silk, is produced in Shan-tung, and exported in steadily increasing quantities from Chefoo. This silk is obtained from a wild black worm that feeds on a different kind of leaf from the mulberry. Rearing silk-worms in China is an exceedingly delicate process, and one which one might almost have supposed unsuited to the natives, for the little worm is most exacting in its habits. It has even been stated that it will refuse either to feed or to work before strangers; and the Chinese aver that it cannot endure the presence of foreigners, or the sounds of barbaric tongues. If in this respect it resembles its masters, it differs from them widely in its abhorrence of uncleanly odours, and indeed in a polluted atmosphere will sicken and starve itself to death. For this reason the Chinese, from the time when the worm emerges from the egg to the moment when it perishes in its own silken robe, must suffer great inconvenience by the compulsory absence of all those strong smells wherein so many of them take an unaffected delight. No wonder, then, if the close of the silk season, when the dainty little toiler has woven its shroud and met its doom, should be one of great rejoicing.

Like the culture of tea, silk—which confers an enormous benefit on China, and has now become an indispensable luxury to the world—is the most modest industry imaginable. Let us cast a glance on the various progressive steps through which the staple passes till it is ready for the looms of China or Lyons.

The eggs are hatched about the middle of April, and the best season to obtain them for exportation is in March, or the beginning of April. The young worms, when hatched are placed on bamboo frames and fed on mulberry-leaves cut up into small shreds. As the worms increase in size they are transferred to a larger number of frames, and are fed with leaves not so finely shred; and so the process continues until, in their last stage, the leaves are given to them entire. The price of leaves runs from four shillings and sixpence to eight shillings a picul (133 lbs). After hatching, the worms continue eating during five days, and then sleep for the first time for two days. When they again wake their appetite is not quite so good, and they usually eat for four days only and sleep again for two days more. Then they eat for the third time for four days and repose for two. This eating and repose is usually repeated four times, and then having gained full strength, they proceed to spin their cocoons. The task of spinning occupies them from four to seven days more; and when this business is completed three days are spent in stripping off the cocoon, and some seven days later each small cultivator brings his silken harvest to the local market and disposes of it to native traders, who make it up into bales.

Leaving popular superstitious influences out of account, the quality of the silk is first of all affected by the breed of the worms that spin it, then by the quality of the leaves and the mode of feeding. As I have already remarked, the silk-worm is injured by noise, by the presence and especially by the handling of strangers, and by noxious smells. They must be fed, too, at regular hours, and the temperature of the apartment must not be too high. The greatest defect in Chinese silk has been due to the primitive mode of reeling, which the natives adopt. Shanghai is the great silk mart, and there, about June 1st, the first season's silk is usually brought down. It is never the growers who bring the silk to the foreign market. These growers are invariably small farmers, who either purchase the leaves, or have a few mulberry bushes planted in some odd corner of their tilled lands, and the rearing of the worm and the production of silk by no means monopolise the whole of their time. It is only a spring occupation for the women and younger members of their families. Chinese merchants or brokers proceed to the country markets, and there collect the produce until they have secured enough to make up a parcel for the Shanghai or Chefoo markets, where it is bought up by foreigners for exportation.

I paid two visits to Chefoo, and must have experienced the extremes of temperature. On the first occasion the heat was intense; but on my return the cold was so severe that my boy Ahong had his ears and nose frost-bitten. We had proceeded to a hill-top to obtain a picture of Chefoo, but the north-west wind, blowing from the icy steppes of Mongolia, was like to freeze the blood in our veins. Having, however, succeeded in taking a photograph, I sent to a neighbouring hut for a bottle of water to wash the negative, but no sooner had I withdrawn the plate from the shelter of the dark tent and poured the water over it, than the liquid froze on its surface and hung in icicles around its edge. In spite of these difficulties we adjourned to a friendly hut, where we thawed the plate over a charcoal fire and washed it with hot water,—wet plate process.

The next place of importance at which we touched on our route north, was Taku, at the mouth of the Peiho. The Taku forts are mud strongholds, which have been often and well described. At the time of my visit these forts had been under repair; still they were not yet properly garrisoned, nor were their guns all mounted. I passed along a stone pavement which leads from the river across the inner extremity of the mud slough. It was here in 1859, that so many of our men were shot down in the unsuccessful attempt to storm the southern fort. We carried the place without much difficulty a twelve-month afterwards. The only entrance into this fort is across a wide ditch from behind. As for me, I passed inside it without a word being asked; for indeed there were only one or two coolies loitering about the enclosure. The walls are of great thickness, and built, as formerly, of mud and millet-stalks—a composition well adapted to resist shot. Within were two batteries of over fifty guns a-piece, one above the other, and commanding the entrance to the stream. Some of them, however, were rusty, badly mounted on their carriages, and altogether sadly in want of repair. Lastly, I noticed two large American smooth-bores lying half-buried in mud in front of the officers' quarters. On the whole the place wore the look of a deserted mud-quarry rather than a fortress. But I have been informed that a great change has since come over the scene—that these fortresses, one on each side of the Peiho, are now armed with Krupp guns and properly garrisoned; so that thus the defence of the capital has been secured after a scheme planned out and decided upon long before the Formosa difficulty cropped up. I myself saw a battery of Krupp guns landed at Tientsin before I left that place of dark memories; and indeed there could be no question that the Chinese were hastily arming themselves with modern weapons, laying up stores of destructive projectiles and ammunition, and addressing themselves to the task of guarding their own shores from invasion. It may be—nay, it must be—that there is a purpose in all this. The Chinese Government have probably not been blind all these years to what has been going on in Japan, to say nothing of the visions they may entertain

15

of possible encounters with more formidable foes. They undoubt-edly still retain the notion that they have an absolute right to do what they like with their own country and in it; and they are probably only preparing themselves to assert or defend this right when a suitable opportunity presents itself. Prince Kung, in despatch about the Woosung Bar at Shanghai, declined to dredge a channel to facilitate trade, and regarded the sand-bank as a barrier set there by Divine Providence to aid the Chinese in the defence of the country and its approaches. He further pointed out that each nation has a right to guard and protect its own territory by the means it alone deems best. It is perhaps very natural to suppose that China was made exclusively for the support of Chinamen, and that no other race has a right to question this divine arrangement, or to seek by the simple dredging of a sand-bar to thwart the plans of a kind Providence, who is thus closing up the river-courses against the commerce which furnishes millions of Chinese with means to feed and clothe themselves that formerly they could never have obtained.

In this narrow policy there is not the faintest recognition of that divine progress which, by a thousand telegraphs, railways and indus-tries, is tending more and more to bind the nations of the earth together in one universal kinmanship, where, by free intercourse and liberal enlightened government, peoples of every nation, kindred and tongue, will be rendered mutually dependent on each other.

The inundations were predicted just as they happened, years before the swollen river burst its barriers at Lung-men-Kan, and might have been easily prevented by keeping clear "what has always been an artificial channel."* The business was put off,

* Journal of the Royal Geographical Society, vol. xl. p. 19.

however, from one year to another, until at last the red flood
burst upon the plains and transformed a fruitful smiling country
into lakes, lagoons and pestilential marshes.

As we steamed up the Peiho, there were many places where
not a trace of the river's banks was to be discovered, and the
further we ascended the more apparent became the ravages of
the flood. The millet-crop was rotting under the water, and
whole hamlets had in many places been swept away. The
village dwellings, like the Taku forts, were for the most part
constructed of millet-stalks and mud; but however well calculated to resist the shots of an ordinary foe, these frail abodes,
one by one had silently dissolved before the invading waters,
leaving nothing behind them but something that looked like
grave-mounds, the melancholy landmarks of each new work of
desolation. We could see the wretched villagers squatting on
the tops of their hillocks, sheltered by scraps of thatch or
matting which they had rescued from the flood. All who had
means were removing to Tientsin, where the authorities were
said to be doing their utmost to relieve the sufferers. Singularly
enough I overheard a Chinaman say that he considered the
flood a punishment for the Tientsin massacre, which had occurred
just a year before.

It is quite impossible to estimate the misery that such disasters
bring upon the toiling poor of the province, who are thus be-
reft of food, shelter and fuel; and that, too, when the winter
was just at hand. The scene on all sides presented one sheet
of water, only broken by the wrecks of villages, and by islands
of mud where herds of cattle were packed and perishing for
want of pasture. Men, women and children were to be seen
fishing in the shallows of their harvest-fields. Fish were
abundant; and this was fortunate, as the people had little else

to subsist on. How they got through the hot days and cold nights, and how many of them survived their hardships only to be subjected to them in the succeeding year, it is impossible to say. We could tell from the bodies drifting seaward that Death was busy among them, relieving the sick and satisfying the hungry in his own sad final way.

The Chinese, like peoples both ancient and modern, have a superstitious dread of disturbing the resting-places of their dead. For many miles around Tientsin the country is one vast burial-ground, and it was pitiful to notice the efforts the living were making to lash the coffins of their dead to trees or to posts which they had driven into the mud. But numbers of the huge clumsy coffins were to be seen floating adrift, with no living relation to care for their occupants. The water was so deep that in many places the tortuous river's channel had been abandoned, and native craft were sailing overland, so to speak, direct from the city.

Our steamer, the "Sin-nan-sing," had great difficulty in turning the sharp bends of the river; her bow would stick in the mud of one bank, and her screw in the other; but at length Tientsin was reached, and there we found the water five or six feet deep at the back of the foreign settlement, and the Peking road submerged.

The foreigners were looking forward to the prospect of soon being shut in by a sea of ice. Here, on the bank of the river, was a British hotel, called "The Astor House," its modest proportions almost concealed by the huge signboard in front. This establishment was constructed of mud, and on one side of it a window had fallen out, while on the other the wall had fallen in. I had a look at this unpromising exterior and some conversation with its proprietor. The latter was an Englishman, and he lamented to me over the wreck of his property. There were still two apartments in front, one containing a billiard-table and the other a bar; but a couple of mud bedrooms had dissolved and could be seen in solution through a broken wall. The stabling in the rear also, out of sheer depression at losing its occupants, had taken a header into the water and disappeared. We next passed out of doors to examine the ravages of the flood in sundry outhouses which had also settled down. In the bar-room I found a Scotchman connected with the Tientsin Powder Factory, saying some very hard things about the peculiar views of a Chinese tailor to whom he had entrusted some "vara guid braid claith to mak a pair of breeks." It appeared that the tailor had found it necessary, on account of family concerns, to remove from Tientsin to another district, and had taken the cloth with him without going through the ceremony of leaving his card.

I slept on board the steamer, and started for Peking on August 29th. Before setting out I engaged a Tientsin man named Tao, or "Virtue," at the rate of nine dollars a month; but this sum was a trifle compared with what he intended to make out of me, as in every transaction, whether it was simply to change a dollar into cash, or to buy provisions, he made a profitable bargain for himself. My own southern men could have managed better, although they were ignorant of the northern dialect, and could only make known their wants in writing. Systematic pilfering, however, I soon discovered to be the common attribute of servants in the north. We engaged a boat to convey us to Tung-chow, the nearest point by water to Peking. This boat carried a wooden house in the centre, which could be shut up all round at night, so as to keep the cold out; and it was just large enough to accommodate my party and baggage. The space

within it was divided into two compartments, and in the after
one stood a clay cooking galley, around which the boys were
stowed. Our crew consisted of a father, Wong-Tsing, and his
two sons, Wong-su and Wong-soon. We had to make our way
up through the city of Tientsin along a narrow ever-changing
channel between thousands of native trading-boats. It was not
without a free use of such poles, and the vilest epithets in the
language, that we got clear of the floating Babel at last. The
left bank, hereabouts, was covered with mounds of salt, piled
up beneath the mat sheds which the salt monopolist had erected
to protect his precious store.

The river at this point was about 200 yards wide, and Tao
pointed out on the right bank the black bare walls of the
Sisters' Chapel that had been burned twelve months before.
There, too, we could see the ruins of the hospital where the
Sisters of Mercy had consecrated their lives to the ministration
of the sick, and to rescuing outcast children; for which good
works they had here been brutally murdered by an ignorant and
superstitious mob. There was still a heap of ashes in front of
the edifice, and the long breach in its wall through which the
murderers dragged their hapless victims to their doom. The
breach had indeed been plastered up with mud, a fitting type
of the unsatisfactory way in which the Chinese sought to atone
for an outrage which was perpetrated almost within sight of
the Governor-General's yamen.

From this point, too, we could descry, at the upper end of
the reach, the imposing ruins of the Roman Catholic cathedral,
the only striking object in the city of Tientsin; and the reflection was forced upon me, from what I know of native superstition, that that noble pile of buildings, standing as it did so
much above what the Chinese themselves hold most sacred in

Night Watchman, Peking.

Chinese Archer.

their yamens and shrines, must in itself have stirred up a bitter feeling against foreigners. This feeling was without doubt greatly intensified by horrible stories, most ingeniously spread abroad by the literary members of society, describing how foreigners manufacture medicines from the eyes and hearts of Chinese children, or even of adults. In the latter case it is to procure silver that these practices are alleged to be carried on; and this we may gather from the accompanying passage out of a native work which was in brisk circulation when the massacre took place. "The reason for extracting eyes is this. From one hundred pounds of Chinese lead can be extracted eight pounds of silver, and the remaining ninety-two pounds of lead can be sold at the original cost. But the only way to obtain this silver is by compounding the lead with the eyes of Chinamen. The eyes of foreigners are of no use, hence they do not take out the eyes of their own people." Further on it says : " The people of France without exception follow the false and corrupt Tien-chu religion. They have devilish arts by which they transform men into beasts," etc.

This pamphlet is full of matter unfit for quotation, and concludes with an appeal to the people to rise and exterminate the hated strangers :—

"Therefore, these contemptible beings having aroused our righteous wrath, we, heartily adhering to the kingdom of our sovereign, would not only give vent to a little of the hate that will not allow us to stand under the same heaven with them, but would make an eternal end of the distress of being obliged to have them ever near us. . . . * If the temporising policy is adopted, this nonhuman species will again increase." The author

* Death-blow to Corrupt Doctrines.

goes on, without mincing matters, to urge the utter extermination
of foreigners and the preservation of the virtuous followers of
Confucius. When we consider that this pamphlet had a wide,
though, as it was pretended, a secret circulation; and above all,
when we reflect on the utter ignorance and superstition, and the
fierceness of the half-starved classes whom it professed to caution
and enlighten, and on whom the calm, moderate and subtle
style of some of its worst passages must have produced a
fearful effect, we cannot wonder at the result.

Tao believed implicitly in the strange stories which he had
heard about the priests and about the poor Sisters, who had
been so cruelly put to death. The ruins now were being carefully guarded by a fleet of native gun-boats; but there were
none of them at hand when succour was really needed, nor did
they reach the spot until long after the deed had been accomplished.

I could not refrain from offering some remarks to my new
man about the miserable mud huts in which his countrymen
dwelt. Whereupon, with a vanity not uncommon in his race—
although it surprised me at the time—he pointed out what he
held to be the advantages of occupying such abodes. His argu-
ments ran something like this:—The materials, mud and millet-
stalks, can be had all over the plain, at every man's doorway
cheaply—for the lifting, indeed; whereas wood and stone are too
dear for poor people to procure. Then, again, with such
materials every man can be his own architect and mason; and
finally, when floods and rain dissolve the tenement, it sinks
down quietly, forming a mound in which the furniture and
domestic utensils may repose, and on which the family may sit
till the waters have subsided and they are able to set to again
and raise up their broken walls.

The river here is spanned by one or two pontoon bridges,

which had to be opened to let us pass through. These bridges form great impediments to the traffic, both on land and by water; for the pontoon is never pulled up to make a passage until about a dozen junks and boats have collected, and their owners, who by that time have been long waiting for the event, are clamouring and fighting amongst themselves to get first through. While the boats are passing through, the land traffic is of course interrupted, and crowds of foot passengers and vehicles are pressing forward on each side of the aperture to await the replacement of the pontoon. One or two of them, unable to make their way back, were driven over into the water and rescued by boat-hooks as we passed. The narrow wooden pavement of the bridge was made still narrower by a throng of shops and stalls, lepers, beggars and jugglers.

As the land rose towards the hills which sweep like a cres-cent around the north of Peking, we emerged from the flooded plains into a less desolate region, where the people were not so destitute of the common necessaries of life, and where the banks were lined with ripe fields of millet. Our boatmen, like the dwellers on land, lived on the flour of this useful cereal, which they season with salt-fish and garlic. The flour is made into bread, or rather cooked and pulled out into strings of hot, tough, elastic dough. This the people consumed in great quantities at meal-times, and always appeared to recover from its effects, although to me it seemed just about as digestible as india-rubber cables. Here we encountered many ponies, mules and donkeys in use; the mules being of an exceedingly fine breed, and having, many of them, zebra stripes across the legs. As for the donkeys, they were thoroughly domesticated, and followed their masters to and fro like dogs.

The huts improved in appearance as we neared Tung-chow,

and the villagers, too, were more robust-looking, although even the best of these, in spite of their willow-shaded dwellings and their harvest-fields, betrayed evidences of a hard-struggling, hand-to-mouth existence.

It was not till the afternoon of the fourth day that we reached Tung-chow, though we made but another halt to visit a village fair, where we saw a poor conjuror perform tricks for a few cash that would make his fortune on a London stage. And yet his greatest trick of all was transforming three copper cash into gold coin. His arms were quite bare, and having taken his cash in the palm of his hand, he permitted me to close the fingers over them. Then, passing a wand above the clenched fist, he opened it again and feasted the greedy eyes of his rustic admirers on what looked extremely like glittering gold. He also killed a small boy whom he had with him, by plunging a knife into his body. The youth became suddenly pale, seemed to expire, then jumping up again, removed the knife with one hand, while he solicited patronage with the other. There was one feat which this conjuror performed with wonderful dexterity. He placed a square cloth flat upon the ground, and taking it by the centre, between his forefinger and thumb, with one hand, he waved the wand with the other; and, gradually raising the cloth, disclosed a huge vase brimful of pure water beneath it.

At Tung-chow our boat was boarded by at least a dozen coolies eager to carry our baggage One of them incautiously lifted a trunk and was making off with it, when he was suddenly relieved of the burden by Tao and hurled pell-mell into the water. This summary procedure on the part of my Tientsin man almost cost him his much venerated tail, for it had nearly been torn out at the roots by the infuriated coolies before I could come to the rescue. Here we engaged carts for the

CHINESE COOLIES.

COLLECTOR OF PRINTED SCRAPS.

metropolis. These carts are the imperial-highway substitutes for our railways, cabs and omnibuses, but they have no springs. A railway is being built from Tientsin to Peking. Notwithstanding this they might be comfortable enough if so constructed as to allow the passenger to sit down, and used only on a perfectly level road. Tao had himself carefully packed into his conveyance with straw, but as for me, not liking the look of the vehicles, I determined to walk at least a part of the way.

There may be passages in what I have still to relate which may seem strange to a European reader, and I may be allowed perhaps, therefore, here to remind him that I am describing only what I actually saw and experienced. Soon we were entering Tung-chow, the carts plunging and lumbering behind us over what at one time had been a massively constructed Mongolian causeway. Gallantly the carters struggled on beneath an ancient archway, when suddenly the thoroughfare was found jammed by a heavily laden cart drawn by a team of mules and donkeys, that had stuck fast among the broken blocks of stone. Straightway the air re-echoed with the execrations of a hundred carters, who found their progress obstructed, and it was full half an hour before we managed to pass. I should think that the distinguished members of the Peking Board of Works can hardly have ventured so far as Tung-chow on their tours of inspection. A few moderate-sized stone walls thrown across the street there could scarcely prove more serious impediments to the traffic than the existing dilapidated pavement. One may now travel on a well-constructed railway from a station adjoining the Taku forts, to Tientsin. This line will eventually be carried to Peking. The rails and plant for the extension were imported during the war. As for the town and its inhabitants, we had ample leisure to inspect them before the carts had struggled clear of their streets. The shop-fronts were of richly carved wood, quite different from what one sees in the south, but seemingly stained with the accumulated dust of ages.

Even outside Tung-chow the roads were knee-deep in mud, in consequence of the heavy rain which had fallen during the previous night, so that I had no further choice, and perforce took refuge in the cart. My driver smelt of sam-shu and garlic, and placed such implicit trust in his mule that, once fairly on the road, he fell asleep on the shaft, and had to be reminded frequently by a shove off his perch, that he might as well do something to extricate his jaded beast and its burden from the pitfalls and mud-pools of the way. At length we made a halt at an inn. These inns supply food for man and beast, and occur at frequent intervals along that road, reminding one in some respects of those similar old-fashioned wayside resting-places which are now dying out rapidly in our own land.

Outside this inn ran a long low wall, whitewashed and inscribed in huge black characters with the sign or motto, "Perpetual felicity achieved." Along the entire front of the establishment a narrow dwarf-table had been set up, and groups of travellers seated round it discussed reeking bowls of soup or tea, and the latest news from the capital. Their cattle they had already made over to the care of hangers-on at the inn.

Tao and my Hainan men had gone on ahead, but I stopped here and partook of a *diner à la Chinoise*, which was served up to me in a bedroom. This apartment contained nothing save a table and a chair, and a bed or *kang* made of bricks. As for the table, it was covered with a surface formation of dirt, into which I could cut like cheese. But I must say that the dinner here supplied me was the best I ever tasted at a Chinese inn. The viands were stewed mutton cut up into small pieces,

THE GREAT BELL, PEKING.

NATIVE PLOUGH.

rice, an omelette, grapes and tea. The room had recently been
used as a stable; and its window filled in with a small wooden
frame and originally covered with paper, was now festooned
with dusty spiders'-webs. Another long *détour* at length brought
us to the Chi-ho gate of the Tartar city.

Before we enter I will run over some of the more general
characteristics of the city at which we have now arrived. It
stands, as we have already seen, on a plain sloping down to the
sea, and is indeed made up of two towns—a Tartar or Manchu
quarter, and a Chinese settlement—joined together by a wall more
than twenty miles round. At the time of the Manchu conquest
these two divisions were parted from each other by a second,
inner wall; the true natives of the soil, at least those of them
supposed to be friendly to the new dynasty, being confined
within a narrow space to the south; while the Tartar army was
encamped around the Imperial palace in the northern city, which
covers a square space of double the area of the Chinese town.

In so far as the features I have just described are concerned,
Peking is the same to-day as it was over 200 years ago, when
the descendants of Kublai Khan mounted the Imperial throne.
There are still in the Tartar city the same high walls pierced
with nine double gateways; the same towers and moats and
fortified positions; and within, the palace is still surrounded by
the permanent Manchu garrison, like that which was established
in most of the provincial capitals of China.

The army was originally divided into four corps, distinguished
by the white, red, yellow and blue banners under which they
respectively fought. Four bordered banners of the same colours
were subsequently added, and eight corps of Mongols and an
equal number of Chinese adherents were created at a later date.
Each corps of Manchu bannermen possesses, or rather is sup-

posed to possess, its ground as originally allotted to it within
the Imperial city; and before the cottage doorways one may
still see square paper lamps, whose colours denote the banners
to which their proprietors respectively belong. But time has
changed the stern rules under which the Chinese were confined
to their own quarter. Their superior industry and their slowly
but surely accumulating wealth have gradually made them masters
of the Tartar warriors, and of their allotments within the sacred
city. In fact, Chinese thrift and commercial energy have conquered
the descendants of the doughty Manchus who drove the Mings
from the throne.

It can hardly be credited by the stranger who visits this
Chinese centre of the universe, that the miserable beings whom
he sees clad in sheep-skins out of the Imperial bounty, and
acting as watchmen to the prosperous Chinese, are in reality the
remnants of those noble nomads who were at one time a terror
to Western Europe, and at a later date the conquerors of the
"Central Flowery Land."

The old walls of the great city are truly wonderful monuments
of human industry. Their base is sixty feet wide, their breadth
at the top about forty feet, and their height also averages forty
feet. But, alas! time and the modern arts of warfare have
rendered them practically nothing more than interesting relics
of a bygone age. A wooden stockade would now-a-days be
about as effective a protection to the Imperial throne within.
They seem to be well defended, however. Casting our eyes up
to the great tower above the gateway, we can see that it bristles
with guns; yet the little field-glass of modern science reveals to
us after all only a mock artillery, painted muzzles on painted
boards, threatening sham terrors through the countless embrasures.
A few rusty, dismantled cannon lie here and there beneath the

Gateway in Imperial Palace Wall, Peking.

gateway, but everything looks out of repair. The moats have become long shallow lagoons, and yonder a train of 100 camels is wading calmly through one into the city. The Government probably know all this, and have turned their attention to the defence of the coast line and frontiers; in the hope perhaps that a foreign foe will never again be able to flounder over the broken highways, and bring warfare to the palace door. A vain delusion truly, unless China is prepared to take to heart the sad lessons of modern battle-fields, and to keep pace with the ever-progressive science that is at work in our European arsenals. How can she do this? She may squander wealth—distilled out of the blood, sinews and sweat of long-suffering labour—upon fleets and armaments; but where will she find the genius to use her weapons to advantage? (Written in 1872.) In the event of a collision with a foreign Power, what good end would the hasty purchase of iron-clads and arms secure? As for the new weapons which they are manufacturing for themselves, we will hope that the rulers may never become so utterly blinded as to place these in the hands of untrained troops to defend the ancient policy of exclusiveness so fatal to progress in China. It will be readily admitted that this forecast has been fully justified by recent events.

But let us hasten our steps and enter the gate to behold this great metropolis. A mighty crowd is pressing on towards the dark archway, and we betake ourselves again to our carts, feeling sure that our passports will be examined by the guards on duty at the portal. But after all we pass through unnoticed in the wake of a train of camels, laden with fuel from the coal-mines not far off. There is a great noise and confusion. Two streams, made up of carts, camels, mules, donkeys and citizens, have met beneath the arch, and are struggling out of the darkness at either end. Within there is a wide thoroughfare, by far the widest I encountered in any Chinese city, and as roomy as the great roads of London. All the main streets of Peking can boast of this advantage; but the cartway runs down the centre of the road, and is only broad enough to allow two vehicles to pass abreast. The causeway in the middle is kept in repair by material which coolies ladle out of the deep trenches or mud-holes to be seen on either side of it. Citizens using this part of the highway after dark are occasionally drowned in these sloughs. Thus one old woman met her end in this way when I was in Peking, so that I never felt altogether safe when riding through the streets at night; while in the morning, when the dutiful servants of the Board of Works were flourishing their ladles, one had to face the insalubrious odours of the putrid mud; and at mid-day again, more especially if the weather was dry, the dust was so thick that when I washed my beard I could have supplied a valuable contribution towards the repairs of the road.

Notwithstanding all this, if there were no dust-clouds to obstruct the sight, the Peking streets are highly picturesque and interesting. Along each side of the central highway an interminable line of booths and stalls has been set up, and there almost everything under the Chinese sun is to be obtained. Then outside these stalls, again, there are the footpaths and beyond them we come upon the shops, which form the boundaries of the actual road. It is a complicated picture, and I only hope that the reader may not lose himself, as I have done more than once, amid the maze of streets. The shops had a great fascination for me. In both cities they are almost always owned by Chinese, for the Tartars, even if they have money, are too proud to trade; and if they have none, as is most frequently the case, they possess neither the energy nor the ingenuity to make a start. The Chinese, on the other hand, will many of them trade on nothing; and some seem capable of living on nothing too, until by patience and thrift, if they ever have the ghost of a chance, they manage to obtain a fair living.

The shops in Peking, both outside and within doors, are very attractive objects. Many of their fronts are elaborately carved, painted and gilded; while as for the interiors, these are fitted up and finished with an equally scrupulous care, the owners ready for business inside, clothed in their silks, and looking a supremely contented tribe. I could discover evidences of distribution of the wealth of the official classes in all those shops which in any way supplied their wants, or ministered to their tastes. On the other hand, signs of squalor and misery were apparent everywhere in the unwelcome and uncared-for poor; all the more apparent, perhaps, when brought face to face with the tokens of wealth and refinement.

I have not space to relate a tenth of what I beheld or experienced in this great capital; how its naked beggars were found in the winter mornings dead at its gates; how a cart might be met going its rounds to pick up the bodies of infants too young to require the sacred rites of sepulture; how the destitute were to be seen crowding into a sort of casual ward already full, and craving permission to stand inside its walls, so as to obtain shelter from the wintry blast that would freeze their hearts before the dawn. There are acres of hovels at Peking, in which the Imperial bannermen herd, and filth seems to be deposited like tribute before the very palace gates; indeed, there is hardly a spot in the capital that does not make one long for a single glimpse of that Chinese paradise we had pictured to ourselves in our youth—for the bright sky, the tea-fields, orange-groves

16

and hedges of jasmine, and for the lotus-lakes filling the air
with their perfume.

Next to the shops, the footpaths in front of them are perhaps
most curious to a foreigner. In these paths, after a shower of
rain, many pools occur—pools which it is impossible to cross
except by wading, unless one cares to imitate an old Pekingese
lady, who carried two bricks with her wherever she went, to
pave her way over the puddles. As in the Commercial Road
in London, crowds congregate in front of the tents and stalls
of the hawkers, while the shopkeepers spread out their wares
for sale so as to monopolise at least two-thirds of the pavement, so also in Peking, in yet greater numbers and variety,
the buyers and sellers occupy every dry spot. Sometimes one
can only get through the press by brushing against the dry
dusty hides of a train of camels, as they are being unladen before a coal-shed; and one must take care, should any of them
be lying down, not to tread on their huge soft feet, for they
can inflict a savage bite. In another spot it may become necessary to wait until some skittish mule, tethered in front of a
shop, has been removed by its leisurely master, who is smoking
a pipe with the shopman inside. Once, as I threaded my way
along, I had to climb a pile of wooden planks to reach the path
beyond, and finding that a clear view could be obtained from
the top of a fine shop on the other side of the road, I had
my camera set up and proceeded to take a photograph.
But in two or three minutes, before the picture could be
secured, there was a sudden transformation of the scene.
Every available spot of ground was taken up by eager but
good-natured spectators; traffic was suspended; and just as I
was about to expose the plate, some ingenious youth displaced
the plank on which I stood, and brought me down in a

TRAVELLING COOK.

CHIROPODIST—PEKING.

rapid, undignified descent, immensely entertaining to the crowd.

Some of the booths close to the foot-way are built of mud or brick, and would indeed become permanent structures, but that their occupants may be ordered at any moment to clear them away, so as to make room for the progress of the Emperor. For I must tell you that whenever the Sovereign is carried abroad, outside his own palace walls, the roads must be cleared, and even cleaned, that his sacred eyes may not be offended with a glimpse at the true condition of his splendid capital. After he has passed by, booths, tents and stalls are re-erected, and commerce and confusion resume their sway. As matters stand, these roadside obstructions are really a great boon to the people. Anything can be bought at the stalls, and their owners are neither slow nor silent in advertising the fact. At one a butcher and a baker combine their crafts. The former sells his mutton cut to suit the taste of his customers, while at the same time he disposes of all the bones and refuse to the cook who manufactures savoury pies before a hungry crowd of lookers-on. Twirling his rolling-pin on his board, he shrieks out in a shrill key a list of the delicacies he has prepared.

Jewels, too, of no mean value, are on sale here as well, and there are peep-shows, jugglers, lottery-men, ballad-singers and story-tellers; the latter accompanying their recitations with the strummings of a lute, while their audience sits round a long table and listens with rapt attention to the dramatic renderings of their poets. The story-teller, however, has many competitors to contend against, and of all his rivals the old-clothes-men are perhaps the most formidable tribe. These old-clothes-men enjoy a wide celebrity for their humorous stories, and will run off with a rhyme to suit the garments as they offer them to the highest bidder. Each coat is thus invested with a miraculous history, which gives it at once a speculative value. If it be fur, its heat-producing powers are eloquently described. "It was this fur which, during the year of the great frost, saved the head of that illustrious family Chang. The cold was so intense that the people were mute. When they spoke, their words froze and hung from their lips. Men's ears congealed and were devoid of feeling, so that when they shook their heads they fell off. Men froze to the streets and died by thousands; but as for Chang of honoured memory, he put on this coat, and it brought summer to his blood. How much say you for it?" etc. The foregoing is a rendering of the language actually used by one of these sellers of unredeemed pledges.

I saw two or three men who were driving a trade in magic pictures and foreign stereoscopic photographs, some in not the most refined style of art; and as for the peep-shows—well, the less one says about them the better; they certainly would not be tolerated in any public thoroughfare in Europe. The original Punch and Judy is also to be encountered in the Peking streets; puppets worked by the hands of a hidden operator, on just the same plan as with us. At night, too, I have frequently seen a most ingenious shadow pantomime, contrived by projecting small movable figures on to a thin screen, under a brilliant light from behind. Capital clay images may be purchased at some of the stalls; but in no part of China has this art of making coloured clay figures reached such perfection as at Tientsin. At that place tiny figures are sold for a mere song, which are by far the cleverest things of the kind I ever saw. These are not only most perfect representations of Chinese men and women, but many of them hit off humorous characteristics with the most wonderfully artistic fidelity.

If I go rambling on in this way over the city, we shall never

Chinese Coster.

Manchu Tartar Lady.

PEKING PEEP-SHOW.

reach the hotel, nor receive that welcome which was so warmly accorded to me by Monsieur Thomas, the proprietor. Thomas was not the cleanest man in the world, but he was extremely polite, which was something. There was, however, about his costume a painful lack of buttons, and its appearance might perhaps have been improved by the addition of a waistcoat, and by the absence of the grease that seemed to have been struggling up to reach his hair, but had not arrived at its destination. His hands, and even his face, in prospect of our coming, had been hastily though imperfectly washed. But then he was a cook, too; and he remarked, when I flattered him on this head, that there was nothing like a little eau-de-vie to enable an artist to put the finishing touches on a *chef-d'œuvre*, either of cookery or painting. Had he confessed to a great deal of that stimulant, he would have been much nearer the truth.

My bedroom was not a comfortable one. How could it be?— it was chiefly built of mud. The mud floor, indeed, was matted over, but the white-washed walls felt sticky, and so did the bed and curtains; a close, nasty smell, too, pervaded the whole apartment, and on looking into a closet, I discovered a quantity of mouldy, foreign apparel. This, as I found out next morning, had been left there as plague-stricken by a gentleman who, some days previously, had nearly died of small-pox in this very room. Fortunately I escaped an attack of the malady.

I paid a visit to the Corean Legation in the Tartar quarter of the city. It was customary before the war for the King of Corea to send an annual embassy of tribute-bearers to Peking. The first detachment of the embassy had just arrived before I quitted the capital. There were but a few members present at the Legation at the time of my visit, and the apartments in which they dwelt were so scrupulously clean that I almost

wished that I had left my shoes at the doorway, in my fear of
soiling the white straw mats. I was also most favourably impressed with the spotless purity of their garments, which were
almost entirely of white. It was with great difficulty, however,
that I secured an illustration, but it was on that account all the
more prized.

After my return from the Ming tombs, H. B. M.'s Minister,
the late Sir Thomas Wall, kindly invited me to stay at the
Legation, but I had promised Thomas to remain in his house,
and although unfortunate in some respects, he proved thoroughly honest, and did his best to make me comfortable.

I bought a Mongolian pony to save me time in exploring the
city, and a saddle and bridle were kindly lent to me by a friend;
but the brute was a large-boned, large-headed animal with a
great round belly, over which, for want of a crupper, the saddle-
girths were always sliding. It had, too, an enormous appetite,
at least, so said the groom whom I employed. The first night
it consumed its bed, and when I examined it in the morning
it seemed to be hungry still, for it had barked the tree to which
it was tethered, and had, besides this, devoured about five shillings' worth of millet-bran, and so forth. I soon found out that
I was being fleeced by the stable-boy, who had a pony of his
own in the next house, and had determined to feed it at my
expense.

The Pekingese have a strange mode of shoeing their horses.
They pull three feet together with cords, and leave the hoof
that is to be shod, free. Then they sling the animal bodily up
between two posts, and so complete the task in comfort and
safety.

In the plan of the city of Peking there is every evidence of
careful design, and this has been carried out minutely, from the

central buildings of the palace to the outermost wall of fortification. The ground-plan of the Imperial buildings is in most respects identical with the ground-plans of the great temples and tombs of the country. So much alike are they, even in the style and arrangement of their edifices, that a palace, with scarcely any alteration, might be at once converted into a Buddhist temple. Thus we find that the Great Yung-ho-Kung Lamasary of the Mongols in the north-east quarter of the city, was at one time the residence of the son and successor of Kang-hi. The chief halls of the Imperial palace—if we may judge from the glimpse one gets of their lofty roofs when one stands on the city wall—are three in number, extending from the Chien-men to Prospect Hill, and in every instance are approached by a triple gateway. The like order prevails at the Ming tombs. There one finds an equal number of halls, with a triple doorway in front of each; while the temple and domestic architecture throughout the north of China is based upon the same plan. In the latter case there are three courts, divided from each other by halls, the apartments of the domestics being ranged about the outer courts, while the innermost of the three is devoted to family use.

It is interesting to observe the evidences which crop up everywhere, showing the universal sacredness of the numbers three and nine. Thus at Peking, the gates with which the outer wall of the Tartar city is pierced form together a multiple of three, and the sacred person of the Emperor can only be approached, even by his highest officers, after three times three prostrations. The Temple of Heaven, too, in the Chinese city, with its triple roof, the triple terraces of its marble altars and the rest of its mystic symbolism throughout, points either to three or its multiples.

The Rev. Joseph Edkins was, I believe, the first to draw attention to the symbolical architecture of the Temple of Heaven, and to the importance which the Chinese themselves attach to the southern open altar, as the most sacred of all Chinese religious structures. There, at the winter solstice, the Emperor himself makes burnt-offerings, just as the patriarchs did of old, to the supreme Lord of Heaven. In the city of Foochow, on the southern side of the walled enclosure, are two hills, one known as Wu-shih-shan, and the other as Kui-shen-shan, or the "Hill of the Nine Genii." On the top of the former there is an open altar—a simple erection of rude unhewn stone, approached first by a flight of eighteen steps, and finally by three steps, cut into the face of the rock. This altar is reputed to be very ancient, and to it the Governor-General of the province repairs at certain seasons of the year as the representative of the Emperor, and there offers up burnt-sacrifices to heaven. In this granite table, covered with a simple square stone vessel filled with ashes, we have the sacrificial altar in what is probably its most ancient Chinese form. The southern altar at Peking bears a wonderful resemblance to Mount Meru, the centre of the Buddhist universe, round which all the heavenly bodies are supposed to move; and there we find tablets of sun, moon and stars arranged around the second terrace of the altar, according to the Chinese system of astronomy.

The city of Peking, or rather the Tartar portion of it, is laid out with an almost perfect symmetry. The sacred purple city stands nearly in the centre, and there are three main streets, which run from north to south. One of these streets leads direct to the palace-gates, and the other two are nearly equidistant from it on either side; while myriads of minor thoroughfares and lanes intersect one another in the spaces between, but are always either parallel with or at right angles to the three main roads. Viewed from any stand-point on the outer wall, the whole scene is disappointing. With the exception of the palace buildings, the Buddhist shrines, the Temple of Heaven, the Roman Catholic Cathedral and the official yamens, the houses never rise above the low, modest, uniform level prescribed for them by law. Much, too, that is ruinous and dilapidated presents itself to the gaze. Here and there we see open spaces and green trees that shade the buildings of the rich; but again the eye wearies of its wanderings over hundreds of acres of tiles and walls all of one stereotyped pattern, and cannot help noticing that the isolation of the Chinese begins with the family unit at home. There stands the sacred dwelling of the mighty Emperor, walled round and round; his person protected from the gaze of the outer world by countless courts and "halls of sacred harmony"; and one can note the same exclusiveness carried out in all the dwellings of his people. Each residence is enclosed in a wall of its own, and a single outer entrance gives access to courts and reception-rooms, beyond which the most favoured guest may not intrude to violate by his mere presence the sanctity of the domicile. There are, of course, tens of thousands of houses and hovels where this arrangement cannot be observed, but where the people, nevertheless, manage to sustain a sort of dignified isolation by investing themselves with an air of self-importance, which the very street beggars never wholly lay aside. These, if they be Manchus, are proud at any rate of their sheepskin coats; or if they be not, then the more fugitive covering of mud, which is all that hides their nakedness, is still carried with a sort of stolid solemnity which would be ludicrous were it not for their misfortunes.

I had the good fortune while in the metropolis to be intro-

duced by Dr. Martin, President of the Imperial Tungwen College, to Prince Kung and the other distinguished members of
the Chinese Government; and they wisely availed themselves of
my presence to have their portraits taken at the Tsungli-yamen,
or Chinese Foreign Office. Prince Kung, as most of my readers
are aware, is a younger brother of the late Emperor Hien-fung.
He holds several high appointments, military as well as civil,
and in particular he is a member of the Supreme Council—a
department of the State which most nearly resembles the Cabinet in our own constitution. He has been for over a quarter
of a century Chief Minister of Foreign Affairs and Chancellor
of the Empire. He is, too, a man esteemed by all who know
him, quick in apprehension, comparatively liberal in his views,
and regarded by some as the head of that small party of politi-
cians who favour progress in China.

The creation of the Tsungli-yamen, or Foreign Board, was
one of the important results which followed the ratification of
the Treaty of Tientsin. Up to that time all foreign diplomatic
correspondence had been carried on through the Colonial Office,
where the great Powers were practically placed on a level with
the Central Asian dependencies of the Empire. This yamen
stands next to the Imperial College, where a staff of foreign
professors is now employed in instructing Chinese students in
European languages, literature and science. Accompanied by
one of these professors, who kindly undertook to be my interpreter, I found myself one morning entering a low narrow
doorway through a dead wall. After making our way along a
number of courts, studded with rockeries, flowers and ponds,
and after passing down dingy corridors in dismal disrepair, we
at length stood beneath the shade of an old tree, and in front
of the picturesque, but purely Chinese-looking, audience-chamber,

MILITARY MANDARIN.

wherein the interests of vast numbers of the human race are from time to time discussed. We had barely time to glance at the painted pillars, the curved roofs and carved windows, when a venerable noble issued from behind a bamboo screen that concealed a narrow doorway, and accorded us a quiet, courteous welcome.

The Prince himself had not arrived; but Wen-siang, Paou-keun and Shen-kwe-fen, members, all of them, at that time, of the Grand Council, were already in attendance. Wen-siang was well known in diplomatic circles as a statesman endowed with intellectual powers of a high order, and as one of the foremost ministers of his age. It is said of him, that, in reply to the urgent representations of a foreigner who was clamouring for Chinese progress, he delivered himself of the following prophecy, which has not yet, however, been fulfilled:—"Give China time, and her progress will be both rapid and overwhelming in its results; so much so, that those who were foremost with the plea for progress will be sighing for the good old times." This transformation may be looming in the far-off distance, like some unknown star whose light is travelling through the immeasurable regions of space, but has not yet reached our own sphere. China has had her ages of flint and bronze; and her vast mineral resources tell us that she is yet destined to enter upon all that is implied in an age of coal and iron.

Wen-siang and Paou-keun are Manchus, while Shen-kwe-fen is one of the Chinese members of the Grand Council of State.

Cheng-lin, Tung-sean and Maou-cheng-he, ministers of the Foreign Board were also present. Tung-sean is the author of many valuable works. One of these, on the hydrography of northern China, was in the press at the time of my visit; and, as the reader will have gathered from my account of the inundations, his treatise is likely to be of great value, provided that its suggestions, if any, for draining the country and restoring the broken embankments can, or rather will, be carried out. The ministers wore simple robes of variously-coloured satin, open in front and caught in by a band at the waist; collars of pale blue silk tapering down from the neck to the shoulders, and thick-soled black satin boots. This costume was extremely picturesque, and what is of far greater importance, the ministers, most of them, were as fine-looking men as ever our own Cabinet can boast. All of them had an air of quiet, dignified repose.

The arrival of Prince Kung on the scene cut short our general conversation. The Prince for a few minutes kept me in a pleasant talk, enquiring about my travels and about photography, and manifesting considerable interest in the process of taking a likeness. He is a man of middle stature, and of rather slender frame; his appearance, indeed, did not impress me so favourably as did that of the other members of the Cabinet; yet he had what phrenologists would describe as a splendid head. His eyes were penetrating, and his face, when in repose, wore an expression of sullen resolution. As I looked upon him, I wondered whether he felt the burden of the responsibility which he shared with the ministers around, in guiding the destinies of so many millions of the human race; or whether he and his distinguished colleagues were able to look with complacency upon the present state of the Empire and its people.

These men have had many and great difficulties to contend against in their time. Foreign war, civil insurrection, famine, floods and the rapacity of their officials in different quarters of the land, have done much to weaken the prestige and power

MEMBERS OF THE TSUNGLI YAMEN, PEKING.

of the great central Government; and her authority now can never be properly felt and acknowledged in the more distant portions of China, until each remotest province of that vast kingdom shall have been united to Peking by railways and by a network of telegraphic nerves.

Perhaps the most grave and distinguished-looking member of the group now before me was Maou-cheng-he. This man's scholarly attainments had won him the highest post of literary fame, and formerly he had been chief judge of the metropolitan literary examinations.

Extraordinary is the honour which the Chinese attach to literary championship, and to the achievement of the Chong-ün or Han-lin degree, which is conferred by the Peking examiners. At the triennial examination of 1871 a man from Shun-kak district, in the Kwang-tung province, carried off the Chong-ün. His family name was Leung. Now this literary distinction had been obtained by a Kwang-tung scholar some half a century before, and he was the first who achieved that success during a period of 200 years. Thus the new victory of their own candidate was hailed by the men of Kwang-tung as a great historical event. It was reported, however, that Mr. Leung had after all obtained the honour by a lucky "fluke." As one of a triad of chosen scholars of the Empire, he produced the composition which was to decide his claims. There were nine essays in all, and these, when they had been submitted to the Han-lin examiners, were sent by them to the Empress Dowager (the Emperor being under age) to have their own award formally confirmed. The work of greatest merit was placed uppermost; but the old lady, who had an imperial will of her own, felt anxious to thwart the decision of the learned pundits; and, as chance would have it, the sunlight fell on the chosen manuscript, and she discovered a flaw, a thinness in the paper, indicating a place in the composition where one character had been erased and another substituted. The Empress rated the examiners for allowing such slovenly work to pass, and proclaimed Leung the victor. The superstitious Cantonese declared that it was a divine choice, that the sunbeam was a messenger sent by Heaven to point out the blemish in the essay at first selected for the prize.

Mr. Leung reached Canton in May, 1872, and was received there by the local authorities with the highest possible honours. All the families who bore the name of Leung (and who had also means to afford it) paid the Chong-ün large sums of money to be permitted to come and worship at his ancestral hall. By this means they established a spurious claim to relationship and as soon as the ceremony was over, were allowed to place tablets above the entrances of their own halls inscribed with the title Chong-ün. An uncle of the successful wrangler, uniting an exalted sense of his duty to his family with a laudable desire to repair his own fortune, forestalled the happy Chong-ün, and acted as his deputy before his arrival, in visiting sundry halls. For such honourable service this obliging relative at times received a thousand dollars, and his nephew, for the sake of the family name, had to sanction the steps thus prematurely adopted to spread his fame abroad. To show the great esteem in which such a man is held by the Chinese, I may add that a brother of Mr. Leung rented a house in Canton, and its owner hearing that he was the brother of the famous Chong-ün, made him a free gift of the tenement.

After partaking of tea with one or two of the members of the Cabinet, and after some general talk on topics of common interest, we rose and quitted the yamen.

Great Gateway, Temple of Confucius, Peking.

I must leave many of the temples and objects of interest in Peking undescribed, as my aim is rather to convey a general impression of the condition of the country and of its people as we find them now-a-days, than to enter into minute details. I can therefore only cast a passing glance at a few places of public importance. The Confucian Temple covers a wide area, and like all palaces, shrines and even houses, is completely walled around. The main gateway which leads into the sacred enclosure is presented in the accompanying picture. This gateway is approached, as were the ancient shrines of Greece and Rome, through an avenue of venerable cypress trees; and the whole establishment forms perhaps the most imposing specimen of purely Chinese architecture to be found among the ornaments of the capital. The triple approach and the balustrading are of sculptured marble; while the pillars and other portions of the gateway are of more perishable materials—wood, glazed earthenware and brick. On either side are groves of marble tablets, bearing the names of the successful Han-lin scholars for many centuries back; and that one to the left, supported upon the back of a tortoise, was set up here when Marco Polo was in China. Within this gate stand the celebrated stone drums, inscribed with stanzas, cut nearly 2,000 years ago, in primitive form of Chinese writing. Thus these drums prove the antiquity at once of the poetry and of the character in which that has been engraved. These inscriptions have been translated by Dr. S. W. Bushell, the gentleman who has also discovered the site of the famous city of Shang-tu, referred to by Coleridge as Xanadu, and spoken of by Marco Polo as the northern capital of the Yuen dynasty. The great hall within simply contains the tablet of China's chief sage and those of twenty-two of his most distinguished followers. The spirits of the departed great are

supposed to reside in their tablets, and hence annually, at the
vernal and autumnal equinoxes, sheep and oxen fall in sacrifice
in front of this honoured shrine of literature.

Close to the Confucian Temple stands the Kwo-tze-keen, or
National University; and there, ranged around the Pi-yung-kung,
or Hall of the Classics, are 200 tablets of stone inscribed with
the complete text of the nine sacred books.

The Observatory has been set up on the wall on the eastern
side of the Tartar city. Here, in addition to the colossal astronomical instruments erected by the Jesuit missionaries in the
seventeenth century, we find two other instruments in a court
below, which the Chinese made for themselves towards the close
of the thirteenth century, when the Yuen dynasty was on the
throne. Possibly some elements of European science may have
been brought to bear on the construction of even these instruments, although the characters and divisions engraved on their
splendid bronze circles point only to the Chinese method of
dividing the year, and to the state of Chinese astronomy at the
time. Yet Marco Polo must have been in the north of China
at about the period of their manufacture, or at any rate John
de Carvino was there, for he, under Pope Clement V., became
bishop of Cambalu (Peking) about 1290 A. D., and perhaps,
with his numerous staff of priests, he introduced some knowledge
of Western art. The late Mr. Wylie (than whom there was probably
no better authority) was with me when I examined these instruments, and was of opinion that they are Chinese, and that they
were produced by Ko-show-king, one of the most famous astron-
omers of China. One of them is an astrolaba, furnished beneath
with a splendid sun-dial, which has long since lost its gnomon.
The whole, indeed, consists of three astrolabæ, one partly move-
able and partly fixed in the plane of the ecliptic; the second

turning on a centre as a meridian circle, and the third the azimuth circle.

The other instrument is an armillary sphere, supported by chained dragons, of most beautiful workmanship and design. This instrument is a marvellous specimen of the perfection to which the Chinese must, even then, have brought the art of casting in bronze. The horizon is inscribed with the twelve cyclical characters, into which the Chinese divide the day and night. Outside the ring these characters appear again, paired with eight characters of the denary cycle, and four names of the eight diagrams of the book of changes, denoting the points of the compass; while the inside of the ring bears the names of the twelve States into which China, in ancient times, was portioned out. An equatorial circle, a double-ring ecliptic, an equinoctial colure and a double-ring colure are adjusted with the horizon ring. The equator is engraved with constellations of unknown antiquity; while the ecliptic is marked off into twenty-four equal spaces, corresponding to the divisions of the year. All the circles are divided into 365¼ degrees, for the days of the year; while each degree is subdivided into 100 parts, as for everything less than a degree the centenary scale prevailed at that period. I take these instruments to be of great interest, as indicating the state of astronomical science in China at about the end of the thirteenth century.

While in Peking I made the acquaintance of many educated and intelligent natives, one of whom accompanied an English physician and myself on an excursion to the ruins of the Summer Palace. With another gentleman, Mr. Yang, I became considerably intimate; and in this way enjoyed some opportunity of seeing the dwellings and domestic life of the upper classes in the capital. Both my friends were devoted to photography; but

17

Yang, not content with his triumphs in that branch of science, frequently carried his researches and experiments to a pitch that caused the members of his multitudinous household no less inconvenience than alarm. Yang was a fine sample of the modern Chinese savant—fat, good-natured and contented; but much inclined to take short cuts to scientific knowledge, and to esteem his own incomplete and hap-hazard achievements the results of marvellously perfect intelligence. His house, like most others in China, was approached through a lane hedged in by high brick walls on either side, so that there was nothing to be seen of it from without save the small doorway and a low brick partition about six feet beyond the threshold—the latter intended to prevent the ingress of the spirits of the dead. Within there was the usual array of courts and halls, reached by narrow vine-shaded corridors; but each court was tastefully laid out with rockeries, flowers, fish-ponds, bridges and pavilions. Really the place was very picturesque and admirably suited to the disposition of a people affecting seclusion and the pleasures of family life; and who (so far as the women are concerned) know little or nothing of the world in which they live, beyond what they gather within the walls of their own abode.

Here I was, then, admitted at last into the sacred precincts of the mysterious Chinese dwelling. Its proprietor was an amateur, not merely of photography, but of chemistry and electricity too; and he had a laboratory fitted up in the ladies' quarter. In one corner of this laboratory stood a black carved bedstead, curtained with silk and pillowed with wood; while a carved bench, also of black wood, supported a heterogeneous collection of instruments, chemical, electrical and photographic, besides Chinese and European books. The walls were garnished with enlarged photographs of Yang's family and friends. In a small

MANCHU TARTAR LADY.

MANCHU LADY AND MAID.

Tartar Lady and Maid.

outer court care had been taken to supply a fowl-house with a steam saw-mill, with which the owner had achieved wonders in the short space of a single day.

The machine, indeed, had never enjoyed but that one chance of distinguishing itself; for the Pekingese, disturbed by the whirr of the engine, scaled the walls with ladders, clustered on to the roofs and compelled the startled proprietor to abandon his undertaking. There, then, stood the motionless mill, with one or two dejected fowls perched upon its cylinder—a monster whom long familiarity had taught even the poultry to despise. I saw the ladies several times while I was teaching my friend how to concoct nitrate of silver and other photographic chemicals. Some of these women were handsome, and all were dressed in rich satins; but the following information which I received from an English lady (Mrs. Edkins), who was much esteemed, and deservedly so, for her good works among the natives, will give further insight into the daily life of the Pekingese ladies.

Many Chinese ladies spend a great portion of their time in gossiping, smoking and gambling—very unlady-like occupations my fair readers will exclaim; nevertheless, these accomplishments, taken either singly or collectively, require years of assiduous training before they can be practised with that perfection which prevails in polite circles in China. Gambling, it is to be regretted, is by far the most favourite pastime, and it is perhaps but cold comfort to reflect that this vice is not monopolised by the ladies of Cathay, but that it is their lords who set them the example. They never dream of playing except for money; and when they have no visitors of their own rank to gamble with, they call up the domestics and play with them. Poorer women meet at some gaming den, and there manage to squander considerable sums of money; thus affording their devoted husbands at the end of the year, when debts must be discharged which they are unable to pay, an excuse for committing suicide.

The married lady rises early, and first sees that tea is prepared for her husband, as well as some hot water for his morning bath. The same attention is also exacted by the mother-in-law; for she is always present, like the guardian angel of her son. As a rule, however, the mother-in-law is not held to be an angel by the wife, who, during the lifetime of her husband's mother, has to be a very drudge in the house. It may be unkind to relate it, but the truth must be told: the ladies in the morning fly about with shoes down at heel—that is, the Tartars do, who have not small feet—dressed *en déshabillé*, and shouting out their orders to the domestic slaves. In short, a general uproar prevails in many Chinese households until everything for the elaborate toilet has been procured.

Each lady has generally one or two maids, besides a small slave-girl who waits on these maids and trims and lights her mistress's pipe. The dressing of a lady's hair occupies her attendants from one to two hours; then a white paste is prepared and daubed over her face and neck, and this, when dry, is smoothed and polished once. Afterwards a blush of rose-powder is applied to the cheeks and eyelids, the surplus rouge remaining on the lady's palm, as a rose-pink on the hand is greatly esteemed. Next they dye the nails red with the blossom of a certain flower, and finally they dress for the day. Many of them have chignons and false hair; but no hair-dyes are used, for raven hair is common and golden tresses are not in repute. Numbers of ladies pass a portion of their time in embroidering shoes, purses, handkerchiefs and such like gear; while before marriage, nearly all their days are occupied in preparations for the dreary event

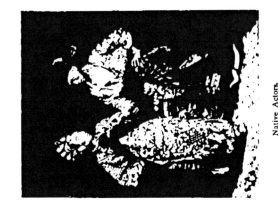

Native Actors.

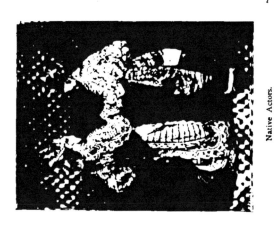

Native Actors.

Bride and Bridegroom.

Manchu-Tartar Bride and Maid.

of wedding one whom probably they have never yet seen, and for whom they can never care. Women of education—there are, alas! but a few—occasionally hire educated widows in needy circumstances to read novels or plays to them. Women capable of reading in this way can make a very comfortable living. Story-tellers and ballad-singers are also employed to entertain them in the courts of their houses.

The evenings they generally spend in their court-yards, smoking and watching the amusements of the children; and on these occasions conjurors, Punch-and-Judy men and ventriloquists are much in demand. The families retire early to rest, the ladies never caring to spoil their eyes by working under the light of a lamp. Opium-smoking is freely indulged in by many women in China. The romance of love is not unknown in the land, although few marriages are ever celebrated where the contracting parties have formed an attachment, or even seen each other, before their wedding-day.

On leaving Yang's dwelling, I had always to make my way across a flooded court, where a steam mining-pump had once been set going and had deluged the premises before it could be stopped. My friend, when I took my departure, was daily expecting the complete apparatus for a small gas-work, to supply his house with gas—a feat which I believe he successfully accomplished without blowing up his abode.

Pekingese Enamelling.—There are but one or two shops in Peking where the art of enamelling is carried on. The oldest enamelled vases were made during the Ta-ming dynasty, about three centuries ago; but these are said to be inferior to what were produced about 200 years later, when Kien-lung was on the throne. Within the last quarter of a century the art has been revived. One of the best shops for such work stood not

far from the French Legation, and was—strangely enough—
kept by a Manchu named Kwan.

The first part of the process consists in forming a copper
vase of the desired form, partly beaten into shape and
partly soldered. The design for the enamelled flowers and
figures is then traced on to the copper by a native artist,
and afterwards all the lines engraved are replaced by strips
of copper, soldered hard on to the vase, and rather thicker
than the depth of the enamel which they are destined to
contain. The materials used for soldering are borax and
silver, which require a higher temperature for fusion than the
enamel itself. The design is now filled in with the various
coloured enamels, reduced to a state of powder and made into
a paste by the admixture of water. The enamel powders are
said to be prepared by a secret process, known only to one
man in Peking, who sells them in a solid form, like slabs of
different coloured glass. The delicate operation of filling in the
coloured powders is chiefly carried on by boys, who manage
to blend the colours with wonderful perfection. After the design
has been filled in, the vase is next subjected to a heat that
fuses the enamel. Imperfections are then filled up and the
whole is fused again. This operation is repeated three times,
and then the vase is ready to be filed, ground and polished.
The grinding and polishing are conducted on a rude lathe, and
when completed the vase is gilt. Some of the largest and finest
vases sell for thousands of taels and are much prized by the
Chinese, as well as among foreigners.

On October 18th I set out with two friends for the Summer Palace at Yuen-ming-Yuen, about eight miles to the
north-west of Peking. One of our party, Mr. Wang, to whom
I have already referred, was connected with the Peking Board of

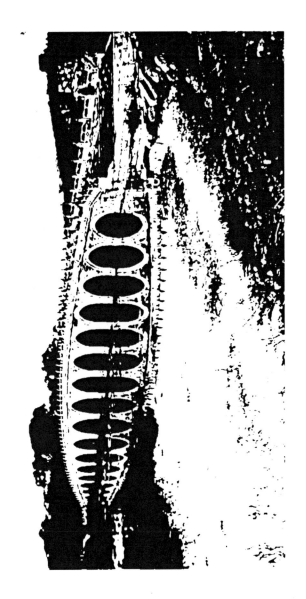

Bronze Temple, Yuen-Ming-Yuen.

Works. This gentleman used his official cart and was followed
by a mounted retainer, while Dr. Dudgeon and I rode ponies.
On the way, near the Imperial Palace, we fell in with a proces-
sion of sixty-four men, bearing a huge sedan, wherein sat
fourteen friends of Wang, his colleagues at the Board of
Works. These gentlemen were testing the strength of the
chair, which they had prepared to convey the remains of an
Imperial princess to sepulture. Something this, on the principle
of placing a railway director in front of every train! A great
vase filled to the brim with water had been set up in the
centre of the sedan in order to train the bearers to maintain
an accurate level. Whether the tea and refreshments and the
general hilarity of the party had anything to do with this
official investigation, I am at a loss to determine, but at any
rate the duties of the Board, apart from their extreme useful-
ness, appeared to be far from disagreeable. Further on the
road I had a race with a cavalry officer, and I managed to
to get ahead of him, but not until the saddle of my trusty
steed was nearly over its shoulders.

By four o'clock we had reached the grounds of the palace,
and there we found a wilderness of ruin and devastation which
it was piteous to behold. Marble slabs and sculptured ornaments that had graced one of the finest scenes in China, now
lay scattered everywhere among the debris and weeds. But
there were some of the monuments which had defied the hand
of the invaders, or had been spared, let us hope, on account
of their beauty. Among these is a marble bridge on seventeen
arches, which spans a lotus-lake. This was still in perfect
preservation; and in the far distance, too, the great temple on
Wan-show-shan could be seen sparkling intact in the sunlight.
At the base of this pile were a multitude of splendid statues,

pagodas and other ornaments, overthrown during the fearful raid of the allies. Enough yet remained, however, to give some faint notion of the untold wealth and labour that must have been lavished on this Imperial retreat. The Summer Palace lay in ruins within its boundary walls, just as it was looted and left. It is a pity that redress for a breach of treaty obligations was not sought by some less destructive mode than this; by some real achievement, which would have impressed the Chinese with exalted ideas of our civilisation as much as it terrified them with the awfulness of our power. If, for example, the capital had been held long enough to show what improvements a wise and liberal administration could, even in a short time, accomplish in the condition of the people and the country; then after a suitable indemnity had been paid for the lesson which we had been forced to convey, we might have withdrawn.

Wang made not a single allusion to the wreck around him. He admired, indeed, what little was left of the former splendour of the palace; but it was impossible to fathom his real sentiments, for a Chinaman, when interrogated, will never disclose what he thinks. The buildings were of purely Chinese design and conception.

At the monastery of Wo-foh-sze, or "the Sleeping Buddha," we found a resting-place for the night. The old Lama here was complaining of bad times. There was not enough land, he said, to support the establishment, and that though every monk enjoyed a yearly grant of twelve taels (equal to about £3 10s. of our money) from the Peking Board of Rites. But of late years there have been but few of the members of the Imperial family to bury—a ceremony for which this establishment receives a fee of some 300 taels. A remarkably beau-

Female compressed foot, and natural foot.

Sculptured Panel on Buddhist Cenotaph, Peking.

Wo-foh-sze Monastery, Yuen Ming Yuen.

tiful place was Wo-foh-sze ; and the quarters of the monks there, though furnished with the usual simplicity, were wonderfully clean and well kept.

There are many institutions and objects of interest in Peking, but to describe even the most prominent among them would require a volume by itself.

The most remarkable, and perhaps the finest, monument in all China is the marble cenotaph erected over the robes and relics of the Banjin Lama of Thibet. This edifice stands in the grounds of the Hwang-She monastery, about a mile beyond the north wall of Peking. When on my way to inspect it I witnessed a review of the northern army on the Anting plain. Some thousands of troops, infantry as well as cavalry, were in the field, and at a distance they made a warlike and imposing show, but nearer examination always seems to me to alter one's ideas of the greatness of human institutions, and more especially so where Chinese are concerned. Thus a close view of one of their river gun-boats revealed to me that a stand of rifles which occupied a prominent place on its deck was all constructed of wood; and the ancient foes of China have more than once in the same way advanced with caution to surprise a tented camp, and discovered that the tents were but white-washed clay mounds in undisturbed possession of the field. Thus also on the Anting plain, beneath the flaunting banners, we found the men armed with the old matchlocks, or with bows and arrows, and carrying huge basket-work shields painted with the faces of ogres, to strike terror into the hearts of a foe. For all that, evidences of military reform were not altogether wanting. Thus there were modern field-pieces, modern rifles, fair target-practice, and above all, desperate efforts to maintain discipline and order. At the same time I could not help thinking of Le-hung-chang (to whom I had the honour of being introduced at Tientsin), the founder of the first arsenal on a foreign type in China, and the companion in arms of Colonel Gordon and Tseng-kwo-fan. Personally Le is tall, resolute and calm, and altogether a fine specimen of his race. Perhaps he entertains an exaggerated belief in the capabilities of his nation; but at the same time he is deeply conscious of the power of Western kingdoms, and apparently desires to fathom the secrets of their superiority. On one occasion, when filled with admiration of the beauty and genius displayed in a piece of foreign mechanism, he exclaimed, "How wonderful! how comes it that such inventions and discoveries are always foreign? It must be something different in the constitution of our minds that causes us to remain as we were." But after all, perhaps he may have intended to compliment his auditors, rather than to give genuine expression to his opinions. He probably knows that for untold centuries there has been little or no opportunity for the development of genius in China. The light of truth has been sought for only in the dark pages of past history; and the Chinese, in their efforts to attain to the perfection of their mythical kings and of the maxims embodied in their classics, have set up an inquisition which perforce suppresses originality and uproots invention like a noxious weed.

We are now at the grand cenotaph; but after all, what is there in its massive proportions, its grotesque sculptures, its golden crown and its shady groves of cypress and pine that will compare in interest with the daily life and aspirations of the meanest coolie who here comes to gaze with reverent awe and to place his simple votive offering before the temple shrine! The story of this building is a short one. The broad white marble base which gleams in the sunlight covers the relics of a Mongol Lama who was esteemed an incarnate Buddha. Yonder

is the vacant throne in the Hwang-Shi, or "Central Hall," whereon this human deity sat in state with his face to the East. In another apartment we see the bed on which his Holiness expired; poisoned, as is said, by a jealous Emperor towards the end of the eighteenth century, the monarch treating his victim with the most stately courtesy to the last, and even worshipping and glorifying him in public, while his sacrifice was being secretly prepared.

The late Mr. Wylie, of the London Bible Society, who was journeying into the Northern Provinces, accompanied me to the Great Wall; and Mr. Welmer, a Russian gentleman, also joined our party. Outside the Anting plain we halted at an inn called "The Gem of Prosperity," and, praise be to the Board of Works I we there found men repairing the roads. At Ma-teen there was a sheep-market, and Mongols disposing of their flocks. It is strange to note the strong nomadic tendencies of this race. In the Mongol quarter at Peking I have seen them actually place their beasts of burden inside the apartments of the house they hired, and pitch their own tent in the court outside. The condition of the sheep testified to the richness of the Mongolian pastures; while the shepherds, clad in sheep-skin coats, were a hardy, raw-boned-looking race. At Sha-ho village, in the inn of "Patriotic Perfection," we made a second halt. Here in our chamber we found the maxim, written up on a board, "All who seek wealth by the only pure principles will find it." Judging by this doctrine our host must have been a sad ruffian, for the poverty of his surroundings bore witness that he, for his part, must have sought after riches in some very questionable channel. We spent the night at Suy-Shan Inn, Nankow. It was truly a wretched place: the "grand chamber" measured about eight feet across, and was supplied with the usual brick bed, having an oven underneath it. In a room of this sort the fire is usually lit at night, and

is made up of charcoal, so that persons sleeping there are apt
to be poisoned by the fumes. Such a calamity indeed at times
will occur. In other respects those who are used to a brick
bed and a billet of wood for a pillow may sleep comfortably
enough; unless by chance the bricks become red-hot, and then
one is apt to be done brown. We left Nankow at six o'clock
in the morning, and followed the old Mongol road formed by
blocks of prophyry and marble. Through the pass our convey-
ances were litters slung between two mules, one in front and
the other behind. Although there is here a great traffic between
Thibet, Mongolia, Russia and China, the road in many places
was all but impassable, not to say extremely dangerous, skirting
as it does precipitous rocks where the slip of a hoof on the
part of either mule might end in a fatal accident. We were
constantly falling in with long trains of camels, mules and donkeys,
all heavily laden, some with brick-tea for the Mongolian and
Russian markets, while others bore produce to the capital from
the outer dependencies of China. At Kew-yung-kwan, an inner
spur of the Great Wall sweeps across the pass; and here, too,
is the old arch which has been rendered famous by Mr. Wylie's
successful labours in translating the Buddhist prayer inscribed in
six different languages on its inner wall. On this arch, too, we
find bas-reliefs representing the Kings of the Devas in Buddhist
mythology. The structure is supposed to have been erected
during the Yuen dynasty, and is said originally to have carried
a pagoda on its summit; but this was afterwards taken down
by the Mings, to propitiate the Mongol tribes. I have on another page drawn attention to the Indian mythological figures
with which this arch is adorned, and Mr. Wylie's notice of the
inscription will be found in the "Journal of the Royal Asiatic
Society," Vol. V., Part 1, pp. 14 *seq.*

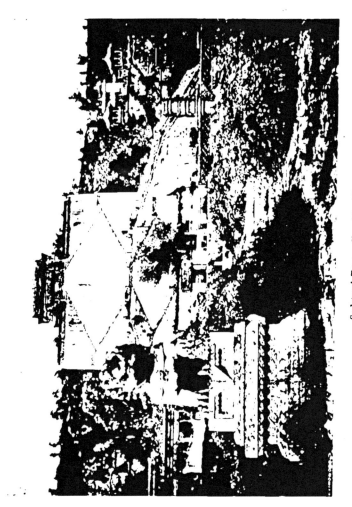

Sculptured Terrace, Yuen-Ming-Yuen.

MONGOLS.

NATIVE LITTER—NANKOW PASS.

It is necessary to be careful in bargaining with the men who take one up this pass, for they will impose on foreigners in every possible way. Thus, when about to struggle through the rough parts of the roughest road in the world, they will ask for a guide a-piece to pilot them over each rock and boulder that has to be crossed. It always happens that these guides are themselves most extortionate characters, and as the way grows more difficult some fresh demand is certain to be put forward. Our friend, Mr. Welmer, had arranged everything with our men before we left Peking, but still they made most pertinacious efforts to extort more money from us.

At the Great Wall I reluctantly parted from Mr. Wylie, who was one of the most distinguished and modest travellers it has been my good fortune to meet.

The Wall has often been described, but I confess that it disappointed me. It is simply a gigantic, useless stone fence, climbing the hills and dipping down into the valleys. At the point I visited it has been frequently repaired, and only attained to its present massive proportions during the Ming dynasty. That piece of it which we see in the Nankow pass at Pan-ta-ling is not so old by several centuries as the outer wall, which was built by Tsin-she-whang, B. C. 213. * In its route of over 1,000 miles there are some portions of the wall which from neglect have now fallen into decay; but it was never much more than a clay mound even in its best parts, faced with sun-dried bricks, and in the passes, as at Pan-ta-ling, with stone. It now only stands as a colossal monument of misdirected human labour, and of the genius which the Chinese have ever displayed in raising costly barriers to shut out barbarians from Cathay. In

* See "Journeys in North China," Rev. Dr. Williamson, ii. 390.

vain were all these toilsome precautions! The danger that was threatening them within the country they all the while failed to guard against, and from this very cause at last the native dynasty had to succumb before an alien race. To understand this we must remember that a rebel wrested the throne from the last Chinese Emperor, and that, when this usurper had been in turn dethroned, the Manchus, taking advantage of the existing disorder, came in and conquered China.

On my return journey I fell in with a gang of convicts, heavily chained and sent adrift to seek a precarious living in the pass. There they spent existence, shut out from the villages and shunned by all. One who had charge of the rest, rode an ass. Half the hair had been rubbed off this poor brute's back by the irons of its rider, and even respectable donkeys as they passed trains, would hold no intercourse with it. Many of the traders we met were fine-looking men, and few went by us without bestowing a kindly salutation.

At Nankow I put up again at the inn, and there found a native merchant in possession of the best room. He politely offered to vacate it in my favour, but this I, of course, refused to allow, contenting myself with an apartment where Ahong, having first obtained the unwilling consent of the landlord, set to with a half-naked slave to reduce the table and chair until they disclosed the wood of which they were made. There were also many spider-webs, but we left these undisturbed, for their bloated occupants were feasting on the flies with which the room was infested. The merchant had a train of fourteen mules, an elegant sedan, and a troop of muleteers, who were carousing in the next apartment. A merry time they had of it! One of them was still gesticulating like a Chinese stage-warrior as I dropped off to sleep.

CHINESE BRONZE LION—YUEN-MING-YUEN.

FUNERAL BANNERMEN.

In the morning I was awakened by the clang of a smith's anvil, and found that the smith was one of the many travelling workmen who abound in Cathay. He was making knives and reaping-hooks, and had contrived a simple forge by attaching a tube to his air-pump, passing this beneath the ground, and then bringing up the end so as to play through the fire which lay in a hollow in the soil. There was also a Mahommedan inn at Nankow, and there the host and his attendants were remarkable for their Indian physiognomies. At the same place, too, I found a guide, who had distinguished himself by show-ing visitors through the pass. This individual had fallen heir to a pair of enormous foreign boots, which he kept on his feet by pads and swathes of cloth. He had, besides, obtained a number of certificates from his patrons, which, almost without exception, described him as a great ruffian. These certificates he presented for my inspection with an evident air of pride. He also said that his sympathies were not Chinese, and pointing to his boots, declared that he was a foreigner like myself.

From Nankow I proceeded on to the Ming tombs. For the information of those among my readers who may still be unacquainted with the great burial-ground where thirteen Em-perors of the Ming dynasty were interred, I will give a brief summary of my experiences in that place.

It will be remembered that Nanking, the ancient capital, where the founder of the Ming dynasty established his court, contains the first mausoleum of those Kings—a mausoleum in almost every particular resembling the tombs of the same line in the valley thirty miles north of Peking. These tombs lie at the foot of a semi-circle of hills, which has something like a three miles' radius.

The temple of Chingtsoo, who reigned with the national designation of Yung-lo, from 1403 till his death in 1424, is by far the finest of these Imperial resting-places. It is approached through an avenue of colossal animals and warriors sculptured in stone, and although some of the figures are in attitudes of perfect repose, well becoming in the guardians of the illustrious dead, yet when we view them as the finest specimens of sculpture which China has to show, we must acknowledge that her ancient art falls short of our own modern standard. I doubt, however, whether Chinese artists of the present day could produce anything, I do not say better, but even so good as these Ming statues. The great tomb may be set down in most respects as a counterpart of the architecture which prevails in the temples, the palaces and even the dwellings in China. I was pleased to find that Mr. Simpson, in his interesting account of his tour round the world, has also noticed this similarity. It must of necessity be so, as the Chinese look upon such a tomb as this as the palace of the spirit of Yung-lo. The animals and warriors form his retinue, while offerings to his soul are annually made at the shrine in the great sacrificial hall. In the same way with their gods : the temples are the palaces wherein the deities reside, and indeed the word "kung," used to designate Taouist temples, signifies "a palace." *

The Emperors of the present dynasty, who drove the Mings from their dominions, still offer sacrifices at the tombs of those sovereigns; and this they do, it may be, out of mere state policy, or perhaps because the spirits of the departed monarchs are supposed to exercise an influence over the Imperial throne.

Although Chinese buildings, in their general plan, present

* "The Religious Condition of the Chinese," Edkins, p. 42.

Avenue leading to the Ming Tombs, North of Peking.

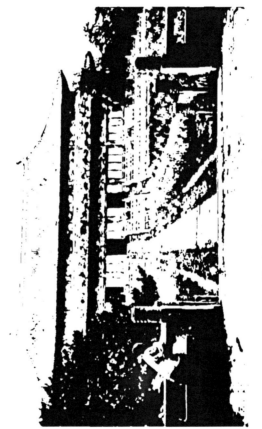

Temple of Ching-tsoo. Ming Tombs.

many points of similarity, differences nevertheless exist in
the number of their courts, and in the details of the various
kinds of edifices. Thus the magisterial yamen has usually four
courts; the first three, with the apartments attached to them,
comprising the various offices required for administrative purposes; while the fourth, with its buildings, is sacred to the
mandarin and his family. But it is impossible to treat, at the
conclusion of a chapter, of a subject which would worthily fill a
volume; nor can I do more than bestow this passing glance at
the Valley of Tombs, which marks the resting-place of the last
Chinese dynasty.

In conclusion, I venture to hope that—so far as my years
of travel and personal observation suffice—I have given the
reader some insight into the condition of the inhabitants of the
vast Chinese Empire. The picture at best is a sad one; and
although a ray of sunshine may brighten it here and there, yet,
after all, the darkness that broods over the land becomes but
the more palpable under this straggling, fitful light. Poverty
and ignorance we have among us in England; but no poverty so
wretched, no ignorance so intense as are found among the millions of China.

A P P E N D I X.

The Aboriginal Dialects of Formosa.

There appears to be no trace of the existence of a written language among the aborigines of Formosa, unless indeed we take into account the use which the semi-civilised tribes have made of Roman and Chinese written characters.

The use of the former was taught by the Dutch over two centuries ago, when they occupied the island. Some singular specimens of Romanised Malay documents are still treasured up among the tribes, although they are quite ignorant of their value, as they are now unable to translate them. These papers are chiefly title-deeds to property, or simple business agreements between man and man.

The Chinese, since the time of the Dutch occupation, have impressed upon the Pepohoan, or 'strangers of the plain', their own language both written and oral. It was therefore only from the oldest members of the Baksa Pepohoan tribe that I could obtain the words set down in the Vocabulary. At Baksa the native language has been superseded by the Chinese collo-quial dialect.

The Shekhoan is the great northern tribe of half-civilised aborigines. They still retain their original tongue, although the crafty Chinese invaders are making rapid inroads on their fertile valleys, and civilising them out of the lands, if not out of the language of their fathers.

In the savage mountain tribes of Formosa—separated as they are from each other by impenetrable forests, rocky barriers, impetuous torrents, and deep ravines, as well as by ceaseless warfare—we have an example of the change which, in time, may be effected in a language by the breaking up of a race into tribes which for at least two hundred years have been, from necessity, for the most part, isolated from each other, and where oral tradition afforded the only means of retaining a knowledge of their original tongue. We find that the numerals of the language, which were probably the sounds most constantly in use, have suffered least change, and the number "five" has retained its original sound. This may be from the fact that among primitive tribes who have no written numerals, the five fingers of the hand are invariably used to solve their simple problems in arithmetic; so notably, indeed, is this the case, that in many dialects "five" and "hand" are synonymous : the hand in that way becoming a sort of — if I may use the expression — rude hieroglyphic signifying five. In the same way "eye", or Mata, is a simple, easily remembered sound; and as it designates the organ of sight — something that has its sign in each human face, that is in constant use, and constantly appealed to to satisfy the savage, as well as the most cultivated instincts — it too has been retained, in nearly its pure sound, in the various dialects. Thus I might go on selecting the words that appear to me to have retained their primitive sounds, simply because they find their visible symbols in the objects which surround the simple abodes of the aborigines.

But the reader, by referring to the Vocabularies, will be enabled to form his own conclusions, and to trace out the affinities, or the opposite, that exist between the Formosan dialects, and also the close family likeness which they bear to the Polynesian languages. (See Polynesian Vocabularies in Crawford's "Indian Archipelago", vol. iii, and the words noted on Table III.)

Fresh evidence of the existence of races on the New Guinea coast who speak the Polynesian dialects has been afforded by the Rev. W. W. Gill, who made three visits to the island in 1872. [1] Thus, he tells us that the word for "eye" with two separate tribes is Mata, for "ear" Taringa and Taia, and for "hands" Ima-ima and Rima-rima. These words are all to be found in the Formosan dialects, and indeed might have been taken from them. As for the numerals in use among the aborigines of Formosa, they would afford but doubtful evidence of the Polynesian origin of the tribes were they not supported by the more direct testimony which the various dialects supply.

[1] Proceedings of the Royal Geographical Society, xviii. 45.

Short Vocabularies of the Dialects spoken by the Aborigines of Formosa.

TABLE I.

NAMES of TRIBES.

ENGLISH	FACHEE	SECGUAN	OBOAL	BANGA	BANTAN-LANG.	SINGAPORE MALAY.
Man	Lalusa	Lamoosa	—	Sarellai	Aoolai	Orang
Woman	Atlain	Maou-spingth	—	Abaia	Abaia	Prampuon
Head	Bangoo	Bangoo	Sapchi	Kapallu	Kapallu	Kapala
Hair	—	—	—	Ussioi	—	Rambut
Tooth	—	—	Nganon	—	—	Gigit
Neck	Guon-gorath	Nipoon	—	Oorohu	Oorohu	Leher
Ear	Charunga	Muttus	—	Charinga	Charinga	Talinga
Mouth	Mussoo	Mata	—	Didisi	Muto-mytoo	Mulut
Nose	Ngoon-goro	Kanum	Nguchu	Coomonu	Ongoho	Idung
Eye	Ooraitla	Tarima	Muchen	Macha	Macha	Mata
Heart	Takaru	Ktlapa	Ramucha	Kasso	Tookuho	Janteng
Hand	Ramucho	Pinassan	Sapchi	Arema	—	Tangan
Foot	Sapatl	—	Tangigya	Tsapku	Amoo	Kaki
Thigh	Bannen	—	—	Danoosa	Laloohe	Pauh
Leg	—	Khap	—	Tiboo-sabossa	—	Betis
Knee	Anasatoo	—	—	Pookuro	Sakaho	Lutut
Leopard	Lakotl	—	—	Likalao	Rikoslao	Animau Kambang
Bear	Chumatu	—	—	Choomattu	Choomai	Bruang
Deer	Putooru	—	—	Silappu	Caliche	Rusa
Wild Hog	Aroomthi	—	—	—	Babooy	Babi-outan
Monkey	—	—	—	—	Mararooko	Monvet

				Dami	Dami	кими
Chief	—	Titan-garchu	—	Tital-abahi	Tailai	Rajah
Bamboo	Baswera	—	—	—	Taroo-lahiroi	Bulah
Cassia	—	—	—	Tara-inai	—	Külit Manis
Tea	Kusang	—	—	Lang-lang	—	Daun Teh
Cooking Pan	—	—	—	—	Palangu	Kwali-Masak
Pumpkin	—	—	—	Tangu-tangu	—	Labū-Fringgi
Fragrant	—	—	—	—	Anaremu	Wangie
Rice	—	—	—	—	Chiluco	Bras
Rice (boiled)	Oaro	—	—	—	Ba-ooro	Nasi
Fire	Apooth	—	Pooju	Curao	Apooy	Api
Water	Satloom	Sapooth	Choomai	Apoolu	Achilai	Ayer
Ring	Tujana	Manum	—	Achilai	Mata-na	Chin-chin
Ear-ring	—	Paklis	—	Tarra	Ang-choy	Krabu
Bracelet	Pitoka	Push-tonna	—	Chin-gari	Issaise	Galang
Pipe	Katsap	Kaconan	—	Uliule	Ang-choy	Pipa
Gun	Taklito	Pavak-sapum	—	Ang-choy	Guangu	Sadapang
Skin Jacket	Nicaroota	Shiddi	—	Guang	Carridha	Bajo-kulet
Cap	Sarapun	Tamoking	—	Amalin	Torra-pungu	Topie
Letter	—	—	—	Tara-pung	Uraome	Surat
Smoke	Worlboroo	Khosalt	—	Senna	—	Asap
By-and-bye	Chuden	—	—	Uburon	Churana	Lagi-sabuntar
Warm	Machechu	—	—	Mechechi	Mechechi	Panas
Cold	Matilku	—	—	Matilku	Malilku	Sajuk
Rain	—	—	—	—	Maisang	Ugan

NOTE.—The Formosa vocabularies, with the exception of the Baksa Pepohoan, were supplied by Dr. Maxwell and the Rev. Mr. Ritchie, Formosa. The Baksa vocabulary was taken down by the author when among the Pepohoans.

TABLE II.

NAMES OF TRIBES.

ENGLISH	SHEKHOAN	MALAY
Man	Mamalung	Grang
Woman	Mameoss	Prampuan
Child	Lakehan / { Lakehan / Mamalung }	Anak
Son	Mamaop	
Daughter or girl		Ano
Father	Aba	Bapa
Mother	Inna	Ma
Elder brother	Abusan	Abang
Younger brother	Soaip	Adik
Sister	Mamaop	
Head	Poonat	Kapala
Hair	Bakus	Rambut
Mouth	Lahar	Mulat
Eyes	Darik	Mata
Nose	Mooding	Idung
Arm	Limat	
Leg	Karan	
Live	Meirad	Idup
Die	Polekat	Mati
Eat	Makan	Mukanan
Eat rice.	Makan-somai	Makan-nasi
Drink	Mudauch	Menam
Drink wine	{ Mudauch / inunsat }	Menam-angur
I or me	Iakok	Aku

NAMES OF TRIBES.

ENGLISH	SHEKHOAN	MALAY
Thou or ye	Isu	Inkang
Good	Riak	Baik
Sun	Liddock	Mata-hari
Moon	Illas	Bulan
Star	Bintool	Bintang
Heaven	Kabu-kanas	Surga
High	Baban	Tingi
Mountain	Binaiss	Bukit
Sea	Anass	Laut
Free	Katxaney	Mardika
Great	Matalah	Besar
Small	Tateng	Kechil
Day	Lahan	Hari
Night	Hinien	Malam
One	Ida	Satu
Two	Doosah	Dua
Three	Tooro	Tiga
Four	Supat	Ampat
Five	Hassub	Lima
Six	Boodah	Anam
Seven	Bi-doosut	Tugu
Eight	Bi-tooro	Da-lapan
Nine	Bi-supat	Simbilan
Ten	Isid	Sa-puluh

NAMES OF TRIBES.

ENGLISH	TRIBE at PILAM	MALAY
Man	Atinbe	Orang
Male	Mainaen	Jantan
Female	Babaian	Batena
Father	Amoko	Bapa
Mother	Abu	Ma
Son	Alak	Anak
Daughter	Abavi	Anak dara
Head	Tungrow	Kapala
Eye	Mata	Mata
Nose	Atingran	Idung
Mouth	Indan	Mulut
Face	Tungur	Muka
Ear	Tungila	Talinga
Hand	A-lima	Tangan
Body	A-liduk	Badan
Feet	Lapar	Kaki
Heart	Ne-rung-arung	Jantong
House	A-ruma	Ruma
Garden	A-uma	Cabun
Vegetables	A-ropan	Siuer
Village	A-tikel	Campong
Wood	Kiau	Kiau
Water	A-tuei	Ayer
Heat	Beaus	Panas

NAMES OF TRIBES.

ENGLISH	TRIBE at PILAM	MALAY
Cold	Litak	Sajuk
Sea	A-nik	Laut
Earth	Darak	Tana or darat
Fire	Apui	Api
Mountain	Adenan	Bukit
Rice	Rumai	Bras
Good	Inava	Baik
Bad	Kaotish	Jahat
Darkness	Aruning	Galap
Strike light	Pulalauit	Dapat-api
North	Ioud	Utara
South	Daiah	Salalan
East	Ameh	Tmur
West	Timur	Barat
One	Itu	Satu
Two	Lusa	Dua
Three	Taloh	Tiga
Four	Sepat	Ampat.
Five	Lima	Lima
Six	Onam	Anam
Seven	Pitu	Tugu
Eight	Aloo	Da-lapan
Nine	Siva	Sambilan
Ten	Pelapsang	Sa-puluh

TABLE IV.

NAMES of TRIBES.

ENGLISH.	BAKSA PEPOHOAN.	MALAY.
Man	Kaguling-ma	Qrang
Male	Ama	Jantan
Female	Enina	Batina
Son	Alak	Anak
Daughter	Yugant nina	Anak-dara
Child	Yugant	Anik
Father	Ima	Bapa
Mother	Ina	Ma
Elder brother	Jaka	Abang
Younger brother	Ebe	Adik
Elder sister	Jaka	
Younger sister	Ebe	
Husband and wife	Maka-kaja	
Head	Mongong	Kapala
Body	Bwan	Badan
Belly	Ebuk	Prut
Beard	Nigh	Jangut
Tooth	Wali	Gigi
Mouth	Mutut	Mulut
Throat	Luak	Lhaer
Hair	Bukaun	Rambut
Hand	Lima	Tangan
Foot	Lapan	Kaki
Finger-nails	Ku-rung-kung	Kooku
Eye	Mata	Mata
Ear	Tangela	Talinga
Nose	Togunut	Idung
Death	Ilapati	Mati
Life	Maonga	Idup
Fire	Apoi	Api
Tobacco	Tabacow	Timbacu
Pipe	Timbakang	Pepo
Stand	Neteku	Burderi
Walk	Daran	Jalan
Sing	Mururou	Ngnia

TABLE IV. (*Continued*). 283

NAMES of TRIBES.

ENGLISH.	BAKSA PEPOHOAN.	MALAY.
Heat	Ma-kinku	Panas
Cold	Ma-hunmoon	Sajuk
Rain	Mudan	Ugim
Stone	Batu	Batu
Wood	Kiau	Kiau
Iron	Mani	Bisi
Flower	Eseep	Bunga
Fruit	Toto	Bua
Earth	Ni	Tana
Water	Jalum	Ayer
Wind	Bali	Angin
Smoke	Atu	Asap
Clean	Ma-kupti	Brisi
Dirty	Ma-luksung	Cotor
Black	Ma-edum	Etam
White	Ma-puli	Puti
Red	Ma-epong	Mera
Rice	Dak	Bras
Rice cooked	Rudak	Bras-masa
River	Mutu	Sungi
Sky	Towin	Langit
Sea	Baung	Laut
To blow	Ayu	Teop
To push	Dudung	Kaki
Banana	Bunbun	Pisang
Cocoa-nut	Agubung	Kalapa
Mango	Mangut	Mampalam
Orange	Busilam	Lemo
Potato	Tamami	Obie
Bad	Masari	Jahat
Good	Magani	Baik
Disease	Maalam	Sackit
To kill	Lumpo	(Kasa-mati ﹤ or Bono
Sun	Wali	Mata-hari
Moon	Buran	Bulan

Comparative Table of the Languages of Formosa, the Philippine, Singapore, New Zealand, &c.

TABLE V.

English.	Paichien Formosa.	Sibucoon Formosa.	Tibolah Formosa.	Banga Formosa.	Bantanlang Formosa.	Samobi Formosa.	Bak. 'epohoan Fo..nosa.	Philippine Iaenla [3]
One	Saoe	Tashang	Chum	Denga	Denga	Itsa	Saat	Isa
Two	Soo	Lusha	Lusa	Noosa	Noosa	Lusa	Duha	Dalat
Three	Toro	Taoo	Tooloo	Toro	Toro	Toroo	Turo	Tallo
Four	Pati	Piat	Supat	Patu	Patu	Sipat	Dapat	Apat
Five	Rima	Tima	Lima	Lima	Lima	Lima	Darima	Lima
Six	Neum	Noom	Nauma	Neuma	Neum	Unum	Danum	Anim
Seven	Pito	Pito	Pito	Pito	Pito	Pito	Dapito	Pito
Eight	Mivaroo	Awoo	Mevaroo	Mevaroo	Mevaroo	Aloo	Kuipat	Ualo
Nine	Siwa	Siva	Chuga	Bangatoo	Cangatu	Siva	—	Siam
Ten	Koomath	Basau	Mat [i]	Poorookoo	Poorooku	Poro	Kating	Samp
Hand [1]	—	—	—	—	—	—	Lima	—

Philippine Bisaya [2]	New Zealand [3]	Des Habitans De Tikopa [4]	Des Papous De Waigiou.	Tonga.	Maw.	Des Harfours De Menado Célebes. [4]	Malay of Singapore.
Usa	Tahi	Tassa	Sai	Taha	Tahi	Essa	Satu
Duha	Rua	Roua	Doui	Oua	Boua	Roua	Dua
Tato	Toro	Torou	Kior	Tolou	Todou	Taiou	Tiga
Upat	Wa	Fa	Fiak	Fa	Wa	Apat	Ampat
Lima	Rima	Lima	Rim	Nima	Dima	Lima	Lima
Uniam	Ono	Ono	Onem	Ono	Ono	Anam	Anam
Pito	Witu	Fitou	Fik	Fttou	Witou	Piton	Tugo
Ualo	Waru	Warou	War	Valou	Wadou	Walou	Da-lapai
Siam	Iwa	Siva	Sion	Hiva	Iwa	Sio	Sambilai
Napulo	Nga-huru	Anhafouro	Somfour	Oulou	NgaOudon	Poulou	Sa-pulut
—	—	—	—	—	—	—	—

[1] I have added the word Lima, or Hand, in the Baksa dialect, in which it also means five 'In many Negro languages Lima also means hand'. See the late Mr. Crawford's Dissertation on the Malay language, etc., p. 236

[2] Essays Ethnological and Linguistic, by the late James Kennedy, p. 74.

[3] Du Dialecte de Tahiti, de celui des Iles Marquises, et en général, de la Langue Polynésienne, Table, p. 101.

[4] Voyage de l'Astrolabe, par M. D'Urville. Paris, 1834.

Lightning Source UK Ltd.
Milton Keynes UK
26 February 2010

150695UK00001B/19/P